# COMING OF AGE IN IRAN

# CRITICAL PERSPECTIVES ON YOUTH

General Editors: Amy L. Best, Lorena Garcia, and Jessica K. Taft

# Coming of Age in Iran

*Poverty and the Struggle for Dignity*

Manata Hashemi

NEW YORK UNIVERSITY PRESS

New York

NEW YORK UNIVERSITY PRESS
New York
www.nyupress.org

References to Internet websites (URLs) were accurate at the time of writing. Neither the author nor New York University Press is responsible for URLs that may have expired or changed since the manuscript was prepared.

Parts of this book initially appeared or draw from the following published articles: "Embedded Enclaves: Cultural Mimicry and Urban Social Exclusion in Iran," *International Journal of Urban and Regional Research* (2019); "Tarnished Work: Dignity and Labour in Iran," *British Journal of Middle Eastern Studies* (2018); "Aspirations, Poverty and Behavior among Youth in the Middle East: Some Theoretical Considerations," *Muslim World* 107 (1) (2017) (originally published as "Studying Disadvantaged Youths in the Middle East: A Theoretical Framework," *CIRS Occasional Papers* (2015)); "Waithood and Face: Morality and Mobility among Lower-Class Youth in Iran," *Qualitative Sociology* 38 (3) (2015). Used with permission.

ISBN: 978-1-4798-7633-4 (hardback)
ISBN: 978-1-4798-8194-9 (paperback)

For Library of Congress Cataloging-in-Publication data, please contact the Library of Congress.

New York University Press books are printed on acid-free paper, and their binding materials are chosen for strength and durability. We strive to use environmentally responsible suppliers and materials to the greatest extent possible in publishing our books.

Manufactured in the United States of America

10 9 8 7 6 5 4 3 2 1

Also available as an ebook

*To Maman and Baba.*

*And to Farzan.*

It could be true that there was another realm hidden within this one and that he might be able to walk and ponder his way into it if he allowed his secret other self to emerge. For the moment, he refused to choose between the two realms. His public views were correct, and so were his private ones; the intentions of the heart and the intentions of words were equally important.

—Orhan Pamuk, *A Strangeness in My Mind*, 2015

# CONTENTS

# A NOTE ON TRANSLITERATION

Throughout this book, I use the scheme outlined by the journal *Iranian Studies* for my transliteration of Persian (and Arabic when applicable). When quoting from speech, I transliterate according to spoken Persian and not the written standard. I use the most common English transliteration for names of individuals or terms known in English. All translations are my own unless otherwise noted.

# PREFACE

When I was a child growing up in the United States in the 1980s and 1990s, my exposure to Iran was largely limited to the four walls of our house, where my parents and I spoke Persian, ate distinctly Iranian cuisine, and listened to the nostalgic music of diasporic Iranian singers who had emigrated, as we had, to the United States. Outside the comforts of my own home, however, being an Iranian was largely the equivalent of being a *persona non grata*. The 1979 Revolution and the subsequent hostage crisis and eight-year Iran-Iraq War did little to ingratiate the émigré Iranians like myself into the social fabric of American society. Public discussions of Iran, when they did occur, revolved around the revolution and the presumed religious fanaticism of Iranians and their propensity toward violence.

As I grew older and entered college, I became exposed to others like myself: Iranian Americans who had to negotiate their identities and navigate between two different cultural realms. Public discussions about Iran became more inclusive and focused not just on the revolution, but its implications for Iranian society at large. This was in no small part due to the 1997 election of Mohammad Khatami, Iran's first reformist president, who ushered in Iran's reform era and emphasized concepts such as civil society, democracy, inclusivity, and individual rights to a beleaguered, war-weary population.

Today, despite these advances, Iran's march toward reform has not worked to drastically change outside perceptions of the country. Media, books, films, and photographs showing the unsavory aspects of life in the Islamic Republic continue to dominate the American imaginary. The Islamic Republic is largely seen as a bastion of repression; Iranian citizens, if not considered complicit in this repression, are seen as victims who attempt to resist and rebel at every chance they get.

Having lived in and traveled to Iran since childhood, I know that this narrative is far removed from the everyday experiences of the many young Iranians I have come to know. In the pages that follow, I detail these realities and attempt to show a different aspect to life in the Islamic Republic, one that is shaped by struggle and hardship, yes, but also defined by acceptance, hope, and the promise of a better life. In showing the richness and complexity of life among ordinary Iranians, I hope that public discussions of Iran can finally evolve from the revolution, state politics, and oppression to something that more closely resembles how ordinary Iranians perceive themselves and their society in the twenty-first century.

Steering through societal expectations is not a practice exclusive to the youth in this book. Like many other Iranian émigrés of my generation, growing up, I had to continually negotiate between a private Iranian culture and a public culture that largely rejected outward manifest signs of Iranianness. In many ways, it felt that I was living two disparate lives until I learned to reconcile my two identities as an Iranian American. In attempting to traverse the two worlds, I finally learned that they were intimately linked, that each one helped to reinforce what I found valuable in the other.

# Introduction

My father always says that the sky is always one color for the
poor, but not for the rich. Whether [the rich] are in the desert or in the forest, they have fun. Whatever country they
live in in the world, the world is to their liking.[1]
—Davud, seventeen years old, laborer, Sari

My first lesson on the illusory character of appearances came on a particularly hot summer afternoon early on in my fieldwork. Driving up a
dirt road to young Mohammad Karimi's house in the outskirts of Sari,
the capital of Iran's Mazandaran province, I came to a one-story concrete
abode with small windows and a rusty red iron gated door that tilted at
its hinges. The house stood derelict. To its right, the dwelling boasted
an equally unkempt garden strewn with rocks and dirt. Tall corn stalks
that bowed violently in the wind were one of the few signs of life in this
small patch of land.

Once inside, I encountered unpainted concrete walls, exposed ceil-
ing bulbs, and a large, furniture-less main living space. And yet, upon
closer inspection, I noticed the artfully placed decorations, revealing the
family's care for their home. Oversized wool rugs with Persian motifs
lay on the cement floors. A large, carefully hung swath of colorful fabric separated the living from the sleeping quarters. Small pots of faux
plants hung above the island separating the tiled kitchen from the living area. A small television set sat on a lopsided wooden entertainment
unit decorated with ceramic tchotchkes. A memento, a framed picture of
Mohammad's father as a young soldier visiting the shrine of Imam Reza,
the eighth Shi'a Imam, hung on the wall.[2] A pot of tea stood brewing on
the samovar in the kitchen, as the family knew they were to be expecting
company. A picturesque warmth percolated the entire house.

As my relationship with the Karimi family grew over the course of my
fieldwork, I learned that the family had saved up enough money to be

eligible for loans to buy a plot of land in this seaside district. Though the house seemed to be run-down, it was actually in the process of construction from the ground up. The slow construction process—which made headway only when the Karimis had enough money to invest—had given the dwelling a deteriorating air that belied the craftsmanship, effort, and cost behind each new building phase.[3] The Karimis were poor, but through sheer perseverance and risk-taking, they had been able to secure a piece of land in a peri-urban area, hundreds of miles away from their rural village in central Iran.

The Karimis are not unique. Throughout the course of my research among members of the young, lower strata of Iranian society, I encountered countless Karimis—people who, according to one Iranian mother, "tried to make the most of the little they had." The shoddy exteriors of their homes often disguised the neatness and meticulous attention to detail of their well-decorated interiors. Their donning of the latest fashion trends and accessories concealed their desperate financial straits and the fact that they sometimes did not have a proper dinner to eat.

This book is about these Iranian youth. It is about how a select group of young men and women between the ages of fifteen and twenty-nine who came of age after the revolution control appearances in order to improve their lot in life. The book examines how those young Iranians who are faced with constant economic deprivation struggle to not only manage their lives, but also to find meaning within them. It is a story of agency, the search for dignity, and the pursuit of face.

## The Universalization of Exclusion

For most of the past half century, scholarly preoccupation with Iran has focused almost exclusively on the country's appearances. The Iranian Revolution of 1979—one of the most historic world events of the past hundred years, which prompted the rise of a constitutional theocracy—has often served as the focal point of this scholarly attention. One of the largest countries in the Middle East and a non-Arab state that has, since the 1979 Revolution, pursued a foreign policy of restricting outside influences and forging strong relations with non-aligned countries, Iran has been viewed as an anomaly among the countries of the region. Scores of articles and books have subsequently focused on the revolution and its various influences in political ideology, civil society, and more recently, in sexual politics and youth cultures.[4] While these studies have done much to heighten awareness of Iranian culture and society in the West, analysts and pundits continue to define Iran in terms of binaries: tradition versus modernity, religious versus secular, rich versus poor—binaries that only reinforce the country's exceptional and almost pariah-like status.

The present book will look beyond the macropolitics of the Iranian Revolution and its publicity to analyze the behavior of ordinary young Iranians. The book moves past the country's public image to unearth what is happening among these youth in the small backstreets, in the local bazaars and shops, and behind closed doors. In so doing, the book reveals how some of Iran's low-income, struggling youth manage the demands of everyday life. The custodians of the Islamic Republic regard this group as the backbone of the regime. However, we have heard little about this population, their struggles to advance, and the ways that they attempt to carve out a meaningful life for themselves.

A large part of the neglect that low-income youth in the country have received has been due to the position of scholars themselves; scholars, given their own backgrounds, have greater access to highly educated youth in Iran's upper and middle crusts. The result has been a tendency to generalize from the experiences of an elite group of young Iranian men and women to encompass all youth in Iran.[5] This universalization, in turn, has led to ethnographies and narratives of exclusion. In this perspective, young men and women in Iran are excluded from productive employment, from marriage and family formation, and from the power to shape their communities due to the structural constraints that characterize Iran itself: formal labor market rigidity and a high youth cohort have created more labor market entrants than there are jobs. Subsequently, scholars argue, young men and women become stuck in a period of "waithood," a period during which they wait with uncertainty for jobs, for housing, and for marriage—socioeconomic benchmarks that have traditionally defined adult status in the Middle East.[6] As a result, youth in Iran create their own subcultures of resistance—reified in their sexual practices, choices of music and dress, and drug use—that undergird their exclusion from formalized institutions of power.

Given the copious amount of attention that studies have placed on understanding the factors that give rise to youth exclusion in Iran and the ways in which this exclusion is reaffirmed by the oppositional practices of certain privileged youth in the country, few works remain that address the experiences of low-income Iranian youth.[7] Consequently, we are left to assume that the latter are similarly alienated, socially excluded, and engaged in oppositional subcultures.

This book will challenge this assumption by showing the variety and complexity of the lives of those youth caught in poverty, a generation that cannot be summarily characterized as repressed, excluded, or defiant. Based on ethnography, this book looks at how the desire to maintain dignity and save face among some young, poor Iranians shapes the way that they go about improving their lot in life.[8] It shows how "making a good showing"[9] of themselves constitutes a culture of acceptance of dominant social norms rather than opposition. Fariba Adelkhah argues that the ethical code of *javanmardi* (chivalry/man of integrity) followed by both men and women in post-revolutionary Iran emphasizes conformity to the social order and to the rules of citizenship.[10] For Adelkhah, the *javanmard* is a product of his community: it is the people around him who bestow "that role on him. . . . He does not really exist outside the recognition, admiration and even concern which society shows for him."[11] Further still, the conformity that the *javanmard* displays not only expands the hegemony of the state into the private realm, but also enables autonomy and increases individual influence on the state.

In a similar vein, this book shows how the ethical code of the face system—of which virtue constitutes a part—emphasizes conformity to the social order, expanding the Islamic Republic's sphere of influence, while nonetheless enabling poor youth to exercise agency and influence their position within the broader social and economic milieu. In abiding by certain authorized cultural norms or rules of behavior revolving around saving face, these youth are able to present themselves in front of others as *javanmards*, as people with moral integrity—good, responsible, and financially secure.

Agency thus lies in the process of subjectivation: social norms that function to subordinate the subject are also the means by which the subject becomes an agent.[12] Through repeated, daily obedience to the face rules, the youth in this book acquire the ability, the agency, to implement change in their lives. As Saba Mahmood argues, agency is therefore predicated on docility.[13] Rather than implying passivity on the part of the compliant subject, daily performative acts of submission become the necessary means by which agency is constituted.[14] How does this happen?

As the stories in this book will detail, those young men and women who comply and save face are able to increase their stock of moral capital, or public perceptions of their moral worth, which they can subsequently exchange for social and economic opportunities.[15] Simultaneously, attempting to live a good life based on a normative code of conduct is central to these young people's understanding of themselves and their relation to others.

The present moment in Iran is a time of great uncertainty. By showing the struggles of a particular group of Iranian youth to live, work, and, ultimately, improve their lives, this book gives an idea of the possibilities for the country's future.

## Resistance versus Conformism

In the social sciences, there is a tradition of studying social marginalization and resistance among lower class youth. Dominant perspectives tend to view poor young people's daily practices as instances of counterhegemony. This harks back to the resistance paradigm pioneered by James Scott.[16] According to Scott, everyday forms of resistance represent the poor's most effective strategy for contesting the hand that they have been dealt. While the specific oppositional practices of the disadvantaged vary depending on context, the end result is argued to be the same: resistance against repressive, all-encompassing rules and regulations imposed from above.

Subcultural studies have a long history of documenting how youth who are excluded from broader structures of opportunity create their own enclaves of rebellion.[17] Between youth studies of the Chicago School, which emphasized the deviancy of these youth as a reflection of their search for individual status, and the Birmingham School, which highlighted oppositional styles as a reflection of a class conflict between these youth and the outside world, poor young men and women have been described as turning to deviancy, gangs, oppositional values, music subcultures, and religious radicalism as a way to deal.[18] All of these paths constitute a series of mediated responses to marginalization that are predicated on these youths' resistance to dominant value systems in an attempt to lay claim to the status, respect, and dignity that are denied to them in the course of their daily lives.[19]

Without undermining the fact that there are disadvantaged youth in Iran as elsewhere who do engage in resistances against mainstream norms, values, and practices in order to reclaim their dignity, I argue that it is a slippery slope to universalize all poor youth as necessarily oppressed and defiant. The search for dignity takes multiple forms, not all of which constitute repudiation of dominant ideologies. Indeed, within sociological studies of urban poverty in the United States, there have been scholars who have shown that adherence to mainstream norms can be a way for the lower classes to maintain their self-worth.[20] The youth I came to know in Iran, youth whom I term face-savers, similarly attempted to maintain their dignity and face by simply trying that much harder to integrate themselves into the broader fabric of Iranian society. While these youth did not refer to themselves as face-savers, I use the term to distinguish them from other youth in the country to whom saving face may not play such a structuring role.

John Hewitt and Randall Stokes contend that people know that based on their actions, they will be "typified" or treated as a certain "kind" of person; to this end, they attempt to present themselves in ways that will lead others to evaluate them as the kind of people they themselves desire.[21] The actions of face-savers were similarly motivated by a desire to be typified in a favorable light. For face-savers, being judged as dignified, respectable, and good were what propelled their day-to-day social interactions. Among these youth, the quest for dignity encompassed cultural definitions of face-saving incorporated around community concerns for self-sufficiency, hard work, purity, and appearance. Thus, a life lived on the margins in Iran can lead to oppositional subcultural practices, but also to acceptance and accentuated conformism.

There are a few explanations for this. Up until the 1979 Revolution, Iran was marked by centuries of monarchic governance, aristocratic influence, and court behavior, and as such, historically, a strong significance has been attached to status recognition.[22] Even after the revolution, as Zuzanna Olszewska argues, "status recognition remains encoded in, and a crucial part of, language, comportment and social etiquette."[23] Consequently, to be perceived as *ba kelas* (someone with class and moral character) as opposed to *dehati* (a peasant) is the ultimate marker of one's person and the manifestation of one's claim to status and dignity. In an extension of the historical importance of status recognition in Iran, the commodity boom that defined the country during the mid-2000s opened Iranians' access to the global marketplace; this forged a pattern of noticeable consumption of luxury goods among Iran's elite and knockoffs by the lower classes in their attempts to pursue the status quo.[24] Mimicry, rather than resistance, became the defining feature for those pursuing a better life.

Finally, for the face-savers in this study who were looking to gain status, overt resistance also had little appeal. In a country where open resistance to social and/or political norms is met with immediate suppression, resistance in the form of marches, protests, collective violence, and other extreme behavior is not common. These young people calculated that their chances of gaining socioeconomic status through daily practices that revolved around the pursuit of face were higher than through antagonistic behavior. This awareness served to temper their involvement in collective acts of resistance. As Farhad Kazemi and Asef Bayat have shown in their empirical research on poor populations in Iran, collective acts of resistance are not a common feature of daily life in the Middle East due to the poor's everyday concerns with obtaining a better life for themselves and their family members.[25] In this sense, localized struggles for advancement become privileged over other forms of action in that they provide both meaning and autonomy to the disenfranchised.[26] Often, it is only when the poor feel that they are at risk of losing the small wins they have made that they can become collectively mobilized in defense of those achievements, particularly when there is a political opening to do so.[27] Overall, then, the crucial significance that status recognition has played in Iranian history has buttressed the importance of localized struggles for saving face among the upwardly mobile aspirant young men and women in this book and has decreased the desire for defiant practices to improve their social standing.

In considering the behavior of these young interlocutors, we must differentiate between intent and practice. There is a tendency to interpret Iranian young people's participation in global youth cultures as a form of defiance toward the moral order instituted by the Islamic state. In this perspective, young women who listen to rap music or wear tight-fitting clothing, for example, present a binary opposition to the woman clothed in a chador who reads the Qur'an, participates in Muharram rituals, and represents the ideal Islamic citizen. In this perspective, young women who listen to rap music, wear tight-fitting clothing, or engage in Sufi rituals, for example, present a binary opposition to the chador-clad, Qur'an-reading, Muharram-participating woman who represents the ideal Islamic citizen.[28] However, there are a variety of motives that propel people to act. A low-income young woman in Iran may position her headscarf so that half her hair is visible; she may wear tight-fitting clothes or a completely made-up face. However, she is not necessarily doing this in an attempt to challenge the moral order. Rather, her motive is much more simple: to look like one of "them"—that is, to look like her wealthier counterparts who surround her on a daily basis in the bazaars, on the streets, and in her classes. As one young woman, Nina, emphatically told me, "I never wanted kids in my school to think that we were poor, so I dressed nicely." For Nina, dressing "nicely" constituted wearing what she perceived was in fashion among her middle-class peers at the time: skinny jeans, loosely wrapped hijab, and a tight-fitting trench.

To be visibly perceived as poor in Iran is to risk losing face. As a result, poverty is often lived in secret. Among face-savers, wealth is a performance: it is a staged production that, like a real play, can win the actor recognition among the audience. Cultural practices—dressing in certain clothes, acting in a certain manner, or socializing with certain people—thus become "chips in the high-stakes game of social mobility."[29] It is upward social mobility or a change to a higher social status rather than subversion of any repressive social order that becomes the ultimate aim for youth like Nina.

The 1979 Revolution in Iran gave birth not only to an Islamic regime, but also to a generation of young people who have no memory of life before the revolution. These young men and women, known as the children of the revolution, today comprise approximately 25 percent of Iran's population.[30] For these youth, an all-encompassing Islamic form of rule is the only form of governance they have experienced; indeed, it has shaped who they are today. Iran's youth boom can be traced back to the 1980s, during the brutal Iran-Iraq War, when increased rates of marriage and childbirth created one of the largest youth demographics in the world.[31] Unfortunately, outsized youth populations create outsized social crises. Despite post-revolutionary increases in social welfare programming and in secondary and tertiary education, youth unemployment has skyrocketed in contemporary Iran, as supply cannot keep up with demand. In 2017 the unemployment rate stood at 26.4 percent for those between the ages of fifteen and twenty-nine.[32] For some youth who have the means, solace comes in the form of attending extravagant house parties, participating in underground music subcultures, consuming luxury goods bought from abroad, using drugs, engaging in sexual practices, and in extreme cases, emigrating from the country itself.

This book is about those youth without the means. How do some young people without ready access to social, economic, and cultural forms of capital go about negotiating the demands of daily life? What is it like to be young and poor in the current global moment in Iran? What can the experiences of the young and the economically struggling tell us about prospects for upward mobility in the country?

These youth constitute the backbone of the Islamic Republic. They are members of the *mostaz'afin*, the dispossessed, an Islamic term that was made all the more significant after the inception of the Islamic Republic when Ayatollah Khomeini's populist revolutionary discourse was made in their very name.[33] The onset of the Iran-Iraq War immediately after the revolution forced *daheh-ye shasti* youth (youth born circa the 1980s), who constituted a large part of my sample, to learn quickly; they had to learn to cope not only with the devastation of war, but with economic precarity, as the war cleaved through the socioeconomic fabric of their daily lives. The learning curve has not yet ended. Iran's young *mostaz'afin* continue to bear the burden of economic inequalities, inequalities that have been exacerbated in recent years with the imposition of biting sanctions on Iran's nuclear program and subsequent rising stagflation.[34] It is the pursuit of a better life within an atmosphere marked by increasing socioeconomic structural constraints that contour these youths' identities in contemporary Iran. This desire for the good life, in turn, has been shaped within a decades-long historical context marked by the interplay of socioeconomic policies from above and struggles from below to make the most of life's circumstances.

## Historical Contingencies

In the 1960s, an unassuming campaign began that found its strength and organizational basis in the modernization policies that were initiated in the 1930s by Reza Shah Pahlavi, and later intensified by his son, Mohammad Reza Shah (known simply as the Shah). Rising oil revenues during the reign of the latter contributed to an intensive program of socioeconomic development—deemed the White Revolution—that led to the rapid industrialization of Iranian cities. Between 1966 and 1976, the presumed widespread availability of manufacturing jobs, coupled with reduced agricultural income and low quality of life as a result of the Shah's mismanaged 1962 Land Reform Program, led more than two million disillusioned rural poor to begin a long migration to capital-intensive urban centers.[35]

The driving force of the Land Reform Program was the Shah's desire to gain a broad base of political support and enhance his own power, thereby preempting challenges to his authority that could destabilize the monarchy.[36] The Shah's land reforms called for the redistribution of land from the landowners who monopolized power and wealth in the countryside to the sharecropping peasants who cultivated the land. The goals were to reduce the power (and ultimately the threat to central authority) of Iran's landholding class while simultaneously presenting the monarchy to its urban reform-minded opponents (as well as to the United States, which was promoting land reform as a cure-all for developmental malaise) as a progressive advocate for economic development, modernization (i.e., Westernization), and agricultural productivity.[37] The monarchy further believed that by enabling peasants to control the product of their labor, it could increase both the nations' and the peasants' agricultural wealth, resulting in a strong base of rural support for the monarchal regime.[38]

In practice, however, land reform turned out to simply deepen class tensions and exacerbate economic frustrations. The power of landholders was simply replaced with the arm of the state. For its part, not only did the Pahlavi state fail to provide basic amenities like electricity and piped water to most of the countryside, but the prices it imposed on agricultural goods, as Ervand Abrahamian notes, "favored the urban sector at the expense of the countryside," thereby lowering incentives for the latter and decreasing agricultural productivity.[39] Most importantly, the regime was not able to gain a broad base of rural support, since only the sharecroppers were the direct recipients of the government's land transfer; agricultural laborers—those who did not have the rights to cultivate the land of others and who were temporary hires who farmed during peak seasons—received no land.[40] Comprising approximately half of the rural population, these agricultural laborers experienced even further economic deprivation as economic competition between themselves and the sharecroppers intensified, since the latter sought the same agricultural work as the former in order to supplement their incomes.[41] At the same time, as Eric Hooglund argues, "the increasing mechanization of agricultural production . . . reduce[d] absolutely both the number of hired workers needed and the total work hours available for those employed."[42]

For many of these agricultural laborers, then, the solution rested in migration to the cities, where they believed that they could make ends meet. Through migration, they hoped to gain high-paying city jobs, which would enable them to achieve greater economic security and greater access to amenities. These pull factors, coupled with push factors including agricultural decline, forced eviction, low wages, and a low quality of life, caused the in-migration of millions of these rural peasants from their villages to surrounding cities, leading many to join the ranks of the urban poor as unskilled workers or laborers.[43] In Tehran, where they were unable to afford decent housing, the majority came to settle in the southern sections of the city, where they resided in residences ranging from squatter communities to small rented abodes.[44] By 1976, more than 46 percent of Iran's population was urban,[45] with the majority (4.5 million) residing in Tehran.[46] The result of this extensive migration was that cities, including Tehran, could no longer provide urban services at a pace that kept up with their demographic growth. Slum areas— characterized by substandard housing and the lack of adequate essential services and facilities—subsequently spread in Iran's major cities.

To ameliorate their economic burdens, the poor turned to self-development initiatives: out of sheer economic necessity, they advanced their socioeconomic claims largely through silent direct actions or "quiet encroachments" such as home squatting, the illegal construction of dwellings, and the tapping of electricity.[47] To foster a sense of collectivity, residents established *hey'at*s, associations based on shared neighborhood or village origin.[48] The spread of radio in the 1950s and early 1960s and the subsequent rise of cassette tapes enabled *hey'at* members to listen to taped sermons, including those made by an exiled cleric by the name of Ayatollah Ruhollah Khomeini.[49] In his taped sermons, Ayatollah Khomeini condemned the Shah's regime for a host of social and economic issues, not the least of which was the Shah's failure to bring basic services to the countryside and his failure to build low-income housing for the new masses of urban poor.[50] Ayatollah Khomeini's pro-*mostaz'afin* discourse was reflected in sound bites that exalted the poor and the slum-dwellers and later became slogans of the Iranian Revolution; "Islam represents the slum-dwellers (*zaghehneshin*), not the palace-dwellers (*kakhneshin*)"[51] and "Islam belongs to the oppressed (*mostazafen*), not to the oppressors (*mostakbaren*)."[52]

While some scholars have emphasized a causal link between these religious sermons and the poor's political mobilization during the revolution,[53] the fact remained that the poor persisted largely on the periphery of the revolutionary operations, recognizing, as Bayat has shown empirically, their own localized struggles as the less costly and more viable alternative than engagement in oppositional politics.[54] It was only near the end of the Shah's reign in December 1978 that the urban poor, particularly young men, became politically mobilized, largely through revolutionary committees including the Islamic Consumer Cooperatives and the Neighborhood Councils.[55] The breakdown in the authority of the Shah's regime at the time provided the political vacuum that the opposition needed in order to consolidate its authority among the masses. A general atmosphere of public disorder, uneven food distribution, and a shortage of basic commodities motivated young, urban poor residents to join the clergy-backed cooperatives and councils in an attempt to secure their livelihoods.[56] Encouraged by Ayatollah Khomeini's populist promises and frustrated by their aggravated employment opportunities, their worsening living conditions, and the growing maldistribution of wealth, many of these new migrant urban poor ultimately came to join the ranks of the opposition forces that helped overthrow the monarchy and usher in the new Islamic Republic in February 1979.

Between 1980 and 1988, motivated by the Iran-Iraq War, Iran's new Islamic state consolidated its power, in large part, by expanding its reach among the poor. Shortfalls in oil revenues and rising wartime expenses led the state to turn to deficit spending, leading to rising inflation rates.[57] In an effort to alleviate the effects of the economic crisis on those most affected by it, the regime targeted its economic policies toward the poorest segments of society. To this end, the economics ministry distributed ration cards so that the poor could purchase basic goods and necessities. The state instituted price controls and provided vouchers. It allocated around 800,000 hectares of agricultural land to approximately 220,000 peasant families in the provinces of Gurgan, Mazandaran, and Khuzestan.[58] It further utilized a quarter of its annual budget to directly subsidize basic foodstuffs such as sugar, oil, and rice and to provide indirect subsidies for electricity, sanitation, and piped water to both the rural and urban poor.[59] Through the recently established revolutionary organization Jehad-e Sazandegi (Construction Jihad), the regime expanded infrastructure, building schools, roads, and libraries in the countryside and providing electricity, piped water, and health clinics to villages.[60] During the war, the regime also extended the scope of social welfare institutions, particularly that of the Imam Khomeini Relief Committee (IKRC), the largest welfare organization in Iran to date; the IKRC was tasked with providing for the needy as well as centralizing relief efforts during the war, coordinating logistical efforts, compensating the injured, and providing aid to the families of martyrs.[61]

The consequences of the regime's wartime developmentalist policies were twofold. On the one hand, its social welfare projects, particularly in the countryside, brought rural populations into the urban fold, as "people, commodities, and sociocultural values and behavior began to move back and forth between rural and urban settings with ever greater ease."[62] As Kaveh Ehsani has noted, desires for upward mobility among many in the lower classes, reflected in their increased literacy, acquisition of jobs in the cities, and purchase of cars and electronic goods, were a direct by-product of the regime's statist developmental push. On the other hand, the lower classes' greater access to basic goods and social welfare as a result of national economic policies meant that their livelihoods became increasingly reliant on the ebbs and flows of the market and domestic economic trends.[63]

This dependency proved tenuous with the end of the Iran-Iraq War in 1988. The subsequent death of Ayatollah Khomeini in 1989 ushered in a new decade of postwar reconstruction and pragmatism under the presidency of Akbar Hashemi-Rafsanjani and the leadership of Ayatollah Khomeini's successor, Ayatollah Ali Khamenei. After a decade of self-imposed economic isolation, Rafsanjani's government—like those of many other countries at the time—endeavored to integrate itself into the new global economy by requesting technical assistance and credit approval from the International Monetary Fund (IMF).[64] The resulting structural adjustment policy recommendations led to official promotion of the standard economic liberalization model; in practice, however, opposition from more statist factions in the government resulted in a contradictory blend of liberalization with state-led economic reform.[65] Indeed, in an effort to maintain and expand on its revolutionary and wartime promises, the new government instituted a set of postwar social protections. This included the expansion of health insurance to previously uninsured segments of the population as well as a universal price subsidies scheme for bread, rice, cooking fuel, electricity, and gasoline. Price subsidies were to alleviate the financial burden created by the new government's loosening of price controls.[66]

Rafsanjani's intention with his economic agenda was to establish a period of growth-oriented planning that shifted the postwar ideological landscape from collective austerity to individual prosperity.[67] As Rafsanjani stated, "Asceticism and disuse of holy consumption will create deprivation and a lack of drive to produce, work, and develop [economically]."[68] In attempting to institute this liberal turn in Iran's economy, Rafsanjani tasked a cadre of experts and specialists to effectively shape Iran's developmental trajectory. Technocratic rule, sequentially, motivated a postwar social order characterized by the popular valuation of educational credentialing, consumerism, and capital accumulation.[69] Iran's march toward a global market economy created expansive urban development and urban migration and the rapid growth of highly affluent social groups. The war-drained economy experienced an upswing.

By 1991, however, the country's economy took a turn for the worse. In an effort to maximize oil production, the government invested $5 billion in the oil sector in 1991; oil revenues nonetheless declined, dropping from $16 billion in 1991 to $14 billion in 1993, straining the economy.[70] Adding to Iran's economic woes, a sharp rise in non-oil imports ($28 billion in 1991) as compared to a moderate rise in exports ($19 billion in 1992) triggered a trade deficit and increased Iran's foreign debts.[71] In order to mitigate the economic crisis, Rafsanjani's government cut subsidies to large families, halved imports, and implemented austerity measures.[72] Rapid upsurges in inflation and unemployment followed, particularly burdening Iran's poor, who found it increasingly difficult to better their livelihoods. Finding that they could no longer afford to not work for pay, many lower-class women began entering the labor force for the first time,[73] leading to a greater feminization of work, a trend I observed during the period of my fieldwork (described in chapter 2).

The Rafsanjani-era economic crisis paved the way for Mohammad Khatami's rise to power in 1997 and the emergence of a new reformist period in Iran. Khatami's message of hope resonated with the disillusioned urban masses, who had come to expect upward mobility in Iran's postwar developmentalist state. Public discourse in Iran now centered on the ideas of civil society, rights, and "dialogue among civilizations."[74] Literacy rates increased, as 97 percent of those between the ages of six and twenty-nine became literate by the year 2000, and women came to constitute the majority (64 percent) of university students.[75] Social justice, a keyword during Khatami's 1997 presidential campaign that alluded to the egalitarian promises of the revolution, was used to legitimate the expansion of Iran's social welfare system, which helped lead to declines in absolute poverty rates.[76]

Nevertheless, Khatami's welfare expansion only did so much to relieve the economic burdens of the disenfranchised. Welfare spending was concentrated on social insurance, a benefit enjoyed mainly by those—namely, the middle and upper classes—who worked in the regulated formal economic sector.[77] Those who worked in the informal labor market, by virtue of their unregulated work, were much harder to enroll in welfare schemes, though some organizations such as the IKRC provided benefits based on need rather than employment status.[78] Simultaneously, the Khatami administration resumed Rafsanjani's liberal economic policies that aimed to incorporate the Islamic Republic into the international market economy. A new five-year plan aimed at the period from 2000 to 2004 called for economic reconstruction and comprised an ambitious program to privatize state-dominated industries, including the financial, telecommunication, and power generation sectors.[79] While the economy experienced growth as a result of the plan, a continued shortage of job opportunities led to persistent unemployment. Similarly, notwithstanding a 3.8 percent increase in per capita income as a result of the government's success in curbing the population growth rate,[80] income inequality and perceptions of social inequality—fueled by thwarted expectations of economic prospects—endured.

The presidency of Mahmoud Ahmadinejad in 2005 once again brought the revolution's populist and conservative politics back to the table. Indeed, Ahmadinejad won on the double platform of reinforcing Iran's national security and executing the populist promises of the revolutionary era in an effort to appease those who had felt increasingly frustrated by the slow pace of economic reforms during the Khatami era. Ahmadinejad positioned himself as a *mostaz'afin* champion by promising to place Iran's oil wealth on dinner tables. He appealed to resource-strapped but upwardly aspirant social groups who saw in Ahmadinejad a way to realize the socioeconomic mobility they had come to expect after years of state developmental efforts.

Ahmadinejad came to office at a time when global oil prices were at a high. This enabled his administration to inject oil revenue into the economy and increase spending on imports and domestic infrastructure projects, much to the dismay of critics who presciently argued that such fiscal policies would only fuel inflation, thereby blunting any benefits that would potentially accrue to the poor.[81] Despite its statist inclinations and initial support of large-scale state subsidies for food and gasoline, the Ahmadinejad administration soon sought the guidance of the International Monetary Fund to help shape its economic policies. A blended populist/private model emerged, whereby the government came to privatize state-owned enterprises, but provide low-income individuals with the dividend shares.[82] The administration also cut price subsidies for petrol and for staple resources and services including bread and public transport, while stating that savings would be distributed to the lower classes.[83] Despite the economic boom of the mid-2000s, by the end of Ahmadinejad's first term in 2009, inflation was at an all-time high and unemployment, particularly among the youth population, continued to plague the economy.[84]

Ahmadinejad entered his second term in office on the heels of a protest movement unseen in Iran's post-revolutionary history. The declared landslide win of Ahmadinejad against his primary opponent, Mir-Hossein Mousavi, prompted thousands of distraught Mousavi supporters—many of whom belonged to the newly emergent middle classes that had been educated through the developmental efforts of the regime[85]—to pour into the streets to dispute the election results, which they believed had been rigged. The unrest surrounding the election carried into the future, influencing the administration's economic policies. In December 2010, the Ahmadinejad government embarked on a subsidies reform plan with the consultation of the International Monetary Fund. Under the targeted subsidies plan, all subsidies were to be gradually liberalized and eventually phased out by 2015.[86] The cuts encompassed key consumer goods, including gasoline, natural gas, electricity, and food, and were "in line with recommendations from global financial organizations which advised Iran to get rid of a heavily subsidized economy if it wanted to boost its economic power."[87]

While the administration initially planned to alleviate the economic burden of the subsidies cuts on the poor by providing targeted cash transfers solely to lower-income households, after the events of 2009, the transfers were universalized to include every Iranian household in an effort to appease Iran's middle-income groups.[88] In 2011 the government began to provide monthly cash transfers in the amount of 45,000 *toman*s (approximately 40 USD in 2011) to each household member.[89] Numerous low-income families I spoke with at the time found the cash transfers useful, but not sufficient to alleviate the difficulty of making ends meet in the wake of Iran's steadily rising inflation. Subsequently, many turned to loans from family members, employers, and/or banks to supplement their incomes, a practice that often mired them in debt.

Incumbent President Hassan Rouhani has continued these transfers while cutting additional subsidies after assuming office in 2013. While cash transfers were initially provided to all households, families deemed high-income by the Rouhani administration have been excluded from the program since 2016.[90] Notwithstanding, due to the plummeting value of the *toman* against the dollar and rising market prices, both intensified by the U.S. withdrawal from the Iran Nuclear Deal,[91] these allowances have lost much of their value for the families they do target.

Indeed, when President Rouhani took office in 2013, the exchange rate was around 3,600 *toman*s. This rate plummeted by 35 percent by April 2018 due to fears of a breakdown of the nuclear deal and a return of sanctions.[92] By May 8, 2018, when U.S. President Donald Trump officially withdrew from the Iran Nuclear Deal, one dollar could be exchanged in Iran's black market for around 6,700 *toman*s, while the government set its own official exchange rate at 4,200 *toman*s, deeming exchanges at any other rate illegal. Washington's phased reimposition of sanctions, which ended in November 2018, led to a precipitous devaluation of the *toman*, which by April 2019 stood at around 14,000 *toman*s per dollar. Over the next three years, the economy is expected to shrink by 1.4 percent as oil exports are predicted to decline to half their current levels.[93] Domestic economic protests—sparked by proposed increases in the price of basic goods in December 2017 and continuing in a more subdued fashion at the time of this writing as a result of increasing inflation—are testament to Iran's weakened economy.[94] Given the current state of economic affairs, cash transfers have grown progressively more inadequate as a social safety net for Iran's low-income groups. Facing one of the greatest economic recessions since the 1979 Revolution and the Iran-Iraq War, lower-class Iranians today, as in the past, shoulder the burden of Iran's economic crisis.

## Moving On Up

However, given the history of Iran's lower strata to not only survive hardship, but to advance, it is not a surprise that rather than accept their fate, the disenfranchised continue the battle for social mobility in the present day by relying on their own initiatives to improve their lot in life. Like those of past generations, the practices of the lower-class youth in this book are shaped not only by their position as underprivileged members of Iranian society, but also by the structure of constraints—and opportunities (described in chapter 1)—that they perceive to be surrounding them. To be sure, the post-revolutionary state's attempts to incorporate Iran into the modern world economy simultaneously worked to raise the aspirations of these very same youth who have now come to expect and struggle for a better life for themselves than their parents had. Individualistic strategies of mobility revolving around facework become the defining feature of these attempts and situate these youth as active agents of change rather than as passive victims wholly susceptible to the ebbs and flows of the economy.[95]

Here, I take as my point of departure Harold Wilensky's consolation prize theory of mobility, which asserts that people climb numerous ladders throughout their lifetime and that "falling behind on one . . . may neither cause an irrevocable loss of social position nor yield much sense of deprivation; some other basis of social differentiation will provide a new start."[96] In this view, people who experience downward mobility in occupation may console themselves through various alternative mobility prizes, including "higher income in a lower-status job, entrepreneurship, intermarriage, [and] horizontal shifts to more pleasant work."[97] In its critique of empirical studies that focus exclusively on occupational transitions, particularly between generations, as the sole metric for social mobility, Wilsensky's theory opens space for incorporating a person's own mobility experiences and status shifts as a source of social change.[98] Early studies by Max Weber and Gino Germani, too, emphasized the importance of more discriminating analyses of mobility—analyses that disclose the multiple moves that a person makes throughout his life.[99] These initial studies argued that expectations of large leaps in occupational and economic success as a prerequisite for mobility gloss over all the other types of "short-distance"[100] movements, both economic and social, that are subjectively meaningful for both the individual and his community. These small but meaningful incremental upward shifts, which I term *incremental mobility*, establish various status hierarchies according to which the mobile actor identifies himself in relation to his peers and perceives himself as doing well. These movements may further exert a significant influence on personal values and behavior.[101] Ethnographic studies in the Middle East, for instance, have shown how struggles to win small socioeconomic gains may confer a sense of dignity to low-income actors.[102]

In the presence of socioeconomic deprivation and perceived structural rigidity, the youth in this book create an alternative basis of social differentiation to improve their lives, one deeply rooted in their attachment to Iranian cultural norms. By publicly abiding by certain socially sanctioned rules of behavior—that is, a moral code[103]—revolving around the cultural practice of saving face, face-savers become moral actors by projecting an image of "goodness" in front of those with whom they "share[] activities, who provide material and emotional assistance, or both, and who receives the same in return."[104] Of course, these youth, in an attempt to define themselves and their place in the world, sometimes question the face rules and act in ways that contradict them in private. Nonetheless, they ultimately believe in the inherent worth of cultivating the moral virtues of the face system, deeming it the "right way" to live.[105] A strongly shared system of values in the urban communities I studied contributed to a deeply embedded process of informal social control that further reinforced the merit of engaging in locally appropriate behavior.[106] Doing so enabled face-savers to maintain their dignity in the face of economic degradation by providing them with moral benchmarks by which they could judge themselves in relation to others and by which others could evaluate their moral worth. Working to demonstrate their "goodness" simultaneously enabled face-savers to incrementally move on up within the social hierarchy of their communities, an opportunity that was denied to those who demonstrably lacked face. In this way, my findings indicate that the cultural homogeneity and cohesiveness that exists in these communities, create, as Jennifer Sherman argues, "greater social pressure on the poor to be culturally acceptable according to the existing standards."[107]

Morality, which is the socially sanctioned set of "norms and prescriptions . . . [that pertain] to personal responsibilies and duties toward others," thus forms the foci of face-savers' social worlds.[108] Drawing from Sherman's framing of moral capital as a tradeable resource used by the economically disadvantaged to gain community rewards, I argue that positive evaluations of their morality provide face-savers with a boost in status that also allows them to secure small yet meaningful social and economic benefits, which, in turn, operate to increase status gains. Such benefits have the net effect of integrating disenfranchised young men who are expected to become the future breadwinners of their families more fully into Iran's socioeconomic scene while simultaneously providing a means by which poor young women are able to stand on a more equal economic footing with their male counterparts. Morality becomes what Pierre Bourdieu terms symbolic capital, a "symbolic boundary marker" that can facilitate access to other forms of real and symbolic capital, such as connections or jobs among those most encumbered by Iran's economic recessions.[109]

Incremental mobility is thus the outcome of a deep socially and culturally patterned process that defines the rules of the face game or, as Peter Gries highlights, the "battle over the zero-sum resource of social status."[110] Acceptance and embrace of the rules become the way to win. The pages that follow will not only explore the face game, its context, and its rules, but also provide an on-the-ground description of the ways that face-savers play by the rules in their day-to-day lives. In the process, it is my hope that this book provides a window into the rich and sometimes contradictory socioeconomic and cultural order that constitutes present-day Iran.

## Fieldwork

This study began with my initial entrance into the field in the summer of 2008, during which time I conducted preliminary fieldwork in the capital city of Tehran for a period of two months. The beginning of my fieldwork roughly coincided with Iran's commodity-linked economic boom and a general atmosphere of increased consumption.[111] In 2010 I moved to the northern Iranian city of Sari to begin the official fieldwork for this project. As my observations of daily life in Iran continued for almost two years through 2012 and persisted for thirteen months between the years 2013 through 2019, I was witness to the increasing imposition of foreign sanctions and an ensuing economic downturn that was marked by unprecedented stagflation. Throughout this time, the youth and the families I came to know looked on as daily life made a turn for the worse; their relentless pursuit of the good life was made that much harder in the wake of Iran's economic crises.

The narratives presented in this study largely come from participant observation fieldwork I conducted in low-income neighborhoods and homes as well as in parks, streets, and shopping sites in the cities of Sari and Tehran. While noting how people expressed their opinions, morals, and attitudes, I strategically positioned myself to observe their behavior as well as to listen to—and many times participate in—their conversations.[112] While there was no fixed sample size in this type of community observational study, over the years that I conducted fieldwork, I spent enough time at various sites to be able to find recurring patterns in people's observable practices and discourses. Unstructured, informal interviews with forty-four low-income youth in Sari and Tehran, largely revolving around individual aspirations, cultural beliefs about saving face, role models, and opinions of family and community, reinforced the observational data and provided additional narratives of how young people managed under conditions of economic hardship.

The youth in this study ranged in age from fifteen to twenty-nine years and predominately came from households where the median monthly income was equivalent to or lower than the minimum wage at the time of fieldwork.[113] Between 2010 and 2019, the minimum wage in Iran ranged anywhere from around 400,000 to 1,500,000 *tomans* per month. Because of inflation and sanctions, the value of the Iranian rial took a tremendous nosedive during the course of my research. While in 2010, 1 dollar was approximately the equivalent of 1,000 *tomans*, in 2019, 1 dollar was approximately 14,000 *tomans*.[114] To compensate, minimum wage rose during this time period, thus accounting for the drastic difference in income levels of the individuals I knew.

Most of the youth I knew were either high school graduates or in high school. Some were high school dropouts. Few were college students. For those who were working, occupations were diverse: peddlers, low-wage service workers in the informal economy, housewives, seamstresses, carpenters, entrepreneurs, and shop and salon apprentices.[115]

The majority of the time I spent in the field in Iran occurred in the northern capital city of Sari in Mazandaran province, located near the Caspian coastline. Of the years I spent conducting fieldwork in Iran, I also engaged in conversations with and observations of residents in the *payin-e shahr* (low-income areas) of Tehran. In both cities, I also found that observations and encounters with residents in the *bala-ye shahr* (uptown areas) provided a more holistic understanding of the norms, values, and practices of the youth I was studying. Using Tehran as an additional site of inquiry allowed me to verify the themes in thought, discourse, and practice that I was observing in the more provincial locale of Sari. I initially chose Tehran and Sari because they differ substantially in size and in economies, are located in two different environmental zones, and have distinct urban configurations. Tehran is the national capital, the heart of Iran's industries, and one of the largest cities in the world. Rural-urban migration to Tehran has created a large urban poor youth population whose experiences are shaped by spatial dynamics not present in provincial cities like Sari. Indeed, there is a distinct geographical divide by class lines in Tehran, with the majority of Tehran's poor concentrated in the southern districts of the capital. Middle classes commonly occupy the middle segments of the city and upper classes reside in the north. Alternatively, the second capital, Sari, is host to a relatively more integrated poor urban youth population that is not nearly as cordoned off geographically according to class, although poor areas do exist in Sari, as I describe in detail below. The presence of these divergent urban configurations in Sari and Tehran thus initially provided an ideal comparative axis for assessing the effect of social-structural contexts on individual perceptions of opportunities and incentives. Despite these structural variations, I ultimately came to observe similar trends in thought, practice, and discourse in both cities that are reflected in the narrative examples and quotes presented in this book.

As other ethnographers have described of their own fieldwork, my fieldwork similarly entailed "hanging out," namely, watching, listening, participating in activities, and/or talking to individuals wherever I turned up,[116] all the while paying particular attention to patterns in thought and lived experience, as evidenced through their conversations and daily practices.[117] I hung out in homes, neighborhoods, mosques, and shops—anywhere I thought that lower-class youth and families lived, worked, or frequented. I used my own personal networks and preexisting friendships in Iran to establish my legitimacy as a trusted member of the community. In so doing, I was able to create rapport with the young men and women, thereby enabling me to hang out and engage in conversations with them.

Hanging out also involved spending time with youth in their homes or in local institutions such as coffee shops, boutiques, and bookstores. At other times, I participated in activities ranging from teaching English to helping out with occasional household chores. I also volunteered on several occasions in four nongovernmental organizations (NGOs) located in Tehran and two NGOs located in Sari whose missions were to provide charitable and educational services to low-income youth and their families. My observations in the NGOs, particularly those located in Tehran, were important in that they enabled me to observe some of the most impoverished districts of the capital city and a large cross section of its members, understanding, in the process, some of their shared struggles, concerns, and values. I also learned of the criteria that some of the more privileged members of the community—the NGO workers themselves—used as benchmarks to measure youth who "succeeded."

In all of these activities, my primary goal was to learn as much as possible about how youth managed their daily lives and how they attempted to improve their lot in life. I shared meals and endless cups of hot tea with families. I walked with youth as they went about their daily errands. I listened to young men and women as they joked, worried, and formulated strategies to deal with school, money, recreational activities, employment, friendships, and relationships. I observed the environments in which they lived, ate, worked, and interacted with community members, with neighbors, with parents, and with siblings. I listened to them as they talked about their desires, hope, dreams, and expectations. As Daniel Dohan has noted, this process of spending time with different residents in a variety of different locations allows the researcher to capture as broad a "cross section of experiences" as possible, thereby enabling a more representative "slice of life" in low-income communities than a more limited ethnographic focus on a specific site or group would have allowed.[118] This data collection strategy of maximizing the cross section of youth I observed informs the analytic ethnographic methodology that lies at the heart of this study.[119]

To be able to navigate within Iran's maze of cultural nuances and its social life, in particular, takes a great deal of perseverance. The fact that I was a middle-class female who did not grow up in the country meant that I was not a true insider and prevented me from being privy to certain conversations and gaining access to certain sites that someone not from my background may have been able to observe. I was seen as comparatively different from the youth that I was studying, someone whose social and economic experiences were fundamentally distinct from those around me. My gender meant that I was not able to engage in many conversations with groups of young men or to sit in teahouses and enter sports arenas, both of which were largely the domain of men. However, my ethnic background as an Iranian and the fact that I was close in age to many of the youth that I came to know made me privy to forms of knowledge that I would not have had access to otherwise. My shared identity and language with my informants and my own past experiences of having both lived in and visited the country growing up ultimately helped me to gain their acceptance. It further enabled me to be sensitive to cultural cues embedded within my informants' behavior that facilitated my analyses.

Being female meant that I was wise to conversations and gained access to realms that were not easily available to men, including women's salons, beaches, and female gatherings. Ultimately, I found that being seen as somewhat of an outsider became an asset to me, as both young men and women were more willing to share personal details of their lives with me, knowing that I would not divulge their information to their friends or families. Through my conversations, observations, and friendships, I became an onlooker to the rhythm of daily life among some of Iran's most disadvantaged. I shared moments of solitude and prayer with them as well as instances of sheer joy, including weddings, social functions, and workplace lunches. In all of this, I was witness not just to their struggles for dignity, but also to their incredible resilience in the face of adversity.

While this book revolves around the theme of saving face, I initially entered the field to understand how young, poor Iranians manage under conditions of hardship. What I eventually came to find as my fieldwork progressed was that normative values revolving around how one should present oneself in front of others exerted a strong influence on these young people's everyday choices and coping strategies, and the way others reacted to them. In short, I found that culture, as manifested through saving face, structured social life among these youth. What this meant for me, as an interlocutor and a participant in their lives, was that I had to learn how to modify my own behavior in order to similarly save face in the settings in which I found myself.

This entailed wearing a *manto* and head shawl even in the privacy of my interlocutors' homes, despite the fact I had grown accustomed to taking these clothing items off among my own circle of friends and family.[120] Saving face also necessitated that I was not seen socializing with unrelated men in public, reserving my conversations with men in family settings, during my tutoring sessions, or through my interviews.

My own subdued mannerisms further helped me a great deal, as they were aligned with cultural expectations of female behavior and facilitated my evaluation as a *ba shakhsiyat* (with character/reputable) young woman.[121] Being the daughter of a *seyyed* (a descendant of the Prophet Mohammad) was also a key factor in the warm reception I received by one community member that I knew of and the tutoring sessions she helped facilitate for me among a group of young men.

Being a doctoral student (and later, a professor) from America constituted one of the greatest facilitators of my acceptance into many of these communities. It was not only a sign of my work ethic, literacy, and perceived financial standing, but, in many ways, my work was associated with being a *farhangi* (cultured) and *ba kelas* (classy) person. As the young men and women I knew held aspirations to advance both educationally and in terms of their careers, I was often seen as a conduit for information about universities, classes, and entrepreneurial ventures in the United States.[122]

During the course of my fieldwork, there were many times when it was not possible to take notes during the course of normal interactions and observations in the midst of casual conversations. During these times, I often resorted to typing detailed, systematic notes of observations, interactions, and conversations immediately at the conclusion of each day's fieldwork, thus averting any lapses in memory that could misconstrue people's speech patterns. I analyzed my written observations by coding themes in my interlocutors' behavior and speech and the meanings that they attributed to their practices.[123] The relationship between saving face and socioeconomic opportunity emerged as dominant in the observations.

As the fieldwork was conducted among native Persian speakers, all of the quotes in this text are my own English translations of the original Persian. Following sociological conventions of informant confidentiality, I have used fictitious names throughout this book to identify people, streets, most neighborhoods, and most establishments. To further protect informants' anonymity, I have also occasionally changed identifying details.

## Sari

While much has been written on Tehran, the capital of the Islamic Republic of Iran and the country's largest city, very few sources have mentioned Sari, despite its historical significance.[124] The capital of Mazandaran, Sari is home to around half a million people.[125] Bordered by the Caspian Sea in the north and protected by the Alborz mountain range in the south, Mazandaran's strategic location meant that it was one of the last regions of Iran to strongly resist, for a time, the conquering armies of the Arabs when they entered the former Caspian coastal provinces of the Sasanian Empire in 650–651 CE.[126]

During this time, Tabarestan—the former name of Mazandaran—was ruled by local rulers or *espahbad* who formed the Dabuyid dynasty of Tabarestan.[127] Farrukhan the Great, the second *espahbad* of the Dabuyid dynasty, founded the seat of the dynasty, the city of Sari.[128] The Dabuyids ruled Tabarestan from their capital in Sari until 761, when they were conquered by the Abbasid empire under the rule of the Caliph Al-Mansur.[129] In the eighteenth century, Sari once again became a significant base, as Agha Mohammad Khan, the founder of the Qajar dynasty, established his center of rule there until 1786, when he transferred it to Tehran.[130]

While it never again served as the imperial heart of Iran, Sari remained an important center. As the provincial capital, Sari was the residence of the governor general (who was often a Qajar prince), associated high-ranking civil and military personnel, and the governor prince's entourage of other Qajar princes and princesses.[131] The presence of these individuals fostered an aristocratic atmosphere in the capital city, and by the early nineteenth century, one could sense a clear social stratification in Sari, with a person's class, appearance, and mannerisms determining the position he occupied in the city's social structure.[132] Indeed, the social structure of the province during this time was similar to that of a cone, with the prince governor occupying the top, subordinate governors and military commanders, merchants, clergy, artisans, and petty landowners occupying the middle, and the peasantry occupying the base.[133] However, by 1843, with the decline of the economy and the removal of the prince governor, the social stratification of Sari, at least at the top of the cone, changed: the landowning class and military force occupied a higher position than the governor general and merchants, who fell in their social position and wealth.[134] Nevertheless, despite these changes at the top of the cone, Sari's distinct social status hierarchy remained intact.

During the reign of Reza Shah Pahlavi (1925–1941), Sari turned into an important site of infrastructural development when it became host to a major railway station on the Trans-Iranian Railway line. Completed in 1938 and constituting Iran's first railway line, the Trans-Iranian Railway connected the northern port of Bandar Shah in the Caspian to Sari and extended to the port of Bandar Shahpur (linked to the city of Dezful) in the Persian Gulf.[135] By going through Mazandaran's mountainous terrain, the line further provided easy access from the provincial capital of Sari to the nation's capital at Tehran. As a symbol of the Pahlavi regime's aspirations for modernization, the railway laid the foundation for further economic development in provinces including Mazandaran. Indeed, by 1941, there were more than fifty thousand wage earners (up from fewer than a thousand in 1925) employed in Iran's large factories, 75 percent of which were concentrated in Tehran, Tabriz, Isfahan, Gilan, and Mazandaran.[136] Rapid industrial growth thus made Mazandaran, like Tehran, a hub of economic growth, paving the way for rural migration to its cities, particularly during the reign of Mohammad Reza Shah (1941–1979).

As in Tehran province, rural-urban migration to the cities of Mazandaran province began in earnest in the 1960s and continues to the present day. Many of the first- and second-generation rural migrants in Sari who constituted the bulk of my research resided in the peri-urban neighborhoods that partly comprise the *payin-e shahr* of the city located behind the city's railway tracks. Others, like the Karimis, resided in the peri-urban, low-income neighborhoods of Aftab Avenue in the perimeter of the city—also considered the *payin-e shahr*—which leads to the Caspian coastline.[137]

Throughout the course of my research in Sari, many migrants would often speak about how they were going to visit their families and homes in their *mahal* (village), suggesting their strong bond with their villages of origin and solid, trans-regional kinship ties.[138] Despite their separation from their extended family members and the economic hardships they faced in Sari, these migrants struggled on in the city, hoping that a move to Sari, widely considered one of Iran's main agricultural, touristic, and farming hubs, would steadily improve their lot in life and distinguish them from their rural counterparts. Many family members who stayed behind in the villages similarly considered a move to Sari as indicative of a better life. "When we go back to Mashhad," Mohammad Karimi's thirteen-year-old sister, Farnaz, told me with a smile one day, "they say, 'oh you're Northerners now!' They don't even know where the North is! When we tell them we went to the sea, they say 'lucky for you!'" Relatives saw the Karimis' migration to Sari and its accompaniments—a house of one's own and trips to the sea—as luxuries attainable to the lucky few who risked making the move. Farnaz, in turn, implicitly mocked these family members for their lack of knowledge and attempted to draw distinctions between her own sociocultural knowledge and that of her more rural kin.

Comprising the main hub of social, economic, and cultural activity in Mazandaran, Sari has steadily urbanized over the years to encompass neighborhoods like the one where the Karimis live and which, at one point, consisted of rural farmlands. Luxury shopping malls, universities, fast-food restaurants, and traditional coffeehouses mimicking those found in the heart of the city have sprung up along Aftab Avenue. Homes like the Karimis' are located on Aftab's side roads, where they stand disjointedly near beautifully constructed villas of the middle- and upper-class Saravi residents who have chosen to move away from the hustle of the city center and live in these more quiet, pastoral neighborhoods.[139]

The heart of Sari itself has grown into a small metropolitan area, where one can find many of the amenities that once existed only in megacities like Tehran. Because cultural institutions dominate in Sari, as they do in Tehran, it was often hard for me to tell the difference between some of the places and services I frequented and used in Sari and their equivalents in Tehran. Online food service deliveries, upscale Western-style cafés, art galleries, bookstores, restaurants, malls, various colleges and universities, cultural houses, music centers, gyms, and museums are scattered throughout the main arteries of the city. Due to its relatively small size, it is easy to traverse Sari by bus and/or inexpensive taxi lines, making the entire city—and these facilities—accessible to a wide swath of the population, including many of the youth I knew.

In 2018, Sari, under the supervision of then mayor Mehdi Obouri, had become a competitive candidate for gaining status as a *kalanshahr* (metropolis), thus opening the way for Sari to become one of Iran's major cities. Many Saravis I knew—regardless of their class background—were proud to call Sari their home and considered living in Sari a step up from living in Iran's other small provincial towns. Youth like Mohammad and Farnaz Karimi saw living in Sari as a manifestation of their upward mobility, and most, like their Tehrani counterparts, had aspirations for a better socioeconomic life than that of their parents. In an attempt to make their dreams a reality, they found it imperative to keep up appearances.

## Face-Savers in Sari and Tehran

While the youth I observed and spoke with over the years were a varied group that included farm laborers, artists, street vendors, hairstylists, and students, despite their diversity, they were all deeply aware of the fact that they had to protect their face from loss in order to uphold their various societal standings.[140] This was not an easy task. These youth constituted part of the bottom rung of Iranian society and were often referred to in the elite's common parlance as *dehatis* from the *payin-e shahr*. In Tehran, this *payin-e shahr* comprises the southern areas of the city, south of Tehran's grand bazaar. Sari, despite its more integrated urban configuration, nevertheless has some neighborhoods where the majority of residents are lower-income rural-urban migrants. While one may find middle-class people who opt to live in these areas because of the low cost of housing and proximity to their businesses, the majority of the inhabitants are rural migrants from the poor and working classes. Poverty has an outward, physical dimension in both cities: the further south one goes in Tehran, the more congested the streets, apartment buildings, and houses become. Physical signs give away one's low socioeconomic status as soon as one approaches the streets that demarcate the southern portions of the capital city. In Sari, poverty is often demarcated by the exposed, unfinished exteriors of houses and apartment buildings, the lack of paved roads, the spotty presence of urban infrastructure, and the presence of domestic fowl in alleyways and residential backyards.

Sari, notwithstanding the presence of these low-income neighborhoods, has a geographically more integrated class structure than does Tehran, the latter which is divided into north-south and east-west axes according to class. This characteristic largely distinguishes Tehran from the traditional Iranian city, where historically both the rich and poor lived in the same neighborhood or next door to one another because the kin structure required more prosperous family members to support those less advantaged: "this prevented any embarrassment that might arise from the poverty and deprivation of a close relative."[141] Despite the recent construction of apartment complexes, highways, and wide avenues, Sari has more or less retained this traditional city fabric.

Alternatively, in Tehran, construction efforts under the Shah led to the creation of a new city fabric in the capital, which can be seen today in the city's sprawling wide avenues and Western-style houses and apartment complexes, as well as in the geographic division of social classes. This north-south/east-west duality, however, has been reduced to some extent in recent years with the construction of highways linking the north and the south. The establishment of cultural institutions and metro stations in the south have further enabled Tehranis from all social classes, like their Saravi counterparts, easy access to various parts of the city (see chapter 1).

Many of the youth I spoke with and who lived in south Tehran or in Sari's lower-income neighborhoods came from rural migrant families who originally resided in the villages surrounding Tehran and Sari. Their migration is one in a long line of rural-urban migration that has characterized Iran for the past several decades. Post-revolutionary (1979–1988) Mazandaran was one of the few provinces outside Tehran that was particularly accommodating to the needs of these low-income migrants, as the Islamic regime, through the Urban Land Organization, transferred undeveloped and abandoned tracts of land to low-income groups that lacked land and housing ownership.[142] The history of land provision in the province coupled with Mazandaran's rich soil and fertile climate has meant that many of these households are economically above the national average.[143] Mazandaran is further home to a vibrant civil society scene; it has the third-highest number of NGOs in Iran,[144] many of which are targeted to improving the quality of life for low-income and marginalized groups. In 2004, for instance, Mazandaran was host to 645 NGOs, comprising 8.1 percent of the total number of NGOs in Iran, while Tehran was host to 1,225 NGOs, comprising 15.4 percent of the total number of NGOs in the country.[145] Indeed, for its part, Tehran is host to the largest share of NGOs in Iran; post-revolutionary economic policy also saw Tehran as the largest distributor of confiscated land.[146]

Unique about such post-revolutionary social empowerment programs has been their ability to normalize aspirations across classes. The motivations, strategies, and choices of some Saravi and Tehrani youth can be explained by their internalization of their desires for a better life—desires that have been actively cultivated in a climate characterized by pro-poor state measures.[147] How do youth act out their ambitions and negotiate their status within such environments? The following pages attempt to answer just that.

## Précis of the Book

The central argument of this book is that within conditions of poverty, cultural practices—in this case, the face system—provide some youth in Iran with an alternative basis of social differentiation to improve their lives. Each of the chapters expounds on this premise. The first chapter of this book explores the history and structure of facework in Iran. Upon examining the interlinkages between saving face and cultural norms of modesty, I argue that face-savers uphold a moral code that is comprised of four rules in order to mitigate threats to their face. These rules, which consist of self-sufficiency, hard work, purity, and appearance, serve as moral evaluative distinctions by which face-savers can measure their own integrity vis-à-vis their peers, and by which others in their community can evaluate the face-saver's moral worth. This leads to a micro-system of stratification within low-income communities, whereby those who have saved face hold a higher status than those who have not. In the absence of clear economic distinctions among poor youth, the face system and the rules it encompasses are an alternative pathway to incrementally moving up the proverbial ladder. The face rules provide the young men and women who successfully abide by them with a form of symbolic moral capital that they can then "trade in" for social and economic benefits.[148] The greater their perceived moral stock, the greater the ability of face-savers to use their moral capital to expand their social and economic opportunities.

Chapter 2 examines the moral norms surrounding hard work and self-sufficiency. The importance of face among face-savers primarily hinges on their ability to be seen as economically self-sufficient, responsible, and hardworking. For young men, evidence of economic self-sufficiency and work ethic is key for proving their worth and masculinity to others in the community. This push to be seen as "responsible enough" or "man enough," in turn, stipulates the prioritization of jobs that pay relatively well over the status of the job. Whether the work itself is morally ambiguous—such as dealing goods in the black market or swindling customers—is not important for saving face as long as young men can get away with a lie. Similarly, for young women, work is one of the primary means by which they can avert threats to their own and their family's face and signal to peers that they are doing well for themselves. While economic deprivation is the primary driver of these women's initial entry into the labor force, the sustained appeal of work is the direct consequence of its ability to enable young women to be seen as good and competent daughters and wives. Those young men and women who can demonstrate that they are self-sufficient hard workers—and have the street smarts, family support, and risk-taking abilities to assist in the effort—are often the first to be incentivized by others.

Chapter 3 turns outward, examining the physical dimension of facework. I argue that the risk of losing face among face-savers hinges primarily on being exposed as poor. The stigma attached to wearing unkempt clothes, not being "with it," having a low-status job, or living in a barely furnished house leads youth to take calculated steps to present a middle-class front to others. Posturing through manipulation of one's mannerisms and physical appearance is the most effective means of doing so. In the acquisition of moral capital, one's physical appearance, knowledge about what's in fashion, and consumption of the "right" things become tokens in the face game. By presenting themselves as *ba kelas* and belonging to middle-class society, face-savers are able to extend their personal networks to encompass the right people: those who can facilitate their actual entrée into the world of the middle class.

Chapter 4 takes us inward, exploring the rise of public moral discourses surrounding the proper Islamic citizen. It describes how the

Iranian cultural sphere has been defined and redefined to produce an image of the model young Muslim. I show how these discourses have been co-opted by face-savers and their communities to give rise to prescriptions about what constitutes morally pure behavior. Since such behavior is perceived by communities to be a manifestation of one's inner moral compass, families discipline face-savers to be hyper-vigilant in their conduct and often discourage them from spending much time in public spaces "hanging out" with friends. Face-savers, too, are hyper-aware of their public behavior at any given moment, taking pains to ensure that they publicly demonstrate their inner goodness and work to hide any deviations from the norm. Ultimately, in proving their purity and differentiating themselves from morally impure others, face-savers are able to gain jobs and access to influential others.

In the conclusion, I discuss the implications of facework for our understanding of morality and socioeconomic mobility in the face of hardship. By imparting incremental social and economic "wins," facework provides a low-cost, high-impact tactic to improve one's lot in life in contemporary Iran. Simultaneously, in playing the face game day in and day out, one comes to embody the moral dispositions endorsed by the game. While it remains unclear how far the game can take a person, what is certain is that facework reveals a new arena for citizen engagement in Iran, one that simultaneously revolves around claims to one's right to dignity and to a better life.

1

# Saving Face

Whomsover thou seest in a religious habit, consider as a
pious and a good man, if you do not know what is hidden
in his mind: what business hath the Mohtesib [guardian of
public virtue] with the inside of the house?
—Saʻdi, *The Gulistan or Rose Garden*, 1865

With the inception of the 1979 Iranian Revolution, veiling became codified. In its literal sense, this meant that women had to wear a chador or
*manto* and headscarf in public and that men were not able to wear neck-
ties, shorts, or short-sleeve shirts—in short, anything that could reveal
their bodies or be considered symbolic of Western cultural influence.[1]
In its metaphorical sense, this meant that both men and women had
to veil certain aspects of their internal selves in public spaces. Public
behavior was subject to scrutiny; you could not be seen holding hands,
conversing with the opposite sex, smoking cigarettes, being boisterous,
or, in general, being too "obvious" in your actions without being rep-
rimanded by the morals police or by neighbors and members of your
community.[2] The Qurʼanic verse "enjoining the right and forbidding the
wrong" (*amr beh maʻruf*) became the official order of the day and everyone was expected to abide by its rules and regulations, which authorized
modesty in both behavior and dress. To be modest, in turn, required
that people censor their instincts if these instincts were not in accord
with socially sanctioned rules; indeed, performing rituals of restraint
was indicative of a respectful person and one whose reputation would
not come under question.[3] Iranian societal ethics, as mandated by the
1979 Iranian Revolution, was thus defined by performative abidance by
the rules of modesty.

While veiling became officially mandated with the establishment of
the Islamic Republic, veiling in its more figurative sense has been an
informal part of Iranian culture for centuries. Iranian culture advances a

principle of contrast that centers on the dichotomy between the external (*zaher*) and the internal (*baten*); this philosophy can be traced to the pre-Islamic religion of Manichaeism, which developed in Iran during the Sasanian dynasty (224–650 CE).[4] At the heart of Manichaeism was the belief that a person's soul held more significance than his physical body. According to this view, the individual soul originates from a transcendent realm and is trapped in the external shell of the body, which is representative of the materialistic, terrestrial world; as such, the soul is constantly searching to escape its physical shell and return to its origins in the transcendental sphere.[5]

It is this focus on the internal soul and spirit of the individual, rather than the external world, that forms the basis of Manichaeism. While the pre-Islamic religion of Zoroastrianism, which predates Manichaeism, also suggests similar concepts such as lightness versus darkness and the transcendent realm in its philosophies, it was Manichaeism that made the duality between the *zaher* and the *baten* explicit.[6] This dichotomy was observed in the various art forms—particularly paintings—that were associated with the religion and that were central to spreading its teachings. Indeed, in one of the most significant Manichaean books, the *Arzhang*, the prophet Mani visually depicts the ultimate objective of the believer to be the release of his inner light from the confines of the darkness that characterizes his bodily material shell: the unrealistic, two-dimensionality of Manichaean art further emphasizes the artificiality of the material world (in contrast to the purity of the inner soul) and, therefore, the inequality between one's external and internal selves.[7]

Manichaeism's emphasis on the importance of the soul and inner self came to be subsequently appropriated into Islamic mysticism.[8] In Sufistic doctrine, the external is considered to be the "outward-oriented," "animalistic," and "materialistic" self, while the internal is where the "real self" resides.[9] Since one's real internal self is the site of passions and thoughts that are often beyond one's control, the external must rein in these desires through "controlled expression."[10] By veiling one's self through norms of modesty and etiquette, one can hold one's "true feelings . . . in check" in public; by successfully manipulating the external in social interactions, one can thus present a "proper public face."[11] To allow the internal self to take over would be to lose one's reputation or *aberu*. Historically, then, Iranian culture is defined by performative abidance by cultural norms or rules that take *aberu* (or, as I define it, face) and personal dignity in direct interactions as its ultimate aim—a goal that continues to the present day under the ruling Islamic regime.[12]

## On *Aberu*

In Iran, it is not uncommon to hear passersby on city streets talk about *aberu*: how they have lost it, how someone else will lose it, or how they can gain more of it. "It would be *aberurizi* [losing face] for me to do that" is a customary line that regularly emerges in casual conversations. Not only a central component of the Persian lexicon, *aberu* is also a crucial concept in the Iranian cultural repertoire. Preserving one's *aberu* preserves one's *baten* from exposure; the *baten*, as a reservoir of one's innermost thoughts and feelings—in a sense, one's truest self—must be protected by an outer shell. As the shield that covers and protects the *baten*, *aberu* thus comes to serve an all-important function in day-to-day interactions.

The term *aberu* in Persian derives from two words: *ab* (water) and *ru* (face, looks, image). Put together, the literal translation of *aberu* is "water of the face." The expression "water of the face," however, is not unique to Iran and finds parallels in the Arabo-Islamic tradition. The Arabic phrase *ma' al-wajh* means "water of the face" and denotes a "happy glowing of a face" as well as moral purity and goodness.[13] Any action or behavior that takes away one's water of the face is seen to bring sadness, dishonor, and shame to the person. In the Iranian popular lexicon, the water of the face refers to a number of interrelated terms such as one's reputation, honor, prestige, respect, and status. However, *aberu* in its most literal sense signifies a veil of water that covers and sheathes a person's external self from the outside gaze.[14] It is only through *aberu* that one can protect the most vulnerable part of one's body—the physical face, that which reflects one's internal truth—from the judgments and valuations of others. Once this water is lost, the face—and all of its attendant weaknesses—is exposed, subjecting the person to potential shame.

Indeed, *aberu*, in Shi'a Islamic doctrine, is seen as "*bozorgtarin tekkiegāh-e shakhsiyat* . . . something that offers the greatest support and that constitutes the most important shelter and stronghold for what is termed *shakhsiyat*," that is, a person's personality, character, and dignity.[15] A person with *shakhsiyat* is considered to be one who has "developed [his] 'ego' along certain lines, around a certain hierarchy of values."[16] Such a person is said to be a person of dignity, one who, according to Maria Ossowska, "know[s] how to defend the values [he] recognize[s], whose sense of self-worth is associated with the defense of these values and who expect[s] to be respected for it by others."[17] A person's *shakhsiyat* is thus shaped by the social world surrounding her and gains its meaning only in context. As one young woman mentioned, "*Aberurizi shod* [I lost face, I was shamed] because I could not repay the loan I took out on time."[18] To lose *aberu*, to lose this protective stronghold of one's metaphorical face, is the equivalent of losing one's *shakhsiyat*; as Magdalena Zaborowska writes, this event corresponds to the destruction of a person's inner self and constitutes a threat to his humanity—that which makes him himself. Indeed, "just as in the situation where there is a lack of water and life slowly disappears and dies, . . . so when human *aberu* is destroyed, man's life is put in danger."[19]

As such, the removal of *aberu*, the removal of the metaphorical veil that covers and protects one's *shakhsiyat* and one's innermost self, is an act that leads to the ultimate sort of poverty: the utter and complete loss of everything a person has.[20] To lose one's figurative face means to lose one's dignity. This, in turn, leads to the loss of one's respect, esteem, and standing among one's peers. A person who is *bi aberu* (without *aberu*) is one who no longer earns trust. As such, he is no longer valued; he becomes a *persona non grata* in the community and cannot hope to forge the connections that will lead him to greater economic or social opportunities. By losing his metaphorical face, he becomes morally bankrupt, a fate worse than simply being materially destitute.[21] To avoid this ruin and protect his face, he must abide by certain moral norms or rules, those "certain hierarchy of values," that become the building blocks of his very existence.[22]

## On Face

In his notable essay on the topic, Erving Goffman describes face as the approved social image or front that a person presents of herself to others.[23] In Goffman's view, all people constantly edit their public image in order to avoid shaming themselves. Conceived in this way, face is a concern that people, regardless of their cultural or socioeconomic backgrounds, are keen to maintain. As such, the dichotomy between the *baten* and the *zaher* and the concern with preserving one's face should not be read as traits specific to the Iranian youth in this study, but universal ones. However, what the practices or rules that govern facework look like in practice vary among people both within and across cultures. In Iran, there are differences in these face rules among rich and poor, young and old, and male and female that are based on a set of evaluative criteria. As Goffman writes, "Each person, subculture, and society, seems to have its own characteristic repertoire of face-saving practices."[24] For example, in Iran, it is not considered immodest for an elderly man to be seen smoking a pipe, while it is considered immoral for a young woman to be seen smoking a cigarette. An upper-middle-class young man's reputation is not necessarily placed under question for holding out for the "right" job. Alternatively, a low-income young man who is no longer in school and unemployed for a stretch of time is thought to be involved with the "wrong" crowd. Face rules thus have different weight or importance depending on one's gender, class, and where one is in the life course.

The face system among the youth I knew was anchored in personal interactions among people in their social and/or economic networks and was dependent on a very public evaluation of the young person's morality or goodness, as measured by his performative success. In other words, the face system can only enforce behavior that is seen on the surface by socially or economically near others. What is done or not done behind closed doors, in a "back region or backstage,"[25] far away from the gaze of one's community is impossible to monitor unless youth are caught in the act. The comments of twenty-eight-year-old Dara, an informal laborer whom I met near Tehran's grand bazaar, are particularly evocative. Struggling to make ends meet to provide for his family, Dara told me how he would often "commit wrongdoings" such as swindling customers to make his "life go round." However, while this was something he readily admitted to people who were not in his social networks (such as myself), he was reluctant to have anyone in his social circles know of his circumstances and misdeeds (see chapter 2).

Indeed, face is an issue only among those who are perceived to be in one's networks because, as Julian Pitt-Rivers contends, they have the same set of expectations for each other and can theoretically compete with one another.[26] It is important to note that those people who comprise a person's networks can further change depending on context. For example, Yas, a sixteen-year-old young woman I knew whose family was in particularly difficult financial straits, saved face among her neighbors by presenting unexpected houseguests with fruit and pastries, which were the best food items that she could afford given her circumstances. When Yas was in another community of hers, her middle-class peers, she prevented threats to her face by dressing in trendy clothes in order to meet the expectations of this other public. Finally, when on city streets, Yas averted eye contact with men and took pains to act modestly in mixed-gender settings such as shops and parks in an effort to not be judged as *porru* (literally, full of face; figuratively, rude) by family friends who may have recognized her.

Thus, youth like Yas match performance with expectation in an effort to safeguard their appearance in the eyes of near others like neighbors, peers, and family friends. If successful, then, according to one young seamstress, "it will go around by word of mouth that you can trust this woman, that she has *aberu*." Alternatively, if youth are to be caught committing "wrongdoings" by people in their personal networks, then they will be sanctioned. However, rarely does the community publicly shame these youth. The etiquettes associated with the face system inhibit communities from criticizing a youth to his face, for then *their* face will be questioned.[27] Rather, community members sanction them in more implicit and circuitous ways: neighbors will gossip behind the young person's back, which will result in the loss of his reputation and lead to economic and social consequences. Other members of the community will be less willing to form ties with him or offer him informal loans, leading to reduced business and social opportunities and, therefore, fewer chances for upward incremental mobility. The young person will no longer be considered a good candidate for marriage, which will then lead to difficulties in forming a household.

Face-savers subsequently make a bid to follow—many times subconsciously—a certain moral code, which consists of a set of four norms or rules revolving around self-sufficiency, hard work, purity, and appearances. The rules enable face-savers to reduce the likelihood of sanctions and allow them to present an image of themselves that is consistent with social expectations. Each rule has different weight or importance depending on the young person's own background and where he is in his stage of life. These rules become moral standards that face-savers consistently follow in an attempt to gain a favorable public evaluation. The face system thus comes to shape their interpersonal relationships, the way they deal with work, and the way they present themselves to the outside world; in short, it becomes a constant organizing force in their lives.[28] It is important to mention here that face-savers themselves did not articulate that they were pursuing a set of four rules in their attempts to create a good impression. Rather, I highlight these four rules as the main constituents of the face system because they emerged as patterns within my interlocutors' discourses, behavior, and interactions. That is, the face rules became habits that youth followed, many times unaware that they were doing so.

Describing the face system as I have, as an image or cover that people put up in front of others, also means that facework can serve as a dissimulation or concealment tactic. In the face game, one's inner moral compass, one's true feelings and beliefs, do not come into play. Rather, appearances are everything. The better showing one is able to make, the more likely one is to win the game. In the face game, it is not necessary for the image one presents to actually align with one's inner self. This process of putting up a front in order to protect oneself from negative repercussions finds similarities in the early years of Islam in Iran, when Iran's Shi'a minority was encouraged to protect itself from persecution from a largely Sunni population through *taqiyyeh*, or religious dissimulation and concealment.[29] The doctrine of *taqiyyeh* is alluded to in the Qur'an, which, while emphasizing the importance of honesty and truthfulness in one's interactions, permits religious dissimulation under extreme conditions. Specifically, both Surahs 3:28 and 16:106 are instances where the Qur'an seems to condone religious dissimulation in order to protect oneself from danger. By concealing their association with Shi'ism, those who practiced *taqiyyeh* were able to avoid the oppression and brutality that were often waged against Iranian Shi'as up until the rise of the Safavid dynasty in Iran in 1501 and the establishment of Twelver Shi'ism as the official state religion.[30] Historically, then, sometimes concealing the truth has been a particularly useful strategy for those looking to improve their lot in life.

## Face and Morality

In the absence of economic markers of distinction, face-savers create a stratification system based on moral status.[31] The moral rules that define the face system come to serve as measures by which others evaluate them and by which face-savers judge themselves vis-à-vis other youth. In short, the rules that define the face system become symbolic boundaries, characterized as the "conceptual distinctions made by social actors to categorize objects, people, [and] practices."[32] Being judged as someone with *aberu*—as evidenced by one's ability to follow the face rules and conceal shortcomings—enables face-savers to maintain a dignified life in the eyes of others. Unlike their wealthy counterparts, these youth are much more vulnerable precisely because of their "lower [socioeconomic] capacity to conceal failures."[33] As Leila, a thirty-year-old woman, stated, "Rich people are comfortable; they can dress how they want, they can get divorced. Even if they go outside naked and even if they're with ten guys, people won't say anything. It's us poor ones who, no matter what we do, are still judged in people's eyes." While an exaggeration of the relative freedom of movement of the rich, Leila's comments reveal the extent to which some poor youth believe that they must always be on guard, as all eyes are always on *them*.

As face-savers and their communities make "conceptual distinctions" to categorize people who do or do not abide by the face rules, they create a form of informal social control:[34] face-savers who are able to adjust themselves by making a good showing are rewarded, while those youth who fail to participate in the rituals of the face game are punished. The constant struggle to adhere to the rules in order to avoid social sanction defines the social reality of face-savers and creates abstract status divisions between "good," "moral" youth and their "immoral" counterparts. It also, however, creates a more tangible distinction of status, since those who are able to save face are also able to monopolize social and economic resources in a way that those who fail to establish a good face cannot. The face system thus finds its strength in both its ability to distinguish "good" from "bad" and its ability to confer meaningful rewards on the "good."

Indeed, positive evaluations of face-savers' moral worth provide them with increments in moral status, which, in turn, can be exchanged for

social and economic capital that results in tangible, incremental im-
provements in these young people's day-to-day lives.[35] Thus, the face
game appeals to those youth who play by its rules not only for its ability
to confer self-worth and reputation, but also for its ability to provide
concrete incentives. Time and time again, I saw how youth who were
meticulous in their appearance and careful in presenting a front of self-
sufficiency, class, and purity became favored in their communities: they
were given jobs, promotions, expensive gifts, and a network of middle-
class connections, which brought with it its own set of perks. Generally,
those who had a more "positive social value"[36] were considered ideal
candidates for community aid, while those who failed to win at the face
game were cast even further to the social and economic margins of their
communities. How low-income youth strategize to live a meaningful life
thus becomes a significant factor in determining whether or not they
can ultimately break free of the hand they have been dealt.

The face game became a vital source of maintaining social order in
the communities I studied because it was often seen as the only way to
make it. Face-savers repeatedly voiced how a person needed connections to make it, and that one should not completely bank on the formal educational or labor market systems to fulfill one's needs. Because
the logic of the economic system in Iran, as well as elsewhere in the
world, promotes the proliferation of one's networks in order to attain
elements of the good life, many youth find it difficult—if not impossible—to secure jobs or to advance without an extensive web of personal
ties. Youth who may be university-educated, but who have not been able
to develop a corresponding network of connections that may help them
to circumvent bureaucracy and secure a well-paying job may be even
more socioeconomically disadvantaged than their high school–educated
counterparts who have an extensive network of (relatively powerful)
friends and acquaintances.

While college education in Iran was once intimately linked with a
lower risk of unemployment, its unemployment premium has now drastically decreased largely due to its unprecedented expansion.[37] In their
quest for advancement, then, many face-savers have come to accept the
premise that it is who they know that necessarily leads to higher returns.
This belief is the result of seeing peers who have succeeded in attaining a
college education but have failed to land a decent job. "What's the point

of going to college?" sixteen-year-old Bashir, a middle school dropout and informal laborer, asked me rhetorically when I inquired about his educational plans. "My cousin went to college and now he's doing the same thing I'm doing. I just want to keep doing this and advance." To advance, in turn, requires a strategic presentation of self that can gain Bashir the reputation and connections he needs to move up.

Essential to this self-presentation is strategically following the work ethic and experiences of people who were once in a similar economic situation, but who have since managed to move on. Often, these people are entrepreneurs or workers in the informal economy. While face-savers want to become solidly middle-class, the gap between where they want to be and where they are is simply too huge for them to cross by just emulating the career trajectories of the middle and upper classes.[38] Face-savers know that in order to attain mobility out of poverty, they have to take incremental steps up the proverbial ladder. The lives of the working class provide them with just the blueprint for doing so.[39] Indeed, this pattern can be observed among the poor in other contexts as well. Martín Sánchez-Jankowski, for instance, has empirically demonstrated that the poor in the United States mimic the working class more than the middle class because the lives of the middle class seem too unattainable for them to achieve.[40] Debraj Ray builds on this concept with his idea of the "aspirations window," which he argues is formed from a person's zone of similar or attainable others.[41] In this view, people use the experiences of their peers or near-peers to form their aspirations and behavior. The comments of seventeen-year-old Davud, a laborer in a poultry farm in Sari, are representative of this perspective:

> Rich kids don't have a care in the world. In our school, there were several rich kids who were really, really up there. Every recess, they would eat three sandwiches. And they always had new clothes. [My role model is] this electrician I worked for when I was in the beginning of middle school. He was an orphan and had a stepfather who harassed him when he was a child. But he worked really hard and made an effort and he eventually became a master electrician. And now he has several cars and a two-story house in our neighborhood and he's really, really up there. He was a good person too. Everyone says he's a good person and I want to be a good person like him. I work a lot and I don't steal. Some kids who

worked here stole chickens at night and got fired and got put in jail. But I want to save money and so I work a lot and want to be a good person.

In emulating the strength of character, strong work ethic, and, at times, even the particular occupation of the former working class, youth like Davud are able to sketch out a plan of action for their futures. Davud implicitly knew that accruing moral capital by working hard and being judged as "good" meant better relations with others, which could eventually lead to greater connections and resources for his career advancement. To this end, he saw hard work and purity as going hand in hand with economic advancement and as constitutive of the source of middle-class success. Mimicry became the ace that he needed to gain the upper hand in the face game.

## Aspirations and Mimicry

It was in a salon in the heart of Sari where I came to understand the fine art of posturing. Amid the curvaceous middle-aged women who came to get blond highlights, arched eyebrows, and fuzz-free faces, there was one young woman who stood out. Nadia was twenty-one and from a lower-middle-class family. I had heard from friends of friends that she had trouble making ends meet. And yet Nadia came into the salon wearing knee-high black imitation suede boots and a long black wool coat, sporting a black leather bag, her face expertly made up in black eyeliner and lipstick. She looked as if she could be right at home in Manhattan rather than in a small city in northern Iran.

Nadia was not the only one. Nina, a twenty-two-year-old homemaker and freelance artist, was dressed in a camel trenchcoat, fake Louis Vuitton crossbody, skinny jeans, and a shawl covering only the bare minimum of expertly coiffed hair when I first met her at a bookstore in one of Sari's upper-class neighborhoods. Her flawless complexion, delicately made up with foundation, a hint of eyeliner and mascara, and clear lip gloss, revealed little of the hardships she faced as a child growing up in poverty on the south side of town. Only her hands, perhaps too tanned and cracked for a young woman her age, betrayed the dishwashing days of her youth, when she worked in the kitchen of an upper-class firm so that she could earn enough money to buy expensive clothes, thereby concealing her poverty from her classmates. "My mother couldn't pay for my clothes, so I started to work when I was sixteen to be able to pay for these," Nina told me. "See, look at my hands, they've already wrinkled."

By manipulating their appearance, face-savers like Nadia and Nina assume certain identities in an effort to mimic those whom they consider superior. These identities, whether expressed through comportment or dress, help these youth to raise their social standing. Self-regulating by appearing to be hardworking and honest, not engaging in drug use, keeping company with the "right" crowd, and being aware of the latest fashions and trends precipitates the bridging of the gap between face-savers' subjective aspirations for a better life and their objective realities.

Mimicry, however, presents its own set of contradictions. Ayatollah Khomeini formed his platform on the basis of the valorization of poverty. As I mentioned in the introduction, during the 1979 Revolution, his allegiance to the poor was reflected in demonstration slogans that exalted the status of the poor and lower classes. Catchphrases including "The poor were for the Prophet; the rich were against him" and "Islam originates from the masses, not from the rich" were testament to the regime's rejection of worldly possessions; indeed, for Ayatollah Khomeini, a truly Islamic society was one characterized by the pursuit of the simple life, untainted by luxury and conspicuousness.[42] How, then, can we explain face-savers' active attempts to mimic middle-and upper-class lifestyles if they live within a social structure that exalts deprivation?

These youths' desires for upward mobility can be understood if we recognize that the Islamic Republic itself has increasingly taken the form of a "propertied middle class republic" over the years.[43] Upon Ayatollah Khomeini's death in 1989, then President Rafsanjani ushered in reforms in the economic, social, and political spheres. An emphasis on social reforms and support for economic practices including laissez-faire, rather than the exportation of the revolution abroad, came to define the economic and political policies of post-Khomeini Iran,[44] policies that have more or less continued unabated through the subsequent presidencies of Mohammad Khatami, Mahmoud Ahmadinejad, and the incumbent Hassan Rouhani.

The most visible of these reforms has been the relaxation in Islamic dress codes with each subsequent presidency; these changes have been further characterized by increasing leniency about the use of cosmetics and colorful headscarves and *manto*s. Early on, to provide justification for the regime's more lenient stance toward public displays of beauty, Ayatollah Khamenei "argued that God liked beauty, that Imam Hasan had worn decorative clothes when praying, and that Imam Ali had taken pride in the picturesque palm plantation he had cultivated outside Medina."[45] Similarly, in his 1997 speech on the occasion of the Iranian New Year, Ayatollah Khamenei stated how "God the Merciful does not want a poor society. . . . He calls for fertilising of the earth, the increase of wealth in society."[46] Official support for middle-class aspirations and lifestyles thus found its validation in religion.[47]

As Abrahamian argues, the regime's shift in rhetoric from praise of the poor and the oppressed to valuation of private property and middle-class standards of living was largely a reflection of political circumstances. Initially, it was necessary for the regime to mobilize popular support against the Shah in order to effectively overthrow the Pahlavi dynasty. Once the Islamic regime came to power, it then became necessary to institutionalize.[48] While the regime always viewed the poor as its primary social base of support, it came to increasingly rely on the propertied middle classes as an essential building block of the Republic. The Iran-Iraq War, in particular, left the Islamic regime with a decline in revenues, a burgeoning youth population, and massive war debts.[49] The state came to recognize that integrating the mushrooming, disillusioned population into a sustainable social and political system necessitated a system funded not by state monopolization and redistribution of oil revenues, but by a partnership between the state and the private sector.[50] Status aspirations among low-income young men and women have been the cumulative result of a thirty-year effort to integrate Iran into the global market economy, propelled by this very shift toward pragmatism and reform. During this time, the Islamic Republic has worked to develop Iran into a middle-income country characterized by rapid urban expansion, high literacy rates, and increased professionalization.[51] The state-enforced Islamization of society and its sex segregation of primary and secondary schools have further encouraged more conservative families to send their daughters to school and/or to join the workforce.

Additionally contributing to the universalization of high expectations has been the regime's establishment of large numbers of institutions for higher education throughout the country. Youth from popular and lower-class backgrounds have often been the direct beneficiaries of state policies that have traditionally set aside 40 percent of university slots to members of the Revolutionary Guard, volunteer militia (*basij*) members, and the sons and daughters of martyrs of the Iran-Iraq War.[52] This has meant that those low-income youth who often lack the resources for gaining entrance into highly competitive universities are now able to join the ranks of the college-educated. For those lower-class youth like Bashir who are unwilling (or unable) to go to college, post-revolutionary governmental and nongovernmental organizations provide welfare support in the form of no-cost or low-cost courses in English, Internet, computer, and job skills; in-kind provisioning of household furnishings; and family planning and public health programs.[53] Charitable foundations, including the Mostaz'afin Foundation and the IKRC, which Adelkhah has termed "public beneficence institutions,"[54] provide welfare services including low-interest loans, job skills training, pensions, in-kind assistance, social security, and health insurance in an effort to "promote a culture of philanthropy, self-sacrifice, [and] good deeds."[55] These public beneficence institutions are evidence of the bureaucratization of the *javanmard* ethos, an ethos "associated with a strategic skill in giving and receiving" and "commitment to others," characteristics that have also come to define the *aberumand* young person.[56] So extensive is the reach of these foundations that they have been called "welfare states within the larger welfare state."[57]

Moreover, the post-revolutionary availability of cultural and leisure activities that were previously the domain of the elite has played a significant role in blurring the boundaries between town and country, expanding the reach of urbanism and urban lifestyles to Iranian villages and increasing expectations of social mobility across wide swaths of the population.[58] In 1991, for example, Tehran's then mayor, Gholamhossein Karbaschi, opened the first *farhangsara* (cultural center) in Tehran, Bahman Farhangsara, in the Nazi Abad quarter (District 16) of south Tehran near the capital's peri-urban periphery. Its location meant that south Tehranis did not have to spend money to travel by taxi or metro to reach it; a short walk would lead them to a vast complex replete with, among other spaces, an exhibition hall, a cinema, a café, classrooms, a music wing, a children's unit, a library, and a gym.[59] Widely considered the heart of south Tehran and one of its poorest districts, Nazi Abad, up until that time, had no established outlet for its youth to gain access to cultural activities. The opening of the Bahman Farhangsara reversed this, enabling youth from the area, and particularly young women (who comprised 65 percent of visitors),[60] to engage in its offerings, including courses in computer skills, art, and music instruction—courses that were often taught by renowned artists.[61] Both rich and poor today rub shoulders in the Bahman Farhangsara, the first and most sizeable cultural center in Iran, as it provides an excuse for wealthy northerners to visit the south and for southerners to interact and socialize in an intimate setting with some of the city's elite.[62] Thus, no longer is south Tehran the exclusive "dormitory" of the poor, nor, given the city's cultural and infrastructural developments, does it manifest the same stark north-south duality that it once did.[63] Tehran's extensive network of expressways and its rapid metro system, with stations in south Tehran, have enabled those living in the southern parts of the city to easily visit, for a small fee, other districts of the capital if they so choose. Indeed, one young woman I knew, Kati, who lived in south Tehran, described how her parents would often take her to galleries in other parts of the city when she was younger, a practice that sparked her interest in art. When I visited Kati in her home, her room was filled with artwork and stuffed animals that she had made, the result of her parents' early instillment of an appreciation of the arts.

Similar cultural developments have occurred in Sari. The Farhang Khaneh-ye Mazandaran (Cultural House of Mazandaran), founded in 1985 by the renowned musician Ahmad Mohsenpour, provides poetry, art, literature, and music classes for little or no charge to the general public. Attracted to its minimal cost of attendance, many people from the lower and lower-middle classes attend the Farhang Khaneh's classes alongside the city's more well-to-do inhabitants. Unlike the Bahman Farhangsara in Tehran, the Farhang Khaneh in Sari is situated on a main commercial and industrial artery, drawing lower-income individuals from Sari's periphery into the heart of town. Because of Sari's small size, taxi rides into town are affordable, thus ensuring that transportation costs for visiting the Farhang Khaneh are also minimal.

As Ehsani points out, the construction of these cultural establishments that provide a leisurely outlet for people from all social classes has had a profound social impact. The casual intermingling of young men and women from different social classes has meant that these cultural centers, along with NGOs established to provide skills training to youth, constitute spaces "free of family and community policing . . . a precondition of the emergence of the modern, autonomous, urban individual. [These] public spaces . . . normalize the secular and individualized norms of the modern middle class and convert such norms into actual needs and expectations."[64] As one relatively well-to-do employee of an NGO mandated with providing job skills to poor youth in Tehran told me, "The youth here did not have any aspirations before we came, but now they want to become doctors and engineers."[65] Herein lies the contradiction at the heart of today's Iran: the cumulative result of the state's efforts to garner popular support have ironically led to the embourgeoisement of Iranian society beyond the middle and upper classes.[66] Aspirations for decidedly urban, middle-class lifestyles and cultural models coupled with attempts to mimic middle-class consumption patterns have become a defining aspect of life for many youth in the lower classes. Having seen and felt the opportunities that can be available to them, many like Nina are no longer content with simply having a working-class lifestyle; indeed, they do not see a contradiction between being a good Islamic citizen and embracing *ba kelas* middle-class aspirations and aesthetics.

## The Pursuit of *Kelas*

One particularly sweltering summer afternoon in 2010, Yas and I took a cab to go to the newly opened coffee shop Café Laleh on Golnar Street in Sari. Yas was outfitted in a tight black *manto*, skinny jeans, and kitten heels. Her gelled hair spilled out from underneath her loosely draped headscarf. The two-story café was the first of its kind in Sari that year. It was established as a gathering place for young artists, students, and intellectuals, and complete with newspapers, books, and, of course, a wide assortment of snacks and caffeinated drinks.

As we were getting ready to go inside the café that day, Yas whispered, "I don't think you can just go in like that." Reassuring her that it would be all right, I walked inside with Yas hesitatingly following me.

The owner, a young man in his twenties, greeted us warmly and led us upstairs to a cozy alcove with wooden chairs and tables, wood-panelled walls, and beautiful stained-glass windows. It was a place fit for Sari's up-and-coming young. Looking on approvingly with a smile, Yas muttered, "I've never seen a place like this in Sari. It's really nice."

Books by Western intellectuals lined the bookcases in this upstairs nook. Kafka held a prominent spot on the shelves. Rifling through the books, Yas eventually picked up the Kafka book, asked me who he was, and started flipping through it. "I have to start reading and studying again for my college entrance exams," she told me wistfully. "Because I'm not going to have much time next year to study." She described how her sister had been admitted to Sari's Azad University, but did not attend, as her mother could not afford it. "But this year, our mom said that she might be able to go." Yas then proceeded to discuss her dreams about going to the United States for college, asking me about the admissions process and what she had to do to get in.

As we spoke, the owner came upstairs to give us the hot teas that I had ordered for us. Once he was out of earshot, Yas started laughing and saying how much she liked his voice. "It's obvious he's *ba kelas* [classy]!" When I offered her the tea that I had ordered for her, Yas began to engage in *ta'arof*, becoming particularly courteous, as she knew that I had paid for it.[67] She initially refused to drink the tea, making excuses about how she did not feel well and how she usually did not drink tea. Yas finally gave in after some prodding on my part.

As we left the café that afternoon, the owner told us how he wanted a certain clientele in his establishment: young intellectuals, rather than the typical teens who populated the other cafés in the city. He gave us several fliers so that we could advertise the opening of Café Laleh to our friends and family. Once outside, Yas started to laugh again. "He's so *ba kelas*. I like that so much."

The relative success of the regime in creating new pathways for upward mobility was clearly visible during the course of my fieldwork. During this time, the pursuit of luxury and *kelas* seemed to characterize a large portion of the population. This pursuit was the product of the aforementioned developmental turn that has characterized Iran over the past several decades. Years of active attempts to transform Iran's socioeconomic landscape led to an economic boom by the mid-2000s. The emergence of a developed economy in Iran today, complete with coffee shops like Café Laleh, luxury hotels, high-speed Internet, social media applications such as Snap (Iran's version of Uber), satellite dishes, high-end boutiques and restaurants, and recreational activities like bowling and paintball, has increased the desire among Iranian youth from varying social classes to belong to the globalized marketplace.

Today, iPhones, multiple ear piercings that showcase diamond studs, and expensive tattoos are ubiquitous among youth in the middle and upper classes. A penchant for Adidas, Puma, and Nike accessories, low-slung sweatpants, and geek-chic clothing define the aesthetic tastes of segments of the hipster communities in Sari and Tehran. Young women wearing skinny jeans, loafers, and Gucci handbags can be seen interspersed among their more drably dressed middle-aged counterparts in north Tehran. Malls and restaurants are populated with young men and women who exchange furtive glances and phone numbers, all the while dressed in their most expensive outfits and perfumed in name-brand fragrances that distinguish them as the "cool," *ba kelas* kids.

For low-income youth like Yas, participation in these activities is tempered by their inability to afford them. In response, these youth turn to more informal, localized means to attain a similar look. The money they earn through their participation in the informal labor market, the connections they forge with neighbors and extended family, and the know-how they attempt to gain help them to bridge this aspirations-means gap. Like Yas, these youth rarely venture into coffee shops like Café Laleh to sample their expensive offerings. However, in their attempts to perform *kelas*, they go to local bazaars and purchase inexpensive designer knockoffs complete with Hilfiger, Versace, and Burberry logos. Young men and women who cannot afford to have a proper meal use their savings to purchase costly gifts for friends and family or smartphones preinstalled with social media applications like Snap, Viber, Telegram, and WhatsApp, all in an effort to give the impression that they are better off than they actually are. Others, like Davud, in their attempts to embody *kelas*, use the money they make to frequent venues that are the domain of their middle-class counterparts. As Davud recalled, "One time, I went with my brother to the pool. It was really fun. It was really fun in the Jacuzzi. And everyone was really *ba kelas*."

Face-savers' cultural mimicry is not confined to consumption. Their assiduous attempts at veiling, in its more abstract sense, are reflections of their desires to abide by norms of modesty in an attempt to appear *ba kelas*. Accentuated behavioral conformism defines their public personas to the extent that they are successful in concealing the less socially desirable aspects of their selves. Some young men con customers by quoting a higher price for goods only when they are sure they will not get caught by their bosses and colleagues; otherwise, they are the picture of hardworking and honest shop apprentices. Others, especially young women like Yas, dress in simple, modest clothing at home in front of religiously conservative family members, only to change into tight *mantos* and the latest fashionable dress the moment they step out in public in order for others, like the café owner, to think they are from a higher social class. A common assumption made by analysts is that makeup, tight *mantos*, t-shirts with Western emblems, and elaborate hairstyles are deviations from the moral and ethical order of the Islamic Republic and as such, represent a form of resistance against the dominant social norms in Iran. However, as I will demonstrate, these practices can also be interpreted, at least among the face-savers in this study, as attempts to maintain their personal dignity and increase their reputation among the different social groups in which they find themselves. The ability to manipulate their selves, to exert control over their appearance and behavior, demonstrates both face-savers' fixation with status recognition and their devotion to social norms.

Of course, face-savers do not always act like "well-programmed social robot[s]."[68] In those instances when they act in ways that place their face at risk, face-savers many times justify their behavior retrospectively by placing blame on others, attributing failure to God's will, and explaining away others' successes rather than their own failures. For instance, being seen alone in public does not reflect badly on the young woman, but on the "backwardness" of those who judge her.[69] Failing one's classes or occasionally slipping and going down the wrong path does not signal one's own lack of skill, laziness, or misjudgment but the ineptitude of teachers and the depravity of coworkers. Take, for instance, the comments of fifteen-year-old Arman, a high school student, and twenty-six-year-old Aria, a stall vendor:

ARMAN: I failed math because my teachers were bad. They keep nag-
ging the students. They'll tell us to fix our collars and then when we
do it, they'll tell us to leave the classroom!
ARIA: There are bad people here in the bazaar. Kids my age shouldn't
work in the bazaar. I've changed so much since coming here. You
learn bad things.

Cultural rationalizations for one's personal failure or those of one's family are also expressed as stemming from the supernatural in an effort, as
Jerome Barkow notes, to maintain self-esteem in the face of a deficiency of
adequate prestige.[70] In this view, failure is delegated to God's will (*khast-e
khoda*). It is God's will, for instance, that one's husband went bankrupt,
that one has to work in menial jobs, or that one has to delay marriage
because one has not amassed enough money. Finally, in addition to supernatural explanations, face-savers often resort to "culturally constituted
rationalizations . . . [that] explain away not [their] own failures but the
successes of others" in an effort to avoid negative judgments.[71] So, for instance, *other* youth are able to do well in school because they have the
time to study since "their schools are closer to where they live."[72] *Other*
young women are able to climb up the educational ladder because "they
don't have the responsibility of a family."[73] Still *others* are able to provide
for their families because they have money and are "*khosh shans* (lucky)."[74]

## Agency

By stage-managing the various external selves that they present in
specific public settings, face-savers engage in a certain performance
of ritual. Some scholars argue that engagement in rituals functions to
limit participants' agency since ritual actions are sanctioned not by
participants, but by a higher authority.[75] In this view, ritual legitimizes
authority and maintains social hierarchy, thereby divesting participants
of autonomy and the ability to produce social change.

Nonetheless, this perspective overlooks the very agency that is the
product of ritual action, whereby, according to Mahmood, submission
to ritual conventions is "a condition for the self to achieve its potential-
ity."[76] The repeated daily practice of certain outward and inward dispositions results in the attainment of particular moral virtues, a habitus

in the Aristotelian sense, that enables ostensibly passive subjects to be endowed with the capacities needed to "enact the world."[77] Mahmood's decoupling of agency from the trope of resistance can be used to explain why everyday public performances of normative modesty are mechanisms by which seemingly submissive, marginalized youth can carve a socioeconomic space through which their agentic selves are articulated. In this way, face-savers conform in order to institute change—however small—in their daily lives. Daily struggles to present an image that is in accord with social expectations, therefore, cannot be viewed separately from desires to get ahead and be on the "up and up." Indeed, following rituals becomes these young people's saving grace. Ironically, public compliance with moral norms also becomes a manifestation of the ingenious ways in which these youth exercise their agency by making use of ritual to realize their telos of a better socioeconomic life.

Nina, for example, by way of forging middle-class aesthetics, was able to establish connections with middle-class women in her city. This, in turn, enabled her to gain access to the booming art scene in Sari and to display and sell her artwork at a renowned atelier. Nadia, for her part, used the friendships she forged with middle-class young women to learn the ins and outs of the salon business, which facilitated her ability to subsequently plan the opening of her own salon. The small, incremental gains that face-savers like Nina and Nadia win by manipulating their public fronts function to weave them into the fabric of their communities. By silently helping themselves through their cultural conformism, these youth affirm their presence, agency, and right to the city. Their incremental advances hold the potential to fulfill their growing aspirations and blur the gap between their ambitions and their objective realities, thereby giving them the leverage they need to move from the bottom up. They may not make the move in leaps and bounds, but they move—slowly and in measured steps—nonetheless. And sometimes that is enough to feel that they are, as one young man put it, satisfied enough.

Understanding how the struggles of these young men and women to conform substantiate, rather than negate, their agency further enables us to shift the terms of the debate from the question of whether or not they are actors to the question of the mechanisms involved in shaping their particular choices and decisions.[78] Why do these youth undertake the actions they do to improve their lot in life in the first place? To fully understand why some youth prefer to undertake certain actions over others, we must place their practices within a larger moral universe that is guided by their conceptions of good and bad. It is here where the moral code of the face system is located.

Morality, as constituted by the face rules, is appealing not simply because it operates as a type of symbolic capital, but because it provides both guidelines and an evaluative code for individual initiative and behavior. Morality thus gives meaning to young people's lives and functions to keep them "socially alive."[79] That is, morality creates a social order that keeps life manageable for them. Youth who find themselves increasingly excluded from formal institutions and structures deploy a set of moral understandings derived from shared cultural norms, religion, and the Islamic regime's own developmental turn that enables them to not simply survive and tolerate their lives, but to find satisfaction and even joy within it. Poverty does not make it impossible to live a fulfilling life, just as wealth does not guarantee it.[80] As Zahra, a twenty-two-year-old housewife, said, "Money doesn't make you have a good life." Rather, the good life is defined by being a moral person, one who has earned the respect of those around him. As such, morality constitutes not only a form of motivation that shapes behavior, but also a form of rationalization that helps people like Zahra make sense of their life decisions.[81] The multifarious forms and functions of morality thus constitute culture,[82] and the moral norms of the face system make up the "cultural toolkit" at face-savers' disposal for managing their day-to-day lives.[83]

Of course, morality is not the only source of influence in these young people's lives. The resources they bring to the table, including their street smarts and preexisting networks coupled with the structural constraints or opportunities they encounter, interact with moral understandings to shape both what face-savers find worthy of pursuing and how successful they are in realizing those aspirations. However, the logic of the face system tends to emphasize ends rather than means. Since youth are evaluated only according to how well they comply by the face rules, communities tend to ignore the variables that may impinge on a young person's ability to conform, such as a lack of familial economic resources or an unsupportive spouse. In this manner, communities in Sari and Tehran tend to replicate framings found in other urban contexts in the Middle East like Cairo, where charity is seen as befitting only those who "[strive] to abide by the moral code."[84] Families, neighbors, acquaintances, and even face-savers themselves end up drawing distinctions between the deserving and undeserving poor, providing aid to the former at the expense of the latter (even though the latter may be the most in need of help).[85] When success is seen as a "Darwinian fight" in which only the most morally fit deserve to advance,[86] the "culture of poverty" perspective,[87] with its inherent attribution of poverty to the culture of the poor themselves, comes to be adopted and reproduced in poor communities. In this way, the face system is neither completely good nor completely bad. Indeed, while an emphasis on morality and being a good, decent, hardworking person can facilitate incremental mobility in certain circumstances, it can also serve as a poverty trap in other instances.[88] Thus, while poor youth can manage the face game to produce a meaningful life for themselves, the game can also prove strong enough to reproduce systems of stratification among them.

Why continue the game, then? It is not simply the drive to garner recognition, a good name, or status that drives face-savers to continue to play the game; it is because youth believe that these motivations define the "correct" way to live one's life that the cultural system espoused by the face game becomes a resilient and ingrained code of conduct. If we are to deal concretely with the complexity of the lived experiences of poverty in Iran, we must first understand the game, how it is played, and how it ultimately comes to provide a sense of purpose to the actors caught in it. The next chapters deal with exactly that.

2

# All in a Day's Work

Boro kar mikon magu chist kar
keh sarmayeh-ye javedanist kar.

(Go work and do not ask what is work
for work is eternal wealth.)
—Mohammad-Taqi Bahar, *Divan-e Ash'ar*, 1989

Maziyar Street, Sari's commercial avenue, is one of the most popular nighttime destinations for Sari's under-thirty crowd. Alongside the fast-food restaurants, coffee shops, and small boutiques that sell both knockoff and original designer goods to the unsuspecting middle- and upper-class youth who make up the majority of Maziyar's clientele, are the street vendors. Often young and male, these vendors lay out their goods on a gunnysack or blanket on the sidewalk and call out into the crowded street, advertising their merchandise. Colorful headscarves, knockoff designer purses, jeans, and t-shirts—goods sold in Maziyar's boutiques for sometimes double the price—are only some of the wares that these young men sell for a bargain on the pavement. The more entrepreneurial and hardworking among them—those who are dressed more fashionably, those who act as personal stylists advising women how nice a particular scarf would look if paired with a certain handbag, and those who work late through the night—are the ones who often have a mass of customers huddled around their small open-air shops. These vendors, by virtue of their bargain prices and expert soliciting skills, eventually end up competing for customers with the apprentices of Maziyar's boutiques, young men and women who at times, not surprisingly, end up making less commission than their street counterparts.

The vendors on Maziyar Street are not unique. Throughout Sari and Tehran, one encounters similar groups of entrepreneurial youth, young men and women who often forgo college, and sometimes even their secondary educations, to work as street vendors, as shop apprentices in boutiques and bazaars, as mechanics, as porters, and as day laborers. "Do you think we would do this if there was no money in it?" quipped a street vendor on Naderi Avenue, south Tehran's equivalent of Maziyar Street. The quest for a better material life is what drives these youth to engage in these autonomous practices, practices that have become increasingly common in recent years as Iran's economic climate has taken a turn for the worse.

Iran's large youth population, the inability of the economy to create enough jobs necessary to absorb the numbers of youth who enter the labor market each year, and the mismatch between the skills emphasized in existing educational models and those needed for productive employment have led to unfulfilled expecations among many of Iran's youth, as they remain without work. For academics, Iran's high youth unemployment rate, on the order of 26.4 percent,[1] means that youth have to endure a period of "waithood," a time during which they can do nothing but wait for their "turn to enjoy the opportunities that the country offers its adult citizens—regular jobs, marriage, and homes of their own."[2] For the youth I came to know, this unemployment rate represented an imminent threat of shame. Sitting idly at home, waiting for their turn for a piece of the pie was simply not an option for those without adequate financial means. Among young men in particular, unemployment signified a lack of responsibility and chivalry, deficiencies that they perceived to impinge on their manhood.[3]

It should be noted that this equation of masculine dishonor with laziness is not new. Indeed, in the nineteenth and twentieth centuries, as Mana Kia describes, Iranian modernists drew from older Persian ideals of "moral refinement as idealized masculinity"[4] to stress the cultivation of zeal, discipline, and the avoidance of sloth, particularly among men, as means by which the Iranian nation could develop, thereby averting shame and "collective abasement."[5] Today, this emphasis on hard work and self-dicipline finds consonance in the Islamic Republic's efforts to promote young people's resolve. In a 2018 speech addressed to university and high school students, for instance, Ayatollah Khamenei stated that the "main need of the country is a noble determination on your part. You, youth, should show determination. You should aim high, work hard, and abandon fear and laziness. This should be accompanied by national zeal. These are the elements which are necessary for our country and our youth."[6] In this perspective, not only will a strong work ethic advance the nation, but it will also cultivate individual moral selves. While the onus for national and familial economic well-being has historically been on men, as I will detail later in this chapter, young women, too, have become active participants in the economic sphere, thereby implicitly challenging its "homo-social gendered order."[7] For both young men and women, work becomes a means by which they can develop their reputations as respectable members of the community.

The stigma attached to being jobless for any length of time means that these youth have to hustle and get creative to bring in money. In response to the difficulty of acquiring jobs in the formal sector, face-savers often resort to individual, informal strategies to make ends meet. Ranging from skills training and portering to sewing and mechanical work, such strategies enable young men and women to present themselves to community members as "hardworking" and "responsible" rather than "incompetent" and "lazy." To avoid the shaming inherent in being seen as a *bikar* (someone without work, often used pejoratively), face-savers engage, or give the impression that they engage, in activities that are widely accepted as having the potential to contribute to their self-sufficiency and to a household income. In this chapter, I examine how work, particularly work in the informal economy, is a medium for face-savers to become incrementally mobile and to exercise agency in Iran's public realm. I argue that the performance of a strong work ethic is a key means of gaining respectability before the public gaze. Before doing so, however, I provide a brief description of the informal economy in which many face-savers labor.

## Informal Work

As mentioned in the introduction, a distinguishing feature of Sari and Tehran's working poor is their rural origin. While cityward migration in Iran picked up after the end of World War II and accelerated in the 1960s and 1970s,[8] it continues to the present day, largely due to migrants' perceptions of the greater structure of opportunities in cities. Indeed, contemporary Iran is host to an urban population that is nearly triple the size of its rural demographic, which in 2017 constituted 26 percent of the country's total population.[9]

Nevertheless, since many migrants lack the skills training needed for the formal labor sector, they have had to turn to the informal sector for work. Better educated than their parents' generations, the sons and daughters of these migrants still face similar job prospects. The youth whom I knew largely worked in a hodgepodge of unregulated informal jobs—jobs that comprise around 36 percent of Iran's gross domestic product[10]—that ranged from secretarial work to apprenticeships to street peddling. While small-scale merchant activities typically constituted the majority of face-savers' work, their informal labor also included mechanical work, painting, tailoring, driving, and carpentry.

Thus, though seemingly insignificant, face-savers' informal activities encompass nearly all the basic skills needed to offer services to the wider population.[11] Far from being marginal or unproductive, the informal sector affords these young men and women with a means to accumulate profit and to engage in productive work.[12] Given the broad clientele that exists for their services, those youth who work hard are able to reap rewards—rewards that range from recognition to larger profits to an expansion of their commercial activities. Informal work, then, in many ways, gives them an edge in life.

## The Street Scene

Naderi Avenue. One of the most bustling commercial avenues in the southern heart of Tehran. A far cry from the northern part of the city, where even the major thoroughfares are characterized by a sense of calm and order. The noise of motorcycles is the first to greet you as you step out of Naderi's train station. The second are the street peddlers standing by the station hawking their goods, the porters hauling heavy burlap bags on their backs, the artisans selling their handicrafts, and the shop vendors who entice you to come into their small stores. On any given day, Naderi is swarming with people, often young, often male, and often eager to make a deal. It is the hustling capital of Tehran, and if you are not careful, you can easily spend hundreds of dollars on the knick-knacks, pastries, household goods, and clothes that are for sale.

Walking along Naderi, one quickly reaches the area known as Shush, commonly referred to by Tehranis as Tehran's "little hell" because of the extreme poverty that characterizes its residents. The many one-story buildings in Shush seem worn-out and tired, unlike the tall, shiny high-rises of north Tehran that glimmer with the money that has poured into the north's land speculation and construction businesses. The vendors in Shush are plentiful. Positioning themselves at strategic points—areas with heavy pedestrian and motor traffic—they frequently display their wares on large pieces of cardboard, makeshift tables, or on the ground over a mat. Others are itinerant, walking from one busy intersection to another and selling more minor goods—toothbrushes, gum, fortunes, and pastries—in cardboard boxes that they have fashioned with a piece of twine into a sort of bulky necklace that hangs from their necks. Relentless in their quest to make a sale, the vendors can be found in south Tehran at almost all times of the day and night; their work hours far surpass those of the sales associates who work in north Tehran's luxury boutiques and malls. Because of their diligence, some have become regular fixtures in south Tehran's street scene. "Go ask the motorcycle drivers how many years the *bamiyeh* seller has been here," quipped twenty-one-year-old Shahpur, an itinerant vendor of Iran's equivalent of sweet fritters.

For the married and single young men like Shahpur who dominate Tehran's bazaar scene, the impetus to work long hours is the necessity of providing for themselves and their families. Time and time again, in my sojourns in Tehran and Sari, I encountered young men who justified their long hours and demanding physical labor on the grounds that there was simply "no other way" to support their parents, to contribute to the household budget, or, for those who were still single, to accumulate enough money to be able to get married. These vendors often served as the primary breadwinners of their families and had to balance their desires to start their own households or to pay for the expenses of their wives and children with the necessity of giving away the little money they made to support the well-being of their parents or nuclear families. Because of their strong work ethic, these men were seen by their families, neighbors, and those in their social networks as models of masculinity.

### Amir Hossein and Bahram

I met seventeen-year-old Amir Hossein outside Naderi's train station. When I first saw him, he was sitting on a curb, organizing the various toothbrushes, tissue boxes, and packs of gum that were strewn over the plastic mat that he had carefully laid out on the landing next to the station. Situated next to a group of vendors selling seasonal fruits, Amir Hossein recounted that he had dropped out of the sixth grade and had gotten married three years ago. His parents had separated due to his father's drug use. With two kids and no familial support, he hesitatingly told me about his job and his financial troubles. Amir Hossein had a starting disadvantage: a family life ridden with poverty—so much so that he was deemed unfit by the State Welfare Organization of Iran to take care of his own children. He believed that overcoming this disadvantage, in turn, required hard work. Looking to the experiences of another who was able to overcome similar economic disadvantage provided Amir Hossein with an example to aspire to:

> I got married when I was fourteen. The Behzisti [State Welfare Organization of Iran] took custody of my kids because we didn't have the money to pay for them. I want to make enough money to get my kids back from them. My wife and I work in shifts selling these things. Right now, my wife is in the metro station and I'm waiting for her to get out and then I go in and start selling. I saw someone before in the metro who sold these types of things and when I asked him about it, he told me that there's good money in *dast forushi* [peddling] and so I thought I would try it out. We bought all this stuff for around 20,000–30,000 *tomans* [18–27 USD]. I also got an apartment on lease for 500,000 *tomans* [450 USD] and now I'm subletting it for 150,000 *tomans* [136 USD] a month.[13] I don't go to north Tehran, no one wants tissues and toothbrushes there. It's better here. I want to improve my life.

A short walk later, I encountered seventeen-year-old Bahram, a high school graduate who worked as a vendor selling kitchen utensils and household items that he would pick up wholesale from his uncle's small housewares shop:

> BAHRAM: I'm content with my life; I have a car, I have enough money.
> MANATA: Do you want to get married?
> BAHRAM: Marriage? Why get married? It costs too much. That kid [you say who got married when he was fourteen] is really *badbakht* [unfortunate]. His wife expects something from him, she didn't just

come from nowhere. What if she asks him for a coat tomorrow? How is he going to pay for it? He is still a baby, his breath still smells like milk!

MANATA: He [Amir Hossein] is a peddler in the metro and he's renting an apartment.

BAHRAM: Oh, well, then he's not that bad off. You know, they make a lot of money. If they sell one toothbrush for 2,000 tomans [1.80 USD] and fifty people buy from him in a day, then guess how much that is? If you make 40,000 tomans [22 USD] a day, is that bad? Of course not!

## Self-Sufficiency

For some low-income youth in Iran who are of working age, saving face hinges primarily on their ability to become economically self-sufficient through work. Among families and communities, I often heard the phrase *dasteshun tu jib-e khodeshun bereh* [their hands should go into their own pockets], to describe the importance that communities placed on self-sufficiency for their youth. To the extent that they can provide for themselves and their families without financial reliance on others, youth are able to maintain their reputations as responsible people. While women do work—particularly if their household circumstances necessitate an additional salary—in Iranian gender ideology, as elsewhere in the Middle East, it is men who are primarily responsible for providing for their families, irrespective of the women's earning potential.[14] Consequently, in being seen as someone who earns money, these youth—and particularly young men, whose masculinity hinges on their ability to provide—are able to gain the admiration of those around them. Young men themselves, too, know the importance of being seen as financially self-reliant. As a man's perceived ability to provide decreases, so does the respect that he receives from others in his social circles.

What Bahram's comments and Amir Hossein's story underline is precisely this importance of being judged as financially self-sufficient even if that evaluation does not square with reality. It is the public display of masculinity—revolving around perceptions of autonomy—that becomes the marker of one's face. Indeed, Bahram did not know how Amir Hossein struggled to make a living. He did not know that the Behzisti had taken Amir Hossein's children because he could not provide. Bahram saw marriage as perfectly acceptable—even for someone as young as Amir Hossein—as long as the person in question amassed the means to provide for himself and his family before marriage. For these young men, the ability to become self-sufficient through work *prior* to getting married is a mark of their character and an indicator of their adult status. "I want to have complete independence so that I can manage a household," twenty-eight-year-old Ehsan, a laborer in a car shop in Sari, stated. "Otherwise, I can't really get married. When I become a father, I want to have the conditions so that I can provide for my kid. Otherwise I'm doing an injustice against my child. Maybe my conditions were difficult. I don't want my child to suffer hardship like I did. [I want to] try to make life easier for my child." To do otherwise, as the story of Bahram and Amir Hossein above indicates, young men like Ehsan risk losing face because they will be considered incapable of being responsible enough to provide for a family. Without financial independence, they are deemed to be the equivalent of an infant.

For young men who are not married, contributing to the income of their parental household also averts threats to their face, as the household and its members are then able to amass enough funds to meet expenses and therefore not be dependent on the economic aid of others. As one young street vendor in Tehran noted, "I had to drop out of school after ninth grade to help my family meet household expenses. We have to meet our bills each month with the money we make. My hope is that we don't become financially dependent on anyone."

The importance of self-sufficiency further extends to people's interactions with welfare institutions. Even individuals who are legitimately entitled to social welfare services by the state and NGOs opt to receive welfare benefits and resources in-house rather than have officials and social workers bring them these goods because, as one NGO official told me, "they don't want neighbors to find out that they are in need of help." Welfare support is seen as a signifying marker of one's incompetence and a breach of the communal norm of self-reliance.[15] This "welfare stigma,"[16] in turn, led one organization I knew to publicize specific dates each month when clients could come to the NGO to pick up school supplies, foodstuffs, and other in-kind goods.

Given the consequences that come with being seen as someone who, like an infant, is reliant on the goodwill of others to survive, being able to find and work in a job that pays relatively well becomes a high priority. Accordingly, many male face-savers work in invisible, informal sector jobs that often pay better than more socially reputable, entry-level jobs in the formal economy, which are more difficult to come by in the first place. Those lucky enough to attain stable formal sector work often supplement their day jobs with informal work at night, such as painting, carpentry, and taxi driving. Others, like Dara, the laborer we met in chapter 1, work solely in the informal economy, believing that economic independence trumps the prestige that can come with a formal sector job. Clean-shaven and wearing a black leather jacket and jeans, Dara was leaning against one of the many motorcycles that lined the main street in Shush when he recounted the following to me:

> [In high school], I majored in electrical work. I know everything about technical work. I know welding, I know mechanics. Whatever technical work you give me, I know how to do it. I used to work for a company [in the formal sector], but since it didn't pay well, I came out. And now I got a pickup truck and haul supplies for customers. When I see that a certain job doesn't bring home the bread, I'll leave it. I have a wife and kids, I have to think of my family. I'll do a job that helps my life go round. My only hope is that I'm able to provide for my kids. Whatever work it is, I'll be able to handle it, but the future of my kids is uncertain. It's enough for me to be able to secure their futures somehow so that I don't come up short [in front of my brothers] for having had children. One brother of mine is working for a cement company and the other is working for a bank. They're doing better than I am. Their financial situation is good. . . . I was supposed to take a motorcycle up north, and the price I quoted the customer was way too high. Don't mention my name. I have acquaintances here and it would be really bad for me if they found out.

For Dara, it is not about the type of work that a person engages in, but his success in bringing home enough money to provide for the needs of his family and being judged economically self-sufficient. In Dara's case, his need to provide for his children so he does not "come up short" in front of his brothers led him to completely give up his formal sector job, join south Tehran's burgeoning informal economy, and engage in morally ambiguous work: swindling customers. However, as long as Dara's acquaintances do not "find out" about his indiscretions, he is in the clear. Maintaining a public face of a hardworking and responsible man pre-empts private immorality. Dara can still preserve his good name if he is able to get away with a lie in front of others in his social and/or eco-nomic circles. Indeed, keeping their jobs a secret and lying about their line of work are commonly used tactics that face-savers employ to keep up their reputations and keep bringing "home the bread."

While the particular job is seen as less important than the money it can bring, face-savers are nevertheless sensitive to the status connota-tions of their jobs. When asked about their line of work, informal labor-ers, for instance, often provide vague answers such as giving the location where they work, stating the type of company they work in, or declaring that they are in *kar-e azad* (self-employed). They never specifically state the kind of work they are engaged in unless prodded. Face-savers are similarly conscious about the status connotations of their parents' jobs, which they see as reflecting on their own reputations. Mojtaba was a twenty-three-year-old pistachio vendor in Shush. Through our conver-sation about his father's line of work, the need to save face became ever more apparent:

MANATA: What does your father do?
MOJTABA: Oh, he works in an insurance company.
MANATA: So, he's an office worker?
MOJTABA: No, he brings tea and stuff.
MANATA: Oh, he's the *abdarchi* [teaman].
MOJTABA: Yeah.

This conversation is particularly illustrative of how face-savers value "company" jobs in the formal sector that are seen as more *dorost hesabi* (valuable, honorable, decent) than jobs in the informal economy. How-ever, because the former jobs often do not pay as well as less "decent" jobs in the informal economy and are more difficult to obtain, face-savers and their families often turn to work in the informal sector, to jobs that will allow them the opportunity to not simply make ends meet, but to advance.

Declines in Iran's social safety nets, in large part due to sanctions, growing inflation, and subsidy cuts, have meant that face-savers have to increasingly rely on themselves, rather than on the state, to improve their life chances. While face-savers rarely confront the problem of actually surviving (a roof over one's head, clothes on one's back, and food in one's mouth), they are constantly faced with the problem of maintaining and increasing what they do have.[17] The dilemma of securing, among other things, furniture, electronic goods, a quality education for one's children, and stylish clothes defines one part of the drive for jobs that can be capitalized on. Participating in reciprocity networks defines the other. For instance, when married youth like Dara are invited to share a meal, they are obligated to return the generosity.[18] As Diane Singerman has observed in Cairo, when houseguests in Iran come to judge a young person's social standing afterward, they will similarly recount his physical adornments, the "quantity and quality of the food and drink offered," the type of furnishings or goods that he had, and the condition of his house.[19] Such norms of reciprocity place a heavy economic burden on youth like Dara and necessitate that they have sufficient financial resources to participate in its rules.

As Marcel Mauss and Marshall Sahlins have argued, gift-giving and exchange can encumber individuals as much as they can reinforce social cohesiveness within a community.[20] Face-savers consider invitations or gifts of material goods as debts that have to be repaid in kind in order to prevent threats to their face. As such, they are not willing to contribute a gift or extend an invitation that may suggest they are struggling with economic hardship. Nevertheless, the extent of reciprocity among these young men and women varies according to how well they know each other. Gift-givers and gift-receivers who are socially close do not feel obligated to return gifts that are the same as the original gift.[21] In this manner, they exhibit Sahlins's model of reciprocity, whereby the extent of their reciprocity varies with social distance. According to Sahlins, as people move away from family and friends to strangers and enemies, they practice generalized reciprocity (altruistic gift-giving), balanced reciprocity (exchange of similar gifts), and negative reciprocity (extreme end of reciprocity that involves theft, deceit, or bargaining), respectively.[22]

Many times in the field, I observed that in exchanges that occurred between youth who were not closely linked, the youth practiced a form of balanced reciprocity. As such, two-hundred-dollar wedding gifts, elaborate rice dishes, and expensive pastries were only some of the items that face-savers went out of their way to purchase in order to save face. To be able to afford participating in these reciprocity networks that pervaded daily life, these youth had to intensify their efforts in the labor market by searching for lower-status but better-paying jobs in the informal sector that would allow them to repay gifts and services in kind. Social structures thus affect what type of work these young people find most sensible.[23] It is not a question, then, of whether or not face-savers value stable, mainstream jobs, but how hustling or informal sector work can enable them to eschew social sanction and to avoid making their already difficult economic lives even more unforgiving.

## Hard Work

While economic independence facilitates face-savers' ability to convey a good impression, these youths' attraction to work cannot simply be explained by the money it can bring. Rather, it is equally important for them to give the impression that they work hard. This serves both an instrumental and performative function. In its instrumental form, working hard reveals to others that a person is responsible enough and has the ability to eventually attain the socioeconomic rewards necessary to successfully achieve full self-sufficiency. As multiple face-savers told me over and over again, "God helps those who help themselves."

It should not go without mention that such references to God's influential presence in a person's life have traditionally been viewed as indicative of a culture of fatalism in Muslim societies.[24] This seeming preoccupation with divine determinism, or the "*insha' Allah* [God willing] complex,"[25] has been contrasted with the principles espoused by the work ethic deemed to be so prevalent in the West.[26] However, as I found, an ultimate resignation to God's will, espoused in phrases such as "whatever God wants" or "first you, then God" is not associated with fatalism or a lack of initiative. Rather, it surfaces as both a source of comfort in the face of uncertainty[27] and, more importantly, a means by which face-savers believe they will reap greater rewards from the divine. While Gary Gregg found that some Muslims express "resignation in the solace of religious fatalism"[28] *only* when they are unable to achieve some end,[29] I found that face-savers express belief in the ultimate will of the divine *while* they are also in the process of undertaking a socioeconomic activity. This belief is grounded in the idea that one has to be content with what God gives—and God will give whatever He wants—so that one can curry God's favor as well as receive divine compensation. As one young woman stated, "Youth should be thankful to God and be content [with what He gives]. If they have qena'at [contentedness], they will get what they want faster."

While face-savers believe that God ultimately controls the consequences of their actions, they also believe that a person plays an active role in shaping that outcome as well.[30] As such, these youth espouse what Joseph Elder terms "theological fatalism" rather than "empirical fatalism," the belief that "empirical phenomena occur for no comprehensible reason, and they cannot be controlled."[31] One face-saver, for example, emphasized how "a person first has to use his senses, and only then will he become lucky [khosh shans]." One cannot know how God will help or the extent to which God will help. This means that one has to exert effort because not doing so will lead one to not be blessed with divine luck (shans). Face-savers, then, believe in the importance of individual agency, as manifested through taking responsibility for one's actions, as the key driving force for success. While these youth believe in the will of the divine, they know that God's will does not simply determine human action, but is also contingent upon it.[32] As one young woman explained, "It is God's will, but a person herself has a brain, ears, a conscience. She has to make an effort." As such, a person must accept what God has in store for him without slowing down his own labor.[33]

In its performative manifestation, such labor denotes the young person's moral purity. As mentioned earlier, those face-savers who do not explicitly manifest a strong work ethic are deemed "lazy" by others, a quality that is considered the moral opposite of "responsible." As Yas noted one afternoon as we passed a group of street musicians, "People are willing to pay these guys because, unlike beggars, they're actually doing something and have a skill." During my time in the field, I witnessed many male face-savers, both those who were in school and those who had dropped out, engaged in some type of labor, either during the week or during their summer breaks. Whether paid, as in Bahram and Dara's case, or unpaid volunteer work for family and friends (particularly if the face-saver is still in school), it is critical that face-savers are seen exerting effort in the public sphere so as to avoid insinuations that they are irresponsible. While not all of these jobs provide monetary incentives, they do provide a means for some youth to build their moral credentials before the public gaze, as the following example demonstrates.

## Karim

Nestled near Sari's main railway is the residential neighborhood of Abadi, a neighborhood of winding roads interspersed with the occasional grocery store and mechanic's shop. The residents of Abadi are mostly informal laborers: housemaids, welders, electricians, and painters. Their children, many of whom I tutored on a weekly basis, attend schools throughout the city. In the afternoons, young men gather in the alleyways to play soccer, catch up with friends, and gawk at the neighborhood's young women who may happen to venture outside at the same time.

One of these soccer players is Karim. Karim, a tall, lanky young man of seventeen, is one of the pride and joys of Abadi. A talented soccer player, Karim is one of the youngest players in Sari's junior league. Confident in his athletic abilities, Karim constantly emphasized to me how, with a little hard work, he just "knew" that he was going to become a successful soccer player. While I was doubtful about his future as a professional athlete, Karim's work ethic was certainly admirable. When he was not in school or in my English class, Karim was on the soccer field, practicing for several hours a day. In the little free time he had, Karim would hang out at one of Abadi's grocery stores that was owned by a family friend of his, Mr. B. As Karim explained to me one day, "I watch over the grocery store when Mr. B is gone. It's a productive way to spend my free time."

Due to his assiduousness, Karim eventually gained a reputation among his neighbors as a hardworking and honest young man. By participating in the performance of work, young men like Karim demonstrate that they do not idle their days away; rather, they are diligent young men serious about their futures. In this way, members of the community implicitly create an important distinction between those who, like Karim, effectively exhibit a commitment to hard work and those who do not. As a local woman noted, "There's something wrong with a kid who doesn't work; maybe he's on drugs or involved with the wrong people." Distinctions between those who manifest a strong work ethic and those who do not become especially important when a young man decides to get married, as community members and the bride's family use evidence of the man's industriousness as an indication of his ability to be a successful breadwinner, a point that I will subsequently elaborate. Young women, for their part, however, do not simply sit around, waiting for the man to provide. Whether single or married, low-income women assert their presence in the public sphere and make claims to dignity by exerting control over their labor power.[34]

## The Feminization of Work

In the tumultuous years immediately following the revolution, women came to constitute a smaller proportion of the labor force than they did in the pre-revolutionary era. This decline has been attributed to a variety of factors, including the imposition of US sanctions and trade disruptions that negatively affected the carpet and handicraft trades, which employed large numbers of young women.[35] Despite this decline in women's work in the immediate aftermath of the 1979 Revolution, over the course of the 1990s and 2000s, there was a rise in women's labor force participation, largely due to the Islamization of the public sphere and the regime's own developmentalist efforts, manifested especially in its expansion of education and more equitable distribution of resources that facilitated access to learning among the population.[36] More conservative women who previously would not have considered entering the public sphere now felt free to learn and work alongside men, as the hijab provided them with a means with which to avert the male gaze. Simultaneously, upsurges in higher education, at least among more middle-class women, led to their growing employment in the professional and technical fields.[37] Many lower-income women also came to constitute Iran's economically active female population, a trend that could be attributed to the increasing poverty that these women and their families faced in the aftermath of the Iran-Iraq War and the economic crises of the Rafsanjani era (see introduction).[38] These women tended to be self-employed and/or work in the informal sector.[39]

Low-income women's entry into the labor force was not unexpected. Indeed, while men's labor was considered the primary source of household income, it became customary for women in poor households to work in order to supplement the domestic revenue and to help meet family expenses—a pattern that has continued to the present day. From my own observations of low-income households during the course of my fieldwork, female participation in the labor force was almost equal to that of men, even though communities continued to judge a man's—and hence, a family's—reputation by whether or not he worked.

As informal labor constitutes the majority of these women's work, they are undercounted in census data, which often report only formal sector work. For instance, in 2006 women's formal labor force participation was estimated to be only approximately 15.5 percent.[40] Ethnographic data can help to elucidate these "missing" women—who they are, why they chose to enter the workforce, and what their experiences have been.[41] The narratives that I highlight in this section help to illuminate these dynamics by underscoring the informal work experiences of young women. This demographic has traditionally faced a much more difficult time in securing work than other social groups, largely due to patriarchal gender norms that privilege males in the workplace and to the rigidity of the formal labor sector that privileges adults by raising costs to employers for laying off older workers.[42] In revealing the strategies some low-income young women deploy to exert control over their livelihoods within these limitations, I show how face becomes a significant heuristic for understanding the choices that these women make.

## Faranak

Rose Salon. Sari. Located on Maziyar Street, Rose Salon is situated on the third floor of a walk-up office building that also houses art classes and physicians' offices. The two-story women's salon does not boast the attractive interiors of salons in north Tehran or those located in the more exclusive neighborhoods of Sari. The chipped walls are plastered with posters of American and European women with pop punk hairstyles: short hair colored in vibrant shades of pink, red, and blue. Red leather chairs, a bit worn out, provide color to the white, clinical space. The downstairs area, where the salon owner, Ms. Zahedi, caters to her more exclusive clientele, is more intimate and spruced up; there is a waiting area with newer chairs and side tables, the clean walls hold fewer posters, and there is a table adorned with hair color charts.

The salon is often crowded with its five young female apprentices. Wearing t-shirts, jeans, and comfortable shoes, the apprentices engage in gossip and chatter as they practice the highlighting and styling skills they learned from Ms. Zahedi so that they can pass the upcoming cosmetology licensing exam. The young women do not get paid for the work they do; rather, they pay Ms. Zahedi a fixed amount (200 USD) to receive training in hair techniques in the hopes that they can start up their own salons or become employed at the salon after their training period ends. For those who are lucky, tips from the salon's clientele provide them with a steady stream of pocket money.

Among the apprentices, Faranak is the most articulate and hardworking. While the other girls take long breaks between clients, Faranak is always on her feet, practicing different techniques. She recounted the following as I was watching her practice one afternoon:

> I lived in Tehran four years ago and I received training in epilation. Now, I epilate ladies from my own apartment. My daughter's room has a ceramic floor and I moved some stuff to the side. I put in a bed there and I bought a warming machine for the wax. For the wax, I use a mixture of sugar that I make myself. If I had my own salon and a sign for my business, I would attract a lot of customers. But right now, it's just through word of mouth. Even still, I get customers. I get at least one or two every day. These girls here, they pay so much money to get training, but they still complain. They come here and don't make use of their time. They still live with their parents so they're not too worried. But when you're married [like I am] and have responsibilities, it's different. You make good use of your money.

At that moment, a young woman walked in and asked Ms. Zahedi if she could receive training at the salon. She said that she was a doctoral student studying pharmacology. "Why would a pharmacology PhD want to become a hairstylist?" I asked Faranak. "She's not really a PhD student. She's just saying that. People like her just want to work. Manata, don't you want to work?"

After a later visit to Faranak's small two-bedroom apartment, I learned that Faranak was so adamant about working because her husband would not share any of the money he made:

He spends it all, and I don't even know how much he makes. I decided to save all my own money and then buy a house [under my name]. I don't want any more kids until I have a huge house. Make sure the guy you end up marrying has money, or at least comes from a family that has money. Money is good. When you don't have money, you end up fighting with each other!

For married young women like Faranak who have a family to provide for, working hard is seen as the only means of making enough money to be able to properly take care of oneself and one's family. This is especially true when husbands are unable to support the household or when husbands are deemed to have the inability to properly handle household finances, as in Faranak's case.

## Parisa

Bazaar Markazi. Sari. Commonly regarded by youth as a *ba safa* (pleasant) place, the bazaar is a fifteen-minute drive from Maziyar Street. Located in a large enclosed space, Bazaar Markazi has dozens of small stalls crammed together. The bazaar is swarming with both sellers and visitors during most days of the week, making the air inside warm even in the dead of winter. The main stalls are often filled with young male vendors who call out to visitors, trying to lure them by enumerating the various products that they have for sale: relatively inexpensive Iranian-made handicrafts and furs, generic makeup, cheap imported tchotchkes from China, and discounted, knockoff clothing items ranging from the latest trendy jeans and tops to headscarves and long Islamic Republic–approved skirts and *mantos*. With its maze-like structure, convivial atmosphere, and abundance of goods, Bazaar Markazi lends itself to wandering, and I often found myself there to stroll and become more immersed in the pulse of the everyday.

During my first visit to the bazaar, I found that I had meandered toward a side of the bazaar cordoned off from the main walkway by a large curtain and a "women only" sign. Curious, I pulled the curtain aside and stepped into a large area filled with stalls that sold women's underclothes. What was remarkable was not the items being sold, but the sheer number of young women who were working at the stalls. Hidden from the predominately male atmosphere of the main bazaar, the women here created their own female milieu. During the winter months, some of the older women who owned the stalls warmed food and soup on the electric stoves that they had hidden in the back of their kiosks. The young women would often congregate together during their lunch hours to share gossip and the latest news. When one of the vendors had to leave, other young women would watch over her stall in her absence. The sense of camaraderie and community that the women had forged in this small slice of Bazaar Markazi was palpable to anyone who entered.

Due to the regularity of my visits, many of these young women and their friends came to know me. Parisa, a married, twenty-nine-year-old high school graduate, was one of them. She sold jewelry and accessories in a tiny stall located right outside the walkway toward the women's lingerie section. Her stall served as a prelude as visitors made their way down the passageway. Parisa worked, in large part, because she wanted herself and her husband to appear "good" before the eyes of others:

I've been married for eight years. I don't want to have children. I found out that my husband was a drug addict while we were engaged, but I didn't call it off because I loved him. [When I would accuse him of being a drug addict], my husband would hit me, saying that he wasn't. It started with opium and ended with crack. He would never tell me. I found out on my own. He doesn't do drugs anymore, but he still takes pills at night to fall asleep. He's addicted to those. He takes whatever pills he can find. I don't want to have kids because I don't know what my husband will do. He's unemployed. I don't know if he'll stay good or bad. I don't want to bring a child into the world when I don't know. I was bored at home, that's why I came to work here, [but] it's not like we don't have financial problems. We rent from Jamileh's [another vendor in the women's section] father. Their financial situation isn't good either; they just have their own house. They live on the upper floor and we live on the bottom floor. Jamileh's father is a laborer. My only hope is that my husband is good. If my husband is good, I'm good too. I want people to say how good I am. I don't want to do anything wrong. And I don't want people to think that I'm doing anything wrong. Don't tell Jamileh my story. I don't want anyone to know. You're the first person I told this much to. I don't want people to see my husband in a different light.

## On the Road to Dignity

What the narratives of Faranak and Parisa reveal are how some female face-savers' work experiences are largely shaped by their husbands' lax participation in the face game. Driven by economic need, these women's entry into the labor force is a direct consequence of their husband's inability or unwillingness to meet various household expenses and thus, to provide for the family. Faranak felt that her husband did not spend the money he made wisely. A bad investment in a get-rich-quick scheme had left him largely bankrupt. In Faranak's view, if he had worked hard and saved, then they would have been able to live in a large house on a nice street, rather than in the tiny two-bedroom apartment they rented in one of Sari's lower-class neighborhoods. Similarly, Parisa's husband was unable to provide for their needs due to a series of unfortunate drug addictions that left him incapacitated to work. Parisa saw her work not simply as an outlet to escape from her home life, but as a means to bring money into the household and convey the impression that nothing was "wrong" before the critical gaze of her community.

Work provided women like Faranak and Parisa with a source of income as well as a means to exercise agency and maintain dignity in their day-to-day lives. While the decision to engage in work was shaped by their marital situations, through work, these women exerted independent control over their bodies and expenses. They made the decision, for example, about whether or when to get pregnant rather than acceding to their husband's desires for children. They no longer had to ask their husbands or extended family members for money for clothes and other incidentals. For instance, during the time I knew her, Faranak would make plans to go to Tehran to buy clothes that were, according to her, "better quality" and "less expensive than clothes you can find in Sari."

Most importantly, work was the means by which these women were able to appear competent and responsible before their community of peers. By attempting to make enough money to buy a large house, for example, Faranak intended to use her job as a way to hide her husband's perceived irresponsibility and to make up for his lack of face among those who knew them. Indeed, while everyone in the salon knew of her husband's failed work history, they looked upon Faranak with admiration. Faranak had formed a reputation in the eyes of Ms. Zahedi, particularly, as an assiduous, hardworking young woman. By the same token, Parisa worked hard in order to save face in the eyes of colleagues like Jamileh and to hide her husband's drug use. She was successful to the extent that no one in Bazaar Markazi knew about her marital troubles and her husband's addiction. Since her colleagues perceived him to be a "good" husband, she was seen to be "good" as well.

The work experiences of the single, low-income women I met were similarly shaped by economic need. However, rather than work to hide their husband's perceived incompetencies, they worked to hide their family's status. Indeed, many, like Nina, the freelance artist and former dishwasher we met in chapter 1, were reticent to give the impression that they were poor. "I didn't want people to think that I dressed badly," one seamstress recounted. Work was seen as instrumental in making the money necessary to present an *aberumand* (dignified, with face), middle-class front. Myriad times I noticed how these young women's earnings made it possible for them to purchase items for their wedding trousseaus, buy fashionable clothing and accessories, and/or procure choice food items to present to guests.

It is through work that young women, like Nina, Faranak, and Parisa, are able to reduce the risk of being exposed for their poverty by signaling to peers and those whom they consider *ba kelas* that they too are doing well, even when the actual evidence indicates that they are not. As it is for their male counterparts, financial need is the primary driver of these women's work experiences and initial entry into the labor force. However, the sustained appeal of work is due to the fact that the money it brings is seen as good, as it assists these women in presenting a socially accepted front and in becoming self-sufficient in the face of unforeseen events. "Even single women need to work because then they can become the hopes of their parents," Sakineh, a middle-aged domestic worker, told me. "What if their future husbands can't provide for them? They have to work to learn a skill in case it becomes necessary in the future. They can't just sit at home." Sakineh—who herself worked because of an unfortunate car accident that left her husband incapacitated—saw a woman's control over her own labor as essential in warding off the risk of future destitution and securing the financial well-being of the family unit. As such, parents like Sakineh will often encourage their daughters who are no longer in school to engage in some type of work activity. Whether this work activity constitutes paid work as seamstresses or unpaid apprenticeships in salons and sewing houses, female participation in the workforce is one means by which daughters can preempt being judged as 'allaf (idle) by community members. It also serves as a way to satisfy parental concerns about their daughters' future financial security and happiness.

Similar to their female counterparts, single male face-savers use the money they earn on the job to present an image of themselves that may not be aligned with their everyday life realities. By spending the capital they accumulate on the job, both male and female face-savers come full circle: they are able to provide for their families, finance a wedding, or buy material goods such as clothing, electronics, jewelry, home furnishings, and cars. All of these activities, in turn, facilitate their quest to safeguard their image from intimations of shame. Through work, face-savers become trustworthy and mature in the eyes of both their economic peers and non-economic unequals like Ms. Zahedi.

However, work—even informal, minor labor—is not available to all who may desire it. For married, female face-savers like Faranak and Parisa, entry into the informal labor force directly stems from their husbands' encouragement or approval. Often, these young women justified their visibility in the public sphere to me by describing how their husbands were "okay" with them working, how their husbands "encouraged" them to work, or how their husbands' income volatility meant that they had to take over the household reins (of course, with their husbands' full knowledge).[43] In a similar vein, some single, working young women knew they had to give up their jobs once they were married because of their fiancé's disapproval. As Mahnaz, a young lingerie vendor in Bazaar Markazi, stated, "My fiancé doesn't want me to work after we get married next month, so I'm going to quit in a month." Mahnaz, a high school graduate who majored in architecture, enjoyed her work and wanted to continue her education, but stated how "in the end, this is what happens." Young women like Mahnaz, who express a penchant for improving their economic situation through work, but who have to confront work barriers imposed by their fiancés, face the difficult choice of working and alienating their future spouses versus not working and minimizing marital discord and conflict. The desire to have a harmonious marriage that garners praise from their family and friends, more times than not, wins out in the end.

Indeed, among some of the families I came to know, a marriage that ended in separation and divorce was perceived to impart shame on the woman and her kin, as she would be judged as being irresponsible and unable to properly carry out her wifely duties and manage her married life. The fear of shaming was so pervasive that some divorced female face-savers were hesitant to reveal their marital status, especially on the job. Ariana, a twenty-six-year-old lingerie vendor in Bazaar Markazi, exemplified this rather poignantly. A divorcée with a nine-year-old daughter, Ariana was reluctant to tell her boss that she was divorced because, as she explained, "It's bad if people here find out. I don't want my boss to find out." By pretending to still be married, Ariana avoided both the social ostracism and economic backlash that may have occurred if the impression she was cultivating was disrupted through the discovery that she was actually divorced.

## Fruits of Labor

Why are face-savers so adamant about embracing work norms? Why do young men and women try so hard to appear hardworking, responsible, and self-sufficient? Is the only reward the ability to hold their head up high in the communities where they live? It is so important for face-savers to help themselves and stand on their own feet because doing so not only enables them to make sense of their lives and maintain their dignity, but also facilitates their access to limited forms of social and economic success. It is this quest for success that is the key driving force behind their work ethic. For my interlocutors, the appeal of saving face through work was not simply to validate themselves, but to augment their reputation and socioeconomic standing.

The rules that govern the face system serve as symbolic boundaries that those who have few other forms of distinction available to draw from can use to distinguish themselves from their peers and live a dignified life in the eyes of others.[44] While middle- and upper-class youth may also share similar values, face-savers are less capable of hiding failures because of their lack of resources, which makes them that much more susceptible to threats to their dignity.[45] In the absence of clear economic distinctions, the face system and the moral rule of work it encompasses become an alternative measure by which some youth can judge themselves vis-à-vis others. These youth understand expectations of self-sufficiency and hard work as the means by which they can facilitate their quest to incrementally move up the proverbial ladder. Their endorsement of and active participation in work play a structuring role in their daily lives. Orientations toward work influence the decisions they make, and the way they view others' social standing.[46] Working subsequently comprises a "cultural background noise" in the day-to-day lives of face-savers, where work is seen as a means to an end.[47]

Work provides those youth who are able to successfully abide by its tenets with a form of symbolic capital that they can then exchange for social and subsequently, economic capital. The pursuit of face through work serves as a mechanism by which some young men and women can secure a positive image of themselves as moral individuals. The greater their perceived moral stock, the greater the ability of face-savers to use this moral capital to expand their social networks. Increasing one's network of associations, in turn, is the most effective tool at face-savers' disposal for preempting destitution.[48] Indeed, "deserving" youth are able to deploy their expanded social ties to heighten their clout over resources that function to incrementally increase their status and standing, as the following cases demonstrate.[49]

### Karim

One afternoon, as I sat with Sakineh, who was also Karim's neighbor, she recalled how Mr. B had gotten Karim into one of the best high schools in the city. The time that Karim spent at Mr. B's grocery store enabled him to foster close ties with Mr. B, who—by way of his connections—was able to get Karim accepted into Mazandaran All Boys' High School. Karim himself was not unaware of the fact that he would be rewarded in kind for helping Mr. B. Karim knew that if he continued to project a good front, Mr. B, by way of his extensive connections in Sari, could help him yet again in the future. As Karim later explained to me in an effort to justify why he would frequent the stuffy grocery store:

> Mr. B knows everyone. He was the one who had a connection and got
> me into Mazandaran's All Boys' High School. He just went in with a letter
> and got me in. One of my uncles only studied until the second grade and

now he is a nurse making 600,000 *tomans* a month [550 USD]. He had connections. You just need connections.[50]

## Nazgol

Nazgol was a twenty-one-year-old apprentice in a bakery located near Sari's south side. Her parents lived in the village that bordered Sari, but she had moved to the city to attend high school and had been living in Sari with her grandmother since then. Nazgol had been working in the bakery for one year when I first met her. She took up the job after she quit her last low-paying job as a salon apprentice. "I used to help my parents, but now I'm just working for my own wedding trousseau." To be able to put together a beautiful trousseau that would bestow prestige upon her, Nazgol worked long hours from the early morning until nightfall. Her dedication to her work did not go unnoticed. Pleased with Nazgol, the bakery owner, Mr. Babak, often invited her to his house for dinner, where she befriended Mr. Babak's daughters. "His daughters treat me like their sister even though I'm just an apprentice."

## Pejman

One winter evening, I visited a family friend, Zohreh. That particular night, Zohreh was preoccupied with finding a carpenter who could create additional shelving to add to a closet. Sakineh, who was Zohreh's maid, suggested that Zohreh hire her twenty-year-old son, Pejman, and his friend, a freelance carpenter whom Pejman worked with. Pejman moonlighted as a carpenter and Zohreh knew that he was considered to be a "good egg" among his neighbors; he had finished high school, enrolled in the military, and was now attempting to amass enough resources to start his own household by working long hours, often into the night. Without hesitation, Zohreh called Pejman that evening and hired him on the spot.

## Hooman

Through Yas, I learned about Hooman, Yas's maternal cousin, a young man in his early twenties. Hooman was able to attain what few others in his family could: a steady, well-paying job in a factory and a car. During the end of my fieldwork, I found out that Hooman had fallen in love with Yas and was getting engaged.[51] While I was surprised that Yas's family raised no objections to her impending marriage, I soon found out that their approval was grounded in the fact that Hooman's work ethic made him a good catch. "He has a job and a car," Yas and her family members would constantly state to me as justification for why he would make a good husband. Yas and her relatives made a cost-benefit analysis, calculating that the benefit that would come to Yas from marrying Hooman would be more than the cost of her marrying at such a young age, as she would most likely not find a better husband.

By attempting to become self-sufficient through work and by showing their diligence, youth like Karim, Nazgol, and Pejman find a way to ingratiate themselves into the social worlds of their middle-class counterparts, who, in turn, provide them with some form of social protection and/or economic support. As I touched on in chapter 1, the painstaking efforts face-savers make to conform to the work ethic stem partly from the belief that it is who they know, rather than what they know, that will ultimately help them in getting ahead. As Amin, a sixteen-year-old high school student, explained, "You have to become friends with people who are well-dressed, organized, and rich. These friends can then be useful to you in the future." In establishing these friendships, face-savers like Pejman often build associations with people like Zohreh with whom they are acquainted. These people constitute family friends, employers, colleagues, neighbors, or extended family members with a wide range of contacts. As these individuals often know of the moral character of the face-saver, they are much more willing to extend economic assistance to him as compared to formal firms and very powerful others who do not have this prior knowledge. Indeed, given their lack of extensive connections and resources, it is nearly impossible for face-savers to receive support from the latter.

The small social and economic gains that are bestowed on reputable young men and women by those in their extended networks help to further raise these youths' profiles in the community. These wins, however minor, create status distinctions among youth that contribute to a micro-system of stratification within the social worlds they inhabit, a stratification system in which those who are judged as upholding the moral principle of work and who incorporate it into their public identities hold a higher standing than those who do not.[52] Upstanding youth then use these interpersonal evaluations to reap the benefits of being favorably evaluated. This is exceedingly important for the face-savers' marriage outcomes, as Hooman's case demonstrated. By being deemed a self-sufficient young man who had a "job and a car," Hooman was able to position himself as an ideal marriage candidate. Young men like Hooman who are able to find and work in a job that pays relatively well, or at least seems to pay well, are considered to have a relatively large amount of financial capital that can protect the face of a future bride and her family in a way that those with smaller amounts of capital cannot. Thus, rather than resist or reject the work ethic, face-savers attempt to embrace it as best they can, secure in the knowledge that through some real effort, they have a chance at improving their socioeconomic situations.

Not all young men and women who experience a rise in status and reputation engage solely in physical labor. Indeed, the amount of effort high school students place in studying hard—largely reflected in the grades they receive—serves as an important measure of their diligence and as a key route to maintaining face. Since school is the focal institution in the daily lives of students, families and community members tend to measure these youths' assiduousness by way of their commitment to studying rather than to work. Communities judge those young men and women who receive better scores, who smoothly transition from one grade to the next, and who ultimately graduate from high school as committed to responsibility in a way that youth who do not study are not.

Knowing that their child's reputation as a good student reflects on their moral character, parents are extremely alert in attempting to ensure that their sons and daughters keep up with their studies.[53] As one mother would constantly state to me, "Farbod [her sixteen-year-old son] only studies for twenty minutes every day. Then he goes to watch television or plays on the computer. I tell him to study in a nice way, and he doesn't listen. I tell him to study in a harsh way, and he doesn't listen. I just don't know what to do!" In a last-ditch effort to help him, Farbod's mother requested that I tutor him. Farbod had failed six of his classes and had gained a reputation in the community as being *tanbal* (lazy).

Farbod's family and neighbors viewed him with concern, as he was seen as having given up on the possibility of achievement through hard work. Having failed so many classes, Farbod's prospects of graduating from high school were equally dim. In the absence of a viable job to fall back on, a failure to graduate meant that Farbod would have a difficult time situating himself as a hardworking and "worthy" member of the community.

Alternatively, those youth who are able to succeed academically are able to secure their reputation as learned individuals. Families are eager to share news about their child's accomplishments to those who are in a position to potentially provide socioeconomic rewards. Sakineh, for example, would constantly boast to Zohreh about Mohammad's (her fifteen-year-old son) accomplishments in school. "He always receives high grades and never wastes time hanging out with the other kids in our *mahal* [neighborhood]," Sakineh would say. Zohreh, for her part, would share this information with me to justify why Mohammad would be a good candidate for my English tutoring classes.

Knowledge of the rewards that can come with academic achievement led many of the students I knew to spend exorbitant amounts of time studying for exams, preparing for their lessons, and negotiating their grades with teachers in an effort to be seen as good students. For example, one young seventeen-year-old south Tehrani young woman, Shiva, would multitask, washing her family's laundry while simultaneously studying from her textbooks. Likewise, Yas would often stay up until the early morning hours preparing for exams. The following reaction ensued after a teacher gave Yas a lower grade than she believed she deserved:

> I've gotten all 20s except for one class. The teacher gave me an 18. It's just ridiculous! How can she give me an 18 just like that on a whim? All the other girls in the class have gotten 20s. My mom said that I just don't have luck. My mom went and spoke to the teacher and the teacher told her that I need to study more. My mom told her that I study enough and I can't study more than I do now. The teacher got quiet after that. I would study until 4:30 in the morning and then I would get up at 6:30 to study more. My mom kept saying that I need to eat. I didn't even eat, I studied so hard for that class.

In an effort to not lose face in front of her peers and to secure her position as a top student, Yas displayed an intense dedication to studying. When I wondered whether her impending marriage to Hooman would put a damper on her educational pursuits, she said emphatically, "One of my conditions was that I finish high school. I told him I wouldn't marry him if I couldn't finish." Not only would her marriage to a "good," "hardworking" young man help Yas increase her status within the community, but her own commitment to the work ethic would help solidify this standing.

## Behavior, Strategies, and Resources

As the preceding representative narratives and cases in this chapter indicate, working hard either in school or on the job equips poor young men and women, who have little else, to save face by presenting themselves as responsible and self-sufficient. However, who people are, the choices they make, and the context in which they live all affect their behavior. As Sherman has noted, some people have an easier time acquiring moral capital through work than others, and this is not random.[54] In a similar fashion, no amount of face-saving is a guarantee that all those who do acquire moral capital will use the social and economic opportunities that they are presented with in the same way and pursue the same ends. Tactics and coping strategies differ among youth, and the particular resources that each youth brings into the game—cleverness, background, and risk-taking abilities—reinforce this.

### Zerangi (Cleverness)

Very often, those young people who are able to easily accumulate moral capital through the performative and instrumental aspects of work are those who are endowed with a certain level of *zerangi*. Those who have *zerangi* are able to skillfully manipulate social situations and individuals to reap the maximum possible personal benefits. *Zerangi*, similar to street smarts, is a set of strategic decisions to maximize one's chances of success and to minimize potential problems; it is a sense that includes knowing how to present oneself in public, how to handle oneself, and how to speak to others.[55] As one of the main strategies to increase one's chances for success, *zerangi* holds a central place in Iranian culture. Indeed, as Erika Friedl asserts, many Iranians believe that "good, honest behavior frequently leads to poverty and hardship—uncritical goodness is foolish."[56] Those face-savers who are able to reap the most rewards from their strong work ethic are those who are able to apply "superior knowledge" in order to sway the odds in their favor.[57] As the representative narratives below indicate, this knowledge can range from "persuasion, bargaining, reasoning and hard work, to deception and dissimulation, lies and outsmarting others."[58]

## *Shahpur*

I met Shahpur, the *bamiyeh* vendor in south Tehran, on a particularly cold evening in the city. At that time of the night, while most of the shops were open, many of the street vendors had gone home. Shahpur, however, was busy walking around the block, calling out to potential customers to taste the hot, oven-fresh *bamiyeh*s that he had expertly placed on a huge platter that he carried as he walked. Whenever he would run out of pastries, he would go back to the bakery where he initially bought them and buy more. By selling the pastries at a higher price, Shahpur would make a small but handsome profit. "I have honey sweet *bamiyeh*s. Come and get them!" Shahpur would cry out as he walked. As he told me, "I've been doing this for ten years. I dropped out of school and started when I was eleven. Ask anyone here who the *bamiyeh* seller is and they will tell you it's me." Shahpur's biggest problem, like those of the other street vendors that he competed with, was the municipality, which, until recently, would constantly shut down his operations since he did not have the proper vending permits. "I started to go to the courthouse to sell my pastries because not only are the former prisoners who come out of there really good buyers, but also because the municipality doesn't bother me when I'm there. I'm going there now."

Shahpur had the astuteness to choose the strategy that brought him the most monetary success. Not only did he work longer hours than his colleagues, but he had figured out who the best clients were (former inmates) and where the best vending site was (the courthouse). His ability to outsmart the municipality and to become the only renowned *bamiyeh* seller in the neighborhood was testament to his *zerangi* tactics.

### Family Support

Face-savers who spend more time fraternizing with friends or working in public venues have a much more developed sense of how to relate to others, how to negotiate, and how to maneuver social situations[59]—in short, a much more developed sense of *zerangi*—than those who spend the majority of their days sequestered in the home. Indeed, recurrent interactions—with clients, neighbors, friends, or employers—reinforce these youths' street smarts and keep it "at the ready" for immediate use.[60] However, the ability to be out in the public sphere is contingent on the supportiveness of the young person's family. It is not random that Karim, whose parents allowed him to spend time in the neighborhood after school, consorting with friends or helping Mr. B, had a much easier time gaining social capital than his friend Mohammad, whose mother, Sakineh, forbade him to socialize in the neighborhood after school, afraid that he would get "caught up with the wrong crowd." Mohammad, while able to accrue moral capital as a result of his work ethic in school, was never able to convert this symbolic resource into the type of social and economic opportunities that Karim had. Indeed, with help from Mr. B, Karim was ultimately able to not only get into college, but also to attend. Alternatively, Mohammad, a stellar student, got accepted into university, but was never able to go because Sakineh could not afford the tuition. Mohammad, for his part, largely spent his time at home, and was not able to foster connections with influential others, like Mr. B, who could have helped him secure the necessary funds to attend college.

Similarly, no amount of saving face is a guarantee that all face-savers will necessarily use the social and economic opportunities they are presented with in the same way. Sara, for example, was a young, engaged woman in her early twenties, who as a consequence of her reputation, work ethic, and subsequent connections, was able to secure an entry-level job at a nonprofit organization, a job that was extremely difficult to come by for someone in her position and one that she was extremely passionate about. But after a year, Sara quit her job and decided to stay at home and become a homemaker.

On the other hand, there was Nina, the freelance artist. Nina decided to start her own art business with the little money she had saved up and through the connections she had formed with her middle-class school peers. Rather than choose to stay at home, Nina was constantly traveling throughout the city, meeting potential customers and gallery owners. She would often critique the young women who were in similar financial straits as herself and who chose to become homemakers, believing that the way for women like her to advance was through education and work. In my last visit to Iran, I learned that Nina was attending university.

What explains the difference between Sara and Nina? As Sara recounted, her fiancé wanted her to be home when he was home and take care of the house. Alternatively, Nina would often remind me that her fiancé actively encouraged her to work and continue her education. As these two examples indicate, the support that comes from influential male figures—often husbands—influences how some young women respond to opportunities that arise as a result of facework. While patriarchal ideology within the family has traditionally been considered an instance of a gender-specific barrier to Iranian women's entry into the labor force, I encountered many young women who were self-employed entrepreneurs who worked from home as seamstresses, hairstylists, or artists. Men who forbade their wives and daughters to work in the public sphere were more willing to accept these arrangements as there was no longer an incompatibility between their wives' or daughters' work and gender roles. Thus, women like Sara who desire to work but do not have their husbands' support are not entirely excluded from the labor force; however, they have less choice to participate in a wider range of employment opportunities than women like Nina who have their husbands' full backing.

### Risk-Taking: Omid's Story

Omid was a successful entrepreneur in Tehran who was Zohreh's family friend.[61] Omid's father passed away when he was in his teens; at the age of sixteen, Omid dropped out of school to work full-time in order to meet household expenses. He soon became an apprentice to a fishmonger in the local bazaar in Tehran and eventually became so adept at gutting fish that another fishmonger decided to hire Omid to work the night shift. Occasionally, Omid would supplement the wages he earned from working these two jobs by taking leftover fish and fish parts that no one wanted to buy so that his mother and sisters could sell them to their neighbors. This little venture laid the groundwork for the start of his own business. While he ran this side business, Omid secured the permission of his night manager to gut fish from home. Enlisting the help of his mother and siblings, Omid was able to gut more fish in a lesser amount of time, earning even more money from this second side hustle. With the money Omid earned from working these jobs, he was able to amass a small savings account.

Eventually, Omid decided to risk losing his entire savings; he went to the south of Iran and spent his savings buying fish directly from suppliers and selling them in the bazaar back in Tehran. When he realized that he was able to earn a rather substantial profit by eliminating the middleman and purchasing fish directly, Omid focused his energies on turning his small at-home fishmongering business into a full-time enterprise. He quit working as an apprentice and went into business for himself, marketing and selling fish in the local bazaar. Since Omid was considered trustworthy and had already proven that he was skilled and hardworking, fishmongers in the bazaar were willing to buy directly from him, even more so than from many of the other wholesale fishmongers. He became so successful that by the time he turned twenty-six, Omid was able to save enough money to buy his former employer's store.

Omid's rags-to-riches story illustrates how the ability to undertake moderate risks is a key factor that influences some face-savers' abilities to convert moral capital to monetary gains.[62] Face-savers like Omid who engage in a certain amount of risk, but who simultaneously take steps to ensure that they do not end up worse than when they started, are often the ones who are able to secure greater social and economic gains than those who simply wait to be discovered by community members or employers. Knowing that their community's job opportunities are limited and that competition is intense, youth like those introduced in this chapter undertake risky practices such as taking out loans, spending their savings on business ventures, or investing money in training opportunities like salon apprenticeships in the hopes that their work ethic and skill will enable them to gain larger amounts of capital in a shorter period of time. As Omid's story indicates, these youth temper the financial risk involved in these practices by working other jobs, enlisting the help of family members, and engaging in low-risk pilot ventures. These calculations ensure that they will not lose everything they have and therefore incur stigmatization if their practices fail.

Work, in all its various manifestations, is a means for some poor young men and women to differentiate themselves as "hardworking," "responsible," and "competent" before the gaze of their communities. It is a way for them to maintain dignity by "defining themselves as successful"[63] despite their daily economic challenges. In embracing socially sanctioned work activities, these face-savers are better able to secure jobs, promotions, or charity than those deemed to be in moral disrepute as a result of their idleness. However, given that such opportunities are generally scarce in the communities in which face-savers live, those youth who have certain preexisting qualities and resources—namely, cleverness, family support, and risk-taking abilities—are able to climb the proverbial ladder much more easily than those who are not blessed with similar strengths and backgrounds.

That developing a reputation as a hard worker is a key prerequisite to building social and economic capital is in line with the cultural belief that one has to work hard in order to receive daily sustenance and to secure one's livelihood.[64] As Shayan, a twenty-six-year-old college graduate, stated,

> If someone is rich, there must have been some effort placed that caused him to be rich. Maybe a seventeen-year-old with a brand-name car under his feet didn't work hard, but his father or grandfather must have worked really hard to get that wealth. When I look at it this way, they're people just like me.

The proverb "From me hard work, from God the blessing"[65] was often repeated by face-savers whenever they described why they did what they did and what they hoped to accomplish. In this view, God is ultimately the one who provides the blessing—social connections, promotions, marriage, or greater income—but the individual has to be resolute enough and work hard enough in the first place in order to secure these rewards.[66] Face-savers believe that they bear the burden of the consequences of their actions. Those who engage in indolence, who do not study or work hard enough, and who do not make use of their skills and the resources surrounding them lose God's blessing and their chances of making it. Work, as a moral principle, therefore represents one pathway to attaining what face-savers view as the "good life." As we will see in the next chapter, appearances constitute another.

Residential alleyways in south Tehran, 2008. Photos by author.

A typical street scene in Sari, 2018. Photo by author.

A young apprentice creating branded magnets in a south Tehran workshop, 2008. Photo by author.

A young man in the outskirts of Tehran picks cherries to sell, 2008. Photo by author.

Friends on summer break in the outskirts of Tehran, 2008. Photo by author.

A young man working in a welding shop in the environs of Sari, 2010. Photo by author.

A young baker with coworkers in a traditional bakery in Sari, 2010. Photo by author.

Informal entrepreneurial copy station in a garage in Sari, 2018. Photo by author.

Friends and vendors gather in front of a traditional teahouse in a bazaar in the heart of Sari, 2017. Photo by author.

Billboard for a men's clothing boutique in Sari, depicting an Iranian man wearing a trendy suit, complete with a vest, handkerchief, and neck scarf, 2016. Photo by author.

A storefront in Sari advertising alternative, fashionable ways of wearing the hijab, 2018. Photo by author.

Storefront mannequins in Sari displaying the latest global fashion trends, 2016. Photos by author.

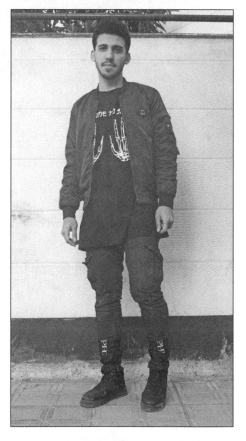

Street styles in Sari, 2011–2019. Photos by Farzin Mahmoudzadeh.

3

## Dress for Success

Khodavand zibast va ziba'i ra dust darad.

(God is beautiful and loves beauty.)
—Hadith

"These *manto*s are being worn by celebrities. In fact, a famous actress made the design for this particular *manto*. The design has more traditional Persian motifs and patterns." This comment, made by a shop owner on Maziyar Street, as he held up a long vest emblazoned with paisley, helped to solidify the sale of a chic, Persian paisley patterned *manto* that was being sold in The Boutique. The many *manto*s sold by The Boutique, priced around 30,000 *toman*s (10 USD) in the summer of 2015, were markedly less expensive than the plainer *manto*s being sold in other boutiques on Maziyar for double the price. The Boutique was doing quite well that summer, as the bohemian look was on-trend: actresses to elite women to ordinary schoolgirls would incorporate elements of "bohemian chic"—a scarf with Persian calligraphy, floral and paisley prints, beaded necklaces, and long, loose, flowing *manto*s with dolman sleeves—into their wardrobes. In fact, The Boutique itself was the embodiment of the chic, "now" Persian bohemian: a modern boutique with wooden walls, parquet floors, and Iranian kilims and pillows lining its walls. On its shelves, The Boutique displayed an assortment of handmade shoes and bags sourced from organic fabrics, linen *manto*s, t-shirts with Persian calligraphy, and beaded jewelry. The shop was constantly filled with a stream of young women—and the occasional man—attracted to its relatively low prices and hipster vibe. To be bohemian chic that summer was to be on point and "with it."

The Boutique is significant because it represents one avenue by which trends can be transmitted to a wide range of Iranians. Indeed, young women and men from more modest backgrounds are among the shop's clientele. Purchasing cheap but trendy clothing items becomes a way of building their cultural capital. Bourdieu developed the concept of cultural capital to encompass the institutionalized (e.g., educational qualifications), objectified (e.g., clothes, books, CDs), and embodied (e.g., ideas, speech patterns) assets that a person has and that can be converted into economic capital.[1] In the case of face-savers, fashionable clothing serves as an objectified and embodied asset that facilitates their attempts to look *farhangi* (cultured) and *ba kelas*. Their self-fashioning allows them to compete in the game of life by staking claim to a certain lifestyle and giving shape to a particular identity.[2] To this I turn below.

## Looks

"I look through books with illustrations of old local, Persian costumes and then I adapt it to contemporary times, make a design, and give it to a tailor to sew for me," twenty-one-year-old Fereshteh explained when I asked her about the uniquely stylish outfits she wore on a daily basis. Often strapped for cash, Fereshteh figured that the most cost-effective way to be on-trend was to have her own clothes made, an option that is often surprisingly cheaper in Iran than buying off the rack. Skinny jeans, distinctive *mantos*, loafers or Converse sneakers, a no-makeup makeup look, and jewelry made of leather, fabric, and various beading comprised the fashion aesthetic that Fereshteh sported on a daily basis. Fereshteh was an apprentice in a modern Barnes and Noble–type bookstore in the heart of Sari; her father was a schoolteacher from the south of Iran, while her mother owned a small clothing shop. Although they were able to save enough money to afford the tuition to send their daughter to college in Sari—itself an astonishing feat for a family of six—they could not provide for Fereshteh's living expenses. Fereshteh worked in the bookstore to be able to pay the rent on the small apartment that she shared with a roommate and to meet her daily expenses. Despite her financial need, Fereshteh would often explain away the reason she worked, attributing it to the culture she was raised in. "Where I'm from, working is an honor. People respect you for working. I don't need the money that badly." Bearing a striking resemblance to a popular Iranian actress, Fereshteh often dreamed of becoming involved in theatre.

In the time I knew her, I noticed how Fereshteh would go out of her way to befriend those youth around her who comprised the upper-middle echelons of Saravi society: the college-aged children of the bookstore owners and their friends and acquaintances. Fereshteh's tactic consisted of giving random gifts of books, poems, and small trinkets, and sending a constant stream of text messages and friendly invitations to hang out. Combined with her fastidious approach to dressing in the unique satorial aesthetic of these well-to-do others, Fereshteh's efforts eventually paid off. She befriended a few young, male bookstore owners, whom she hung out with on a regular basis after her shift at the bookstore would end. She eventually became close friends with Naghmeh, the bookstore cashier, a job Naghmeh took up not out of financial need, but to spend more time with her boyfriend, the bookstore manager. Through Naghmeh, Fereshteh became even more integrated into Sari's hipster, affluent crowd. She came to befriend others—theatre actors, university students, and small business owners—and was eventually able to land a role in a small theatre production in Sari. Throughout the time I knew her, I could not help but think how Fereshteh was the poster child for how far the "right" look could take a person.

## Posturing

As I discussed in chapter 1, face-savers know that by manipulating their *zaher* to conceal their socioeconomic backgrounds and their often desperate financial straits, the possibility of befriending and eventually becoming part of middle-class society becomes infinitely more real. As William Beeman notes, the word *ru* (literally face, looks, image) is widely used in Iran to speak about one's reputation because it is one's face that is external and visible, and as such, it becomes the ideal medium for discussing social, external issues like one's reputation.[3] To preserve face, then, what better way than to safeguard and cultivate the most discernable, most external vehicle of one's face: the body?

When a face-saver is not able to secure a job, her public image becomes the instrument by which she can protect her reputation. When a face-saver has a job, fashionable tweaks to her physiognomy can project a certain cultural capital that can help her to conceal her particular line of work, attract customers and friends, or secure a promotion. In this view, the body comes to be used as a type of commodity, as an arena to display to others who can confer status and respect, the type of self-image that face-savers want to convey. The commodification of the body—a practice that is an offshoot of the modern, consumerist era[4]—enables the body to serve as the platform by which a person can display her possession of certain coveted goods and services like clothing, surgery, and exercise regimens. The body, as Joanne Finkelstein elaborates, can be contoured, tweaked, and stage-managed to be made into an emblem of the person's character, successes, and potentials.[5] As such, the body becomes the means by which a person can control others' evaluations of herself, that is, the means toward impression management.[6]

Appearance and reality thus come to coalesce in the eyes of the beholder: face-savers' appearance becomes an authenticating narrative for their relative power, status, or class without necessarily being an accurate reflection of their lives. Physical posturing represents one of the most efficient and effective ways for youth to strategically fight to turn the odds of winning the face game in their favor, as Nina describes:

> You know, an iron doesn't cost that much, washing your clothes doesn't cost that much, taking care of your appearance doesn't cost that much. I take really good care of my skin. What cream do you use, Manata? ... These kids around me, they have no hope for the future and are always trying to knock down those who do. But I always think to myself that my fiancé and I will have a big house in a garden. And I know that we'll get it. A scholar once wrote that what you think is what will happen. So I try to think positively. Even though I suffered a lot of hardship, I know it won't always be like this. If you see the world one way, that's how the world will treat you. You become what you think.

Thinking positively, in Nina's case, translated to imagining herself as wealthy and living in a large house in a good part of town. Part of Nina's strategy to make her dreams a reality was to present herself as moneyed. Every time I saw her, she was dressed in a different style of well-ironed fashionable *manto*, a pair of skinny jeans, heels, sunglasses with faux diamonds encrusted on the sides, and a faux Versace bag. Her makeup was done expertly and she made sure that she showed just the right amount of hair underneath her strategically placed loose shawl. She used the little money she had to join a local gym, so that she could maintain her modelesque physique. Even the way she spoke was well-measured, without a hint of the Mazandarani accent that often tinged the speech patterns of her lower-class neighbors.[7]

Not only was Nina able to fool her classmates into thinking that she was not poor, but through her dress and mannerisms, she was able to form close friendships with them. Indeed, her schoolmates were the ones who bought Nina, an aspiring artist, her first paint set. As Nina grew older, by way of her appearance and mannerisms, she was able to forge connections with other middle-class women whom she met through family and friends or through her gym memberships. She subsequently gained access to Sari's burgeoning art scene, forming acquaintances with writers and emerging artists. In time, Nina's engagement in middle-class society led her to become acquainted with, and eventually engaged to, a young businessman whose father was a bank manager. "Everyone was surprised that I married into a relatively well-off family," Nina told me. Nina, however, knew that it was not dumb luck, but rather her steadfast adherence to a middle-class way of life—shaped by her donning of fashionable clothes, skillfully applied makeup, engagement in artistic productions, and involvement in health, literary, and artistic circles—that gave her an edge over her working-class peers who were not as vigilant in expressing their adherence to the symbols of middle-class status.

By following the rules associated with saving face, youth like Nina find a way to become integrated into the social worlds of their well-heeled counterparts. These connections, in turn, enable face-savers to increase the diversity of people they know and the activities they engage in. Face-savers consider these connections to be important because as Amin, the young man we met in chapter 2, stated, they can be "useful" to them in time.

This notion of utility is a particularly salient incentive. Much literature on the politics of the poor in the Middle East documents how networks of exchange and aid are invaluable for both managing hardship and facilitating social mobility.[8] In Iran, face-savers' vertical ties with those who are doing better than themselves in some socioeconomic dimension often prove to be exceedingly valuable in enabling them to secure various non-economic resources that contribute to their projection of a certain *ba kelas* appearance. In these instances, vertical exchange networks, or informal networks that operate between face-savers and those who hold a higher socioeconomic position, enable face-savers to gain access to material goods or resources free-of-charge in exchange for their labor.[9] Simultaneously, as discussed earlier, embodying an admired front facilitates these young people's ability to form vertical associations in the first place.

Yas's excursions to the seaside villa of her mother's upper-class employer are a fruitful example. I accompanied Yas once on these trips to the elite seaside subdivision that she would make every summer, by virtue of her mother's position as a housemaid and the employer's own admiration of Yas's character. During my time with her, I noticed how Yas, while helping her mother with daily chores, would also participate in the leisure activities of the neighborhood's elite youth.[10] The activities—swimming, biking, and shopping—that Yas engaged in not only provided her with a form of social entertainment, but also functioned as opportunities for her to observe the behavior of affluent youth at the seaside resort. From these advantaged others, Yas was able to learn the fashions and cultural cues of Iran's upper and middle classes, including the types of clothing that were in style that season, the exercise routines and gyms that were in vogue, and even popular courting rituals. As Yas explained to me while we were walking around the resort one morning, "Guys here usually follow girls around! Guys will drive up to girls that are driving around and try to talk to them and do a car race with them. Just drive and see what happens!" This type of knowledge not only helped Yas among her own peers by allowing her to give the semblance that she was "with it," but also helped her navigate the world of the middle class by giving her a common language and identity through which she could communicate with socioeconomic unequals like myself.

During my time in the field, I rarely witnessed face-savers not groomed to perfection, not well-mannered, or dressed in anything but their finest clothes in public. Among these young men and women, bodily aestheticization became the basis for performing class.[11] Even though Yas, whom I noticed was well dressed on a daily basis, emphasized that visible signifiers of one's class status did not come solely through one's appearance, what she noted most about others' socioeconomic standing was precisely their looks:

> You can just tell if someone is rich. It's not always just in the clothes, but
> also in the mannerisms, the way they talk, everything. Do you see that

guy over there with the headphones on his ears listening to music? A poor person wouldn't have that. Or those girls, dressed up all nicely? They're in a good position. Look at that woman dressed up all nicely over there with the baby carriage. She's upper-class because a poor person wouldn't have a baby carriage. My mom's side of the family is rich, while my dad's is low-class. My mom always encourages us to buy the more expensive items of clothing so that we can save face in front of her family.

When Yas could not afford an expensive item of clothing or accessory, she often relied on loans from friends and family. On more than one occasion, I noticed Yas wearing outfits that marked her accultuturation to admired, middle-class sartorial norms. I later found out that she would conveniently borrow these ensembles from her friends. By catalyzing young people's ability to keep personal expenses to a minimum and to appear fashionably on-trend, horizontal exchange networks like these that occur between people from similar socioeconomic backgrounds enable youth to live by the moral code of the face system. As Yas explained to me, "I only have around three or four *manto*s, but I exchange with my sister and her friends. The one I'm wearing now is my sister's friend's *manto*! If you change your outfit daily, people will think you have a lot of money!"

This deliberate tweaking of the self extends to the costly gifts that face-savers purchase for family and friends. It extends to the rhinoplasties that they undergo (a well-sculpted nose is a marker of middle-class status) at the expense of buying a home. It extends, too, to older, married face-savers' acquisition of valuable household furnishings and electronic goods that means that they will have to sacrifice in other, less publicly visible expenses, such as proper meals and diapers for their infant children. It even extends to the non-physical markers of *kelas* that Yas hinted at when she admired the accent of the Café Laleh owner we met in chapter 1: the tweaking of their intonations to hide their rural origins.

It is through these deliberate manipulations of self—the slipping on of modish outfits, the wearing of expensive perfume, the enhancement of one's physical features, the modification of one's accent and mannerisms, and the decoration of one's residential space—that face-savers are able to signal their cultural capital. Without taking care of their appearance, these youth cannot lay claim to the respect that is offered to those who do, thereby incurring censure in the process. During afternoon prayers at a mosque one summer evening, Yas, for example, derided a young woman who was wearing winter boots. "She probably can't afford another pair of shoes!" she exclaimed to me. Similarly, Nina would make fun of a cousin for not wearing a different coat every winter season: "We went shopping and she wanted to buy a coat that she could wear next year as well! She just doesn't take care of herself."

As is the case with other social groups the world over, face-savers construct their sense of identity by distinguishing themselves from who or what they are not. As the comments of Nina and Yas reveal, to be able to posit themselves as *ba kelas*, face-savers need to create an unpolished, *dehati* other: one who has, according to Nina, "no hope for the future." The latter are found among face-savers' own neighbors, acquaintances, and economic circles. Drawing boundaries between themselves and these "other" youth enables face-savers to give significance to their own successes and failures;[12] face-savers define themselves as having achieved superiority in the realm of *kelas* when they can readily identify those who have not.

Discerning who is *dehati* and and who is *ba kelas* is not a practice confined to face-savers alone; middle- and upper-class youth use similar categories to distinguish themselves from their alleged uncivilized, backward, *dehati* and/or *bi kelas* (without class) counterparts.[13] As twenty-four-year-old Hanna, an upper-middle-class woman in Tehran, told me in an upscale coffee shop one afternoon, "The guys who come here are all *ba kelas*. *Ba kelas* people don't make their hair spike up and all that stuff. They tend to be more intellectual, they read books, they're well-mannered." For upper-class young men and women, the divide between *ba kelas* and *bi kelas* does not just extend to institutionalized assets like one's education, but also encompasses even the most minute details. For instance, during one particular afternoon at the bookstore where Fereshteh worked, Naghmeh and her friend Bamdad were complaining that some people just throw presents in a gift bag without knowing how to wrap tissue paper around the present properly. "They just place the folded tissue paper on top!" they exclaimed. "They're *dehati*, what do you expect," Naghmeh asserted.

Among youth like Naghmeh, Bamdad, and Hanna, adherence to the codes of civility and *kelas* necessitates a holistic, detailed knowledge of how to dress, how to act, and how to be. *Kelas* in this sense is not just about possessing a certain look or having material goods, but also encompasses one's communicative style and manners. It is not enough to simply know about what is fashionable, for example, in gift-giving etiquette or in hair trends, but to perform that knowledge, and perform it in accordance with a set of specific rules of propriety. Those face-savers who are the most successful in positioning themselves as *ba kelas* are the ones who have acquired the appropriate cultural capital and "know-how" that can earn them status and respect in the eyes of their middle class peers. In the latter's perception, then, the truly *ba kelas* person is the one who has the insitutionalized, objectified, *and* embodied assets associated with cultural capital.

## The Production of *Kelas*

One day, strolling on Maziyar Street, I notice Yas pull out her smartphone and start snapping pictures of the expensive *manto*s on display in the shop windows. "Are you going to buy one?" I ask her inquisitively, surprised that the $100 price tag was not deterring her. "No. I take pictures of the nicest *manto*s and then give the pictures to my cousin so she can sew an exact replica. She's really good! If you want, I can have her make one for you too. She only charges around $10."

To successfully know and embody what is "on point" is a costly endeavor. Not only does it necessitate investing a certain amount of money, but it also demands investing one's energies. Face-savers make strategic investments of time, effort, and money in order to facilitate their access to knowledge of fashion and fitness trends, social etiquette, popular self-help books, and hip, *denj* (cozy) venues in the city.

Among face-savers who have a job, it is not uncommon to spend what little money they make on the latest "it" jeans, smartphones, or makeup. Of course, to be au courant with the latest trends entails a certain time investment. Many of these young men and women dress in their finest to spend part of their days mingling in the commercial streets and centers of Sari and Tehran in places like Maziyar Street that are the heart of fashion and high culture. Seaside restaurants and sites are another popular location to observe "chicness." "Those sunglasses that guy is wearing are so chic!" exclaimed Yas, as we were hanging around by the Caspian coastline in Sari one summer afternoon. Staring at a young man wearing sleek black shades, Yas observed, "It's obvious they're brand-name, around 50–60,000 *tomans*." Although unable to afford many of these and similar items, face-savers window-shop or observe the crowds, taking inventory of the latest trends, which they later replicate with knockoffs or do-it-yourself methods. Sunglasses, designer *mantos*, iPhones and Samsung smartphones, Versace, Gucci, and Burberry emblems, t-shirts emblazoned with foreign words, and Nike, Converse, or Vans sneakers are but a few markers of status that face-savers either regularly sport or long for.

Strolling city streets further familiarizes them with the latest and most popular cafés, bookstores, and hangout venues in the city. Nevertheless, strolling is an activity that male face-savers are able to do with more laxity than females due to greater restrictions on young women's movements.[14] During my fieldwork, face-savers repeatedly made it clear that it was inappropriate for young women to be seen alone in public by those in their social circles, for to travel alone placed a woman's character in question and implied sexual misconduct. "These things don't matter for the rich," Yas once told me. "Among my family, though," she continued, "being seen alone is inappropriate." The importance communities place on young women's movements in public is related to the *visibility* of public conduct and how it will be perceived by one's peers rather than to its intrinsic (im)morality.[15] In these instances, young women learn what styles are "in" by emulating the fashions of their more well-off friends and acquaintances at school or those of their peer groups at private get-togethers.

Face-savers who are either unemployed or in school and who have little of their own money to spend on achieving the "look" deploy various tactics to attain the same ends. Strategies range from borrowing up-to-the-minute items from family and friends, saving up cash gifts that they receive from extended family in order to make costly, visible future purchases like gold jewelry or smartphones, and in the most extreme cases, diverting funds from the household to their own coffers. An example of the latter case comes from Mina, a young woman in her early twenties who is Yas's older sister. As Yas recounted:

> All of Mina's friends are wealthy. They're from the Darya neighborhood [one of the wealthiest areas in Sari]. Mina's expectations are really high—

just the fact that she got a 1.2 million-*toman* [1,000 USD] nose job. We're building a house in the village on land that we have there. Mom took out a loan for it and she said that half the house is mine and half is Mina's. And Mina started arguing with mom, saying that she doesn't want the house and for mom to give her share of the house in cash now. And mom agreed. That's how Mina was able to afford her nose job.

While Mina's particular strategy was an exception among the youth I knew, it is particularly suggestive of how far some face-savers are willing to go in order to attain the look of wealth. Redirecting funds meant for the household to one's self-investment takes many forms. The most common instances are when young women spend markedly less on publicly invisible but necessary everyday expenses in order to buy publicly discernable makeup, clothes, or costly wedding gifts that will help preserve both their face and that of their families among their communities. A phrase I would hear in conversation during my fieldwork, "*Agar mikhayi rosva nashi, hamrang-e jama'at show*" (If you don't want to become disgraced, become one with the crowd), encapsulates the reason these young women go to such lengths to perform class. Having one's poverty exposed results in the complete and utter loss of one's reputation, leading to *rosva'i*, or disgrace. As such, these young women believe that they have to sacrifice in certain, less visible realms in order to be able to afford the public image that conforms with mainstream standards of *kelas*.

Like Nina, female face-savers are also acutely aware that in the absence of social and economic forms of distinction, the physical embodiment of *kelas*—as defined through the enhancement of the self through makeup, fashion, speech, and etiquette—can serve as a way to differentiate themselves from their peers by physically exhibiting their moral worthiness and integrity. In beautifying themselves, young women associate bodily refinement with status. As Nina and her sister, Baharan, once told me, "Most of the [poor] kids around us don't take care of themselves. The rich go to the gym, they take care of their skin." In similarly embodying these bodily markers of *kelas* such as exercising and engaging in certain beauty rituals, face-savers ward off stigmatization, claim social status, and display that they are morally worthy of friendship and even marriage to the socioeconomically better off. Thus, as Finkelstein notes, physical appearance becomes equated with social status and serves as the means by which individuals can forge a new identity—one they believe is better and more refined than their current selves.[16]

So deeply do face-savers believe in the importance of conforming to particular standards of *kelas* that without fashioning this better self, they feel they cannot enter the realm of the *ba kelas*. The following conversation I had one evening at a local park in Sari with Yas and her twenty-something cousin, Atoosa, is particularly revealing:

> MANATA: Let's go to the *sofreh khuneh* [traditional coffeehouse restaurant] over there.
> ATOOSA: *Ba kelas* people usually go to *sofreh khuneh*s.
> YAS: Girlfriends and boyfriends go there with their high-heeled shoes and cars. They'll look at us weird if we walk up there without a car.
> ATOOSA: [And] I don't have any makeup on.

To Yas and Atoosa, not having the proper look meant that they could not have access to this other realm composed of perceived chic, classy people who drive cars and wear makeup and high-heeled shoes. To see and be seen means that one has to first invest in the proper accoutrements. "*Ba kelas* men are looking for *khoshgeli* [prettiness]," said Yas that same evening. As her comment reveals, the proper look also means a fighting chance for marriage mobility. Without looking the part, these young women felt that they would not be able to access the social capital they needed to succeed in the marriage market.

This belief was not just expressed by women. Karim, the football player from chapter 2, once emphatically told me how "wealthy women want to marry someone who's *khoshtip* [handsome]." Yas, Nina, and Karim, then, become invested in this equation of beauty with prestige as they attempt to navigate their present and make plans for their futures. To reject this narrative is to expose oneself to stigmatization and isolation. As such, tweaks to clothing, makeup, and general outward bearing become strategies that face-savers use to control the impression that they give to others. Indeed, this impression management, as Goffman has pointed out, ensures that actors do not experience shame, embarrassment, or anomie as they go about their day-to-day lives.[17] That face-savers' struggles to create a more attractive image go hand in hand with tangible socioeconomic advantages like a wealthy spouse further indicate that they are not the efforts of the vain. Karim and Nina implicitly know what economists like David Hammermesh have empirically shown to be true: there is a beauty premium.[18] Those who are considered more attractive are more likely to secure loans, have a job, make more money once in the labor market, and even have more educated spouses with greater earning power.[19]

Thus, in the eyes of my interlocutors, wearing boots in the summer, not plucking one's eyebrows, wearing the same clothes over and over again, or not paying attention to trends all become ways to attract the critical gaze and gossip of others, smearing one's reputation while simultaneously lowering one's chances for employment or economic security in the marriage market. To avoid these blowbacks, face-savers become invested in this authenticating narrative of how one's character and moral worth are embodied in one's physical image. Trendy clothes, cosmetics, exercise, and rhinoplasties become strategies that face-savers use to mold their bodies into a public indication of a better self.

However, in doing so, face-savers can also, at times, be singled out among Iran's middle-upper-class elite.[20] In these instances, small giveaways, such as a too-tight t-shirt, overly styled, "spiky" hair, not carrying a smartphone, or simply being seen as trying too hard in their pursuit of fashion lead to whispers about how they are from the *payin-e shahr* or *dehati*. Nevertheless, as face-savers attempt to become more socially aware and to gain upward mobility through education, work, and/or the use of social media, they make small tweaks in their appearance that over time can lead them to become indistinguishable from their more well-off counterparts: they become, as Olszewska writes, "some combination of Iranian, Islamic, *and* inexorably modern."[21] The social success of face-savers in this realm became particularly evident when middle-upper-class community members in Sari would mention to me, upon hearing that my research was largely among the rural-urban migrant poor in Sari, that I would be hard pressed to find subjects because "there are no poor people in Sari." There was a prevalent—albeit incorrect—assumption among Sari's elite that rural migrants to the city all had land, which served to mitigate poverty. While these claims were simultaneously offset by comments—such as those by Naghmeh and Bamdad—that implied that rural migrants were backward or lower in class, the existence of this myth substantiated the extent to which some youth were successful in hiding their poverty through their deliberate appropriation of admired cultural forms of capital.[22]

## Gendered Beauty

Walking the streets of Sari and Tehran, one notices how the quest for a "better" self is largely physically embodied by women. While men can easily hide their class origins by donning a t-shirt, jeans, a nice pair of shoes, a smartphone, and perhaps a clean-cut hairstyle, women must invest much more of themselves—and their finances—into producing the "right" look. In addition to the jeans, the shoes, the hairstyle, and the electronic accessories, female face-savers must also ensure that their makeup, the style of their *manto*, the purse they carry, and the jewelry they wear similarly convey the "right" message.

Why is this? Social theory tells us that historically, women's looks have a larger influence on their life trajectories than men's and that it is women, rather than men, who are more likely to exchange their looks for economic security.[23] As detailed in chapter 2, intense social pressure with regard to male work and breadwinning means that women do not face the same social stigma as men for not being able to perform a strong work ethic.[24] Indeed, young women can often get away with being unemployed and not being in school for a period of time, whereas the masculine imperative to work means that the slightest indication of idleness among men is cause for an immediate loss of face. In the absence of being able to distinguish themselves through their work ethic, these young women, then, become reliant on the only immediate, visible feature of the self that can denote their moral worth: their physical appearance. Appearance, too, becomes the main means by which many female face-savers can secure their futures; an attractive appearance makes them competitive in the marriage market and makes it more likely, as Yas stated, to marry *ba kelas* men.

The moral imperative to work, in turn, means that low-income young men—such as car mechanics, painters, and carpenters—who are judged to be models of masculinity through their hard, physical labor are not sanctioned for not always being put together, particularly while on the job. Even in the absence of a smart exterior, these jobs become visible proof of one's moral virtue encompassed by a commitment to responsibility and an assertion of manliness. Alternatively, poor young men who are known to be unemployed and keep up appearances simply by aestheticizing their external selves become subjects of gossip and slander, ill-reputed as doing "nothing" and being *bi kar* (without work). "We have a saying for boys like that," Sakineh once told me. "*Jib-e khali, poz-e 'ali* [empty pocket, full pretense]."

## *Khareji* Tastemaking

To understand the image imperative among female face-savers, and to a lesser extent, males, we must turn to history. Preoccupation with modern, Western fashions finds its roots as early as the late nineteenth century during the Qajar period in Iran. Encounters with European state structures and cultural models not only provided the foundations for the Constitutional Revolution of 1906, by which a constitutional monarchy modeled after the European system of governance was established, but also ultimately led to the modernizing initiatives of Reza Shah Pahlavi.[25] In the 1920s and 1930s, with the reign of Reza Shah, Iranians began to experience a visible influx of luxury goods into the country, signaling the arrival of a consumerist beauty culture based on the importation of clothing and beauty products from the West, particularly from the United States.[26] Iranian Occidentalism during the Pahlavi era came to conflate notions of what constituted modernity and high culture with Western fashions and beauty practices.[27]

The high value and appeal of a distinctly *khareji* (foreign) beauty culture in Iran were assisted by Reza Shah's Women Awakening Project (1936–1941), which, in an effort to both liberate and control Iranian women, banned the wearing of the veil and promoted an image of the moral and "modern" Iranian woman defined by her embrace of "wholesome" Western clothing and mannerisms.[28] As Camron Amin notes, education, patriotism, fitness, employment, and "simple" (i.e., Western) fashion became the hallmarks of this new Iranian woman.[29] These ideals were reinforced by advertisements for cosmetics, clerical jobs, and Western hairstyles and clothing in some of Iran's major official newspapers and magazines, including Iran's main newspaper, *Ettela'at* (Information), and the young adult magazine *Mehregan*.[30] Men, too, were not immune from being cajoled into *khareji* tastes, fashions, and sensibilities. By 1935, in an effort to present a thoroughly modern image of Iran to the world, the Pahlavi state required men to wear the fedora in public and mandated certain government officials to wear uniforms modeled after those worn by the British during official receptions.[31]

Criticisms of the Pahlavi state for equating Westernization with progress formed one of the main underlying bases of the 1979 Iranian Revolution. Under the newly established Islamic Republic, the "modern" Iranian was no longer the citizen who embraced Western culture, but the one who embraced Islam in its entirety; enforced veiling, a modest dress code, and minimal use of cosmetics became the order of the day. Blue jeans, t-shirts with Metallica and Iron Maiden emblems, Chicago Bulls hats—in short, anything that could potentially be suggestive of an invasion by Western, particularly North American, secular culture—was expressly prohibited. To ensure that youth adhered to the Islamic dress code of modesty, Islamic squads dressed in military gear, squads such as Goruh-e Zarbat, were assigned to watch over areas where youth congregated—including Maziyar Street in Sari—and take in those who flouted the rules. The Qur'anic principle of enjoining the right and forbidding the wrong (*amr beh ma'ruf*) was officially institutionalized in Iran in the late 1980s in the form of the Setad-e Amr beh Ma'ruf va Nahy az Monkar, a state agency tasked with ensuring that Islamic morality was observed by citizens. Setad forces—many dressed in plain clothes—patrolled major urban thoroughfares, looking especially for signs of youth moral misconduct and indecency, such as intermingling of the sexes and bad hijab.

Demands for social and economic reforms beginning with the 1997 election of the reformist president Mohammad Khatami resulted in the Islamic Republic visibly opening social space for Iranians, especially young Iranians, to exercise greater freedom of dress—a freedom that persists to the present day. Billboards and advertisements for the latest European-style men's clothing shops, Tag Hauer watches, Dolce and Gabbana accessories, and Samsung smartphones can now be found on highways and storefronts. The clothing, headscarves, makeup, and accessories advertised by salesmen as the "best quality" that are displayed on storefront mannequins and that are today coveted by rich and poor alike are those that are either *khareji* or mimic *khareji* fashions and have

Western brand names: Apple, Nike, Swatch, Zara, Chanel, Louis Vuitton, Clinique, and L'Oreal. The Zarbat group no longer exists and the Setad has visibly scaled down its activities. The Islamic Republic's morality police, Gasht-e Ershad, too, is now largely visible on city streets only in the summer months, when soaring temperatures mean more exposed body parts, and a greater risk of pushing the boundaries of what is considered "decent" dress. The Islamic principle of 'efaf, defined broadly as self-restraint from temptation, has now become as promoted as the principle of hijab. Whereas in the past, one would find billboards that mainly instructed women to observe their hijab, today one can now find these billboards alongside those that caution men to control their gaze. Shortly after being elected, the incumbent president, Hassan Rouhani, stated in a news conference in Tehran:

> If a woman or a man does not comply with our rules for clothing, his or her virtue should not come under question. . . . In my view, many women in our society who do not respect our hijab laws are virtuous. Our emphasis should be on the virtue.[32]

The implicit message is clear: one can be a moral, Islamic citizen while simultaneously being attuned to the latest *khareji* fashions and trends and actively co-opting and shaping them according to one's own vision. A globalized commercial culture, despite the best intentions of the early Islamic regime, has seeped into Iran, changing notions of Islamic modernity. Iran, today, is characterized by an alternative modernity, or what Lara Deeb has termed an "enchanted modernity"—that is, a modernity that is simultaneously both cosmopolitan and pious.[33] Material culture, encompassed in the nation's drive to improve its material conditions, goes hand in hand with very public displays of Islamic piety such as veiling or participating in Ashura processions, and comes to influence the image of modernness that is now effectively on display in the streets of Sari and Tehran. Material progress and spiritual development have both become integral in defining what it means to be a modern, civilized person today.[34] In the Islamic Republic of Iran, Islam and modernity, then, become wholly compatible.

This historical trend toward *khareji* tastemaking can today be found in the emphasis on *ba kelas* and *khareji* fashions among face-savers. As an Iranian who lived abroad, I became somewhat of an object of appeal and emulation among these youth. My popularity was due to the perception that I, being from the United States, was the source of knowledge about *khareji* trends. Upon finding out that I lived abroad, some male face-savers would ask me about certain phrases or words in English or the best toiletry brands. Young women would also ask about where I purchased my clothing or what beauty items I used. The outpouring of questions was not simply because of my *khareji* status, but because of the dominant (and dominating) idea that *khareji* taste stands for everything cool, *ba kelas*, and "now."[35] For face-savers, the body became a site of control, of aesthetic labor, made to become "cool" and *ba kelas* in order to conform to what was widely considered good (i.e., *khareji*) taste.[36]

What is considered in, *ba kelas*, and cool is not only advertised through boutique windows and the street style of Iran's middle and upper classes, but also through satellite television, home shows, and social media. Once a luxury only among the upper classes, satellite television, since its introduction to Iran in the early 1990s, has become ubiquitous today due to the relative affordability of a satellite dish and receiver.[37] Although officially banned by the government, various Persian-language channels broadcast from abroad stream hundreds of programs, including music videos, American television series and movies, and Turkish soap operas, to millions of households in Iran today. While not all low-income families—particularly those from more conservative households—have satellite television, considering it to reflect lifestyles and norms that are in contradiction with their everyday lives (see chapter 4), many do and are thereby able to gain knowledge of the latest global trends at any time of day or night. By showcasing contemporary global fashions and consumer goods in their programs, these channels "help cultivate a more [global] aesthetic sensibility toward everyday life"[38] among face-savers.

In recent years, in an effort to establish a more culturally appropriate, local alternative to satellite, the state has sanctioned the production and direct-to-DVD distribution of home shows (*namayesh-e khanegi*).[39] These shows, which encompass reality shows (e.g., *Sham-e Irani*), romantic historical drama series (e.g., *Shahrzad*), and comedy series (e.g., *Shahgush*), have much freer rein to play with the rules of hijab and fashion (albeit in an Islamically sanctioned mold) than television shows produced by the Islamic Republic of Iran Broadcasting (IRIB), the official organ that oversees all television and radio programming. Like cinema, home shows are under the purview of the Ministry of Culture and Islamic Guidance (MCIG), which as Saeed Zeydabadi-Nejad explains, provides a relatively open platform for negotiations between Iranian artists and the authorities.[40] By bypassing television altogether, home shows can therefore exist "within the space of freedom that was so far only allocated to cinema."[41] As such, they feature Iranian celebrities wearing globally fashionable clothing and accessories tweaked to suit an Islamic milieu, thereby enabling face-savers to learn how to creatively engage in the *khareji*, consumerist market in culturally sanctioned ways. For those unable or unwilling to expose themselves or their families to satellite television programming, home shows thus provide a more contextually relevant alternative that exemplifies Iran's innovativeness in responding to "initiatives and pressures from below."[42]

Simultaneously, the rise of social media in contemporary Iran has offered face-savers yet another window into how to adapt global trends to fit the Iranian public sphere. Numerous Instagram accounts, for example, have arisen in recent years in Iran that present an image of Iranian youth at drastic odds with the stereotypical look usually associated with the Islamic Republic by Western media outlets: veiled women in black chadors and bearded men in conservative, ill-fitting suits. These social media accounts in Iran act as echo chambers, amplifying ideas about good, *khareji* taste onto the youth who espouse them, reinforcing their importance in the minds of these young men and women.[43] Since many accounts are publicly accessible, and therefore subject to governmental scrutiny, they largely observe the hijab mandates of the regime. Nevertheless, as they are under the purview of individuals, rather than the state, these same accounts reflect a much looser interpretation of the rules than do home shows.

In the style of famous street style blogs in the United States such as The Sartorialist,[44] social media accounts become platforms for young people dressed in the latest "it" trends and accessories from the United States and Europe to showcase their wealth, all the while conforming to the Islamic Republic's dress code of modesty, albeit in a more risqué manner. A popular Instagram account, "Rich Kids of Tehran," defies the regime's dress code altogether, posting pictures of wealthy (or at least upwardly mobile aspirant) young men and women at mixed-gender parties and social gatherings, wearing swimsuits, cocktail dresses, and revealing designer clothing.[45] Most social media accounts, however, depict images that fall perilously close to the red lines: headscarves cover the minimal amount of hair, *manto*s are left unbuttoned, exposing designer tops and accessories, and jeans are sometimes ripped, exposing parts of one's knees and thighs.

While Iran's middle and upper classes have the most access to these various forms of social media, face-savers are also ardent users. The ubiquity of smartphones and the ability to purchase Internet access in Iran through one's SIM card have enabled youth from the lower classes to gain access to these relatively private realms of thought, practice, and meaning-making. Social communication apps like Telegram, too, have become major mediums through which many face-savers become knowledgeable about the latest news, events, and trends happening in Iran. In evening out the playing field, then, satellite television, officially sanctioned cultural productions, and new media technologies have all facilitated these young people's access to the cultural knowledge necessary to successfully participate in the face game.

Even though the particular cultural trends of dress espoused by many face-savers (and many youth in Iranian society at large) often go against the normative dress code advocated by hardline custodians of the Islamic Republic, this need not be interpreted as defiance to authority. Rather, as Olszewska has emphasized, similar dress styles or behavior may have completely different meanings when they are transported across social classes.[46] In this sense, aspiring to or mimicking the venturesome fashions and consumption practices of their upper- and middle-class counterparts can be read as an attempt on the part of the lower classes to fit in and to reify their middle-class aspirations. In describing the aesthetic labor that low-income Tehrani youth engage in as they frequent high-end malls in Iran, for example, Shahram Khosravi notes how their ways of acting and dressing can be read as an "attempt to dissociate themselves from their poor working-class neighborhood. They come to Golestan [a high-end shopping mall] to imagine being part of a 'better' life than their own. Golestan represents a dream of economic and cultural capital."[47] For the face-savers in this study, embodying a certain look likewise represents the pursuit of a better life. Indeed, among face-savers who dressed more daringly, none justified their apparel in political terms. Rather, they couched explanations for their self-aestheticization in phrases such as "being chic," "protecting *aberu*," or "not wanting to seem poor." One eighteen-year-old, Ajang, for example, stated that a person should dress "in a style that isn't the object of laughter or ridicule."

Despite the importance of following fashion trends, face-savers know they have to adjust their self-presentation based on the particular public they are going to be exposed to. As Davud stated:

> People here [in my neighborhood] aren't very cultured. Kids my age grow their hair long and everyone laughs at them and says "The girl is coming" and these types of things. It's *bi farhangi* [uncultured-ness]. If I want to go to Maziyar Street on Thursday nights or I style my hair and these types of things, the people in my neighborhood keep telling my dad, "Stop your son."

Similarly, Yas's other cousin, Niousha, a seamstress in her twenties, told me how she could not wear a toe ring she wanted in the public sphere of her neighborhood because "people will make fun. It's like the village here, they won't understand." "They're going to look and say, *what* is *that*?" Yas interjected. As these comments indicate, face-savers often pointed to the perceived backwardness or conservativeness of their neighbors when explaining why they could not wear a particular trend around certain neighbors or family members. To do otherwise would be to subject oneself, as Davud had, to rebuke. "I can't wear these heels in the village. They'll look down on me," Yas once told me when I asked her why she had to change her shoes to go to her extended family's residence.

The fashioned selves that Yas, Davud, and Niousha created to save face walking the streets of Maziyar were not aligned with the image that was needed to present a front of propriety in the backstreets and alleyways of their own neighborhoods and villages. Styles that are in fashion in main streets, such as high heels, bright red lipstick, and men's skinny jeans and tunic shirts, are looked down upon in the more conservative, peri-urban neighborhoods where many face-savers live. Face-savers themselves, too, often negatively evaluate those in their communities who are made up in a less conservative manner.

Yas and Atoosa, for instance, mocked a young woman wearing a short *manto* and matching pants for being *jelf*, or dressed in a way that attracted too much attention. "I would love to see a person who is simple-looking," said Atoosa, referring to someone who dressed in a chic, refined manner. "I saw a group of people once, and the way that one of them was dressed, the way he did himself up, he really stood out," a twenty-nine-year-old man, Abbas, recounted. "We call these people *nokhaleh*. People like this think they're better than others." Another critique was expressed in an exchange I had with Karim's friend Ashkan:

ASHKAN: We have an English teacher who plucks his eyebrows!
MANATA: Why do you think he does that?
ASHKAN: Because he's a woman![48]

A person has to tread carefully, then, between distinguishing himself from others through his appearance and mannerisms and distinguishing himself so much that he becomes a social outcast and subject to derision. Among face-savers, the best "look" is one that is chic, clean, and *ba kelas*, but not *jelf* or too trendy.

To avoid insinuations of impropriety, most face-savers adjust their physical appearance for different publics, wearing more modest and conservative hairstyles, clothing, and makeup choices among their primary public such as family, intimate friends, and neighbors, while reserving their more fashionable choices in hair, makeup, and clothing for those in their secondary public (everyone else).[49] Nevertheless, there are some youth like Davud who still knowingly break with convention from time to time. In these particular cases, dressing up to go out means that neighbors may see their more "daring" dress choices if youth do not actively work to hide them. It is also possible that more conservative-minded family members and friends will see—and chastise—face-savers as they mingle with friends on the main streets of town, dressed in the latest fashions, as the following excerpt from my fieldnotes illustrates.

## "Backward" Others

Sari, July 7, 2010. At the park this evening, Yas and her cousin Atoosa had dressed up considerably; Atoosa was even wearing heels. After some time in the park, Yas noticed a few conservatively dressed family friends from her village walking around. She did not venture to greet them, but rather just stood where we were looking at them. At one point, one of their family friends, a young woman with a small child, came up to Yas. "Are you here alone?" she asked. "Why did she want to know?" I asked Yas later. "They're *rusta'i* [villagers]!" Atoosa exclaimed. "Their minds are a bit backward." Yas explained, "Usually, girls [like us] don't come to parks without their families."

By casting their family friends as "backward," Yas and Atoosa did not simply justify their own behavior, but placed themselves on a higher moral rung than these economically near "others." In their view, the benefits that could potentially come from socializing with those out-side their families and from presenting a more fashion-forward front outweighed the cost of these rebukes. As their dream was to be a "part of a 'better' life than their own,"[50] emulating what they perceived to be the behavior of the middle and upper classes encapsulated the imagined possibility of making that dream a reality. Simultaneously, this emula-tion created a very real distinction between youth and some members of their community. By aestheticizing their bodies and mimicking admired behavior, face-savers manifest the "contradictory twin imperative for sameness and difference, to simultaneously fit in and stand out."[51] Face-savers' desires for imitation function to unify them with well-off others while simultaneously segregating them from other groups, a dualistic process that is reflective of the history of human societies.[52]

## Bodily Capital

In using their bodies to perform *kelas*, face-savers deliberately work to tilt the odds of winning the face game to their favor.[53] In such a way, as described earlier, the body becomes a type of commodity: some-thing that can be shaped, fashioned, and even surgically altered to reflect the particular social world that face-savers aspire to be a part of. Face-savers, then, become what Loïc Wacquant has described as "entrepreneurs in bodily capital," working to convert their corporeality into a certain "look" that can gain them status, friendships, relationships, and even jobs.[54] Like body entrepreneurs, face-savers have to face the gaze. Unlike Wacquant's pugilists or the supermodels studied by Ashley Mears, however, face-savers' livelihoods are not wholly dependent on their physical characteristics: looks are not everything for my interlocutors. As outlined in the last chapter, one's work ethic and the subsequent community judgment of one's work ethic also play significant roles in determining who gets ahead. Indeed, if one is not deemed self-sufficient and hardworking, one's appearance means little. As detailed earlier, if community members know that youth, principally young men, do not have the means by which to support themselves or their families, they are called out as "posers." However, those youth who are able to both perform a strong work ethic *and* display the right look become extremely competitive in the race for economic and social opportunities in communities where both jobs and networks are scarce.

Like Mears's supermodels, the young men and women I knew were often under intense scrutiny.[55] Neighbors, family members, friends, acquaintances, and even other face-savers implicitly evaluated them, looking for clues about their competence, responsibility, and character in their appearance. The more positive the clue, the more likely face-savers were to get the job, the contact, or the resource. During fieldwork, I observed many such instances of discrimination based on physical looks—that is, lookism. The following case is representative.

*Faranak*

Sari. March 13, 2011. Rose Salon. This morning as I was watching Faranak style a customer's hair, I noticed how the other girls were starting to speak in hushed whispers. "It seems like Ms. Zahedi wants to have a private conversation with Faranak," they kept saying. Sure enough, within the hour, Ms. Zahedi called Faranak downstairs to talk. After the conversation, Faranak told me that Ms. Zahedi had offered her the opportunity to run the salon. Ms. Zahedi was leaving for a few months and wanted Faranak to take charge.

To be able to make rent on the salon, Faranak started to deliberate on who she could potentially choose as a partner. "You need someone chic and *ba kelas* to run a place like this. Samaneh [one of the other salon apprentices who was also hardworking] isn't the type to do it." Unlike Faranak, who made sure to have impeccable posture and wear trendy clothes on a daily basis, Samaneh often wore baggy clothes that were considered more conservative than chic, and walked with a distinct hunch. Samaneh was also reserved and barely spoke to customers. Faranak, on the other hand, was articulate, without a trace of the Mazandarani accent that tinged the intonation of her colleagues. In Faranak's view, being able to run a salon meant being able to physically embody, as she did, everything the salon aspired to stand for: modish and *ba kelas*.

The gaze is pervasive. It not only defines the way that community members and employers like Ms. Zahedi scrutinize those who work for them, deciding who is the most worthy for a promotion. It also defines how face-savers themselves view the youth around them. Like Faranak, face-savers internalize the gaze, reflecting its mirror image onto themselves and their peers. They use markers of physical distinction, including dress, posture, and speech, to determine the moral worth of their counterparts and to assess others' shortfalls and correct their own. In doing so, face-savers make implicit comparisons between themselves and others, providing justification for their own sense of moral uprightness or those of their peers. Examples abound. Nina and Baharan would critique relatives and acquaintances who did not "take care of themselves," who did not pluck their eyebrows or change up their clothes. Faranak judged her colleagues as being unworthy of a promotion because they failed to measure up to the face standards of the job. Twenty-five-year-old Morteza, a young man who lived in south Tehran, actively worked to change his provincial accent to a Tehrani one so as to not give away his social origins as a *shahrestani* (literally, someone from one of Iran's *shahrestan*s or provinces; sometimes pejoratively used in Tehran to describe a non-Tehrani, particularly someone who is seen as less cultured).

Face-savers are disciplined, then, to shape their bodily capital through the act of exposure,[56] and, in turn, become dependent on this exposure in creating their public personas and securing the benefits that come from this public image. The gaze therefore functions to create a symbolic boundary, an invisible barrier between youth like Morteza and other youth who have a similar economic standing, but who have failed to follow the face rule of appearance. For Morteza, this symbolic boundary placed him in a subjectively higher status than these other youth whom he would call *dehati*. In this view, *dehati* became synonymous with unworthy.

Moral discourses surrounding one's image also have very tangible consequences. Just as judgments of one's work ethic become a form of symbolic capital, so too, do moral evaluations of the physical image that one embodies. The gaze becomes a "formula" for social control, dictating norms of self-presentation.[57] Michel Foucault writes that the calculated, disciplinary gaze "establishes over individuals a visibility through which one differentiates them and judges them."[58] As such, the gaze enables qualification, categorization, and, ultimately, punishment of others. Face-savers, then, knowing that they will be watched, monitor themselves, cautious to conform to the expectations of the various publics in which they find themselves in an effort to avoid the ultimate punishment: shaming and the subsequent loss of their reputation. These youth "must strike a strategic and sometimes paradoxical balance between discretion and self-display, and pitch [their] behavior at just the right level, embodying society's values."[59] Whether they succeed or fail to adhere to these norms, in turn, has concrete social and economic repercussions, as the cases of Samaneh and Faranak clearly illustrate.

In this way, the gaze, as embodied in judgments of morality, functions to reproduce cycles of micro-stratification among poor youth. Those who have the "proper" look are ranked by employers, colleagues, and peers as subjectively higher in status than those who do not. Subjective rankings, in turn, determine objective rewards, with those who manipulate their external selves to embody norms of *kelas* being able to secure "the" promotion, "the" contact, or "the" spouse. The strive to conform can create upward socioeconomic mobility while it concurrently works to reify difference.

Thus far I have shown how certain young people in Iran use appearance as an external indicator of inner character. The fashioned image becomes conflated with the real self. Traditional perspectives of materialism argue that when more value is placed on the visible attributes of one's self than on one's inner character, the result is the complete commodification of the self.[60] In this view, consumerism and the valuation of performance, rather than reality, subvert an understanding of the world around oneself. The person becomes so concerned with how she looks and how she presents herself in public that she becomes a non-actor, content with the status quo.

However, this perspective neglects how the political and social are inscribed onto the actual process of image-making itself. Among face-savers, the manipulation of one's external self is seen as a means of bringing about social and economic change, however small. By manipulating their physiognomy, face-savers are able to present themselves as "competent" and "classy" individuals, thereby averting the shame that comes with revealing their poverty. Their new fashioned selves constitute a type of marketable capital that then has the potential to bring them certain opportunities such as a better job or a more well-off spouse. In this way, the image-making that face-savers engage in becomes a form of dress politics: how face-savers dress has clear implications for the way that community goods, services, and resources are allocated to them. We can therefore read image-making as a political act—whether or not the youth themselves intend to act politically—because it leads to a "distribution and redistribution of public goods and services,"[61] relieving conditions of poverty for the actors involved.[62] Daily decisions about how to act and how to be "add up incrementally to create the boundaries and interests" of the economic order in these communities.[63]

Though saving face through the maintenance of a *ba kelas* appearance does not guarantee socioeconomic mobility, the prospect exists nonetheless; it is precisely this chance for a better life that drives face-savers forward, pushing them to spend their limited time, money, and resources on dressing well.[64] By presenting themselves as hardworking, self-sufficient, *and* chic, they become closer to winning the face game. But there is a final rule that they must abide by: purity. Without purity, face-savers cannot hope to even be eligible to play the game. For those who are able to effectively follow all four rules, they will have shifted the odds of victory in their favor.

# 4

## Be Good, Do Good

One day in the bath a piece of perfumed clay came to me
from the hand of a friend; I said to it, "Art thou musk, or an
artificial compound of sweets? For I am charmed with thy
delightful odor." It answered, "I was a worthless piece of clay,
but having for a season associated with the rose, the virtue
of my companion was communicated to me; otherwise I am
the same identical earth that I was at first."
—Sa'di, *The Gulistan or Rose Garden*, 1865

"Sometimes, I go down the wrong path. Well, I won't lie, not sometimes,
but most of the time. Rather than going down the right path, I go down
the wrong one. Because people struggle with some issues, their identity has become two-sided: they go down the right path and sometimes
you'll see that they'll go down the wrong path. It's not in their hands
either; it's become a habit. They've become polluted, but they pretend
not to notice. People may say that they're not into [bad] things, but
they're lying. I'm a truthful person. If you ask anyone, if so and so is
good, they may not say my bad things, they may talk about my good
qualities. But I tell you, my bad qualities are more than my good qualities. This is the truth. To the extent that I can, I try to take care of my life,
especially now that I have a wife and kids. I won't let the smallest thing
hurt it. But there are some things that I have to do wrong—small things
to big things" (Dara).

How can one be considered "good" when one does the "wrong" thing?
What counts when one is trying to save face by being good: one's intent
or one's practice? The answers to these questions are contingent on the
differentiation between two different aspects of the self: one's hidden,
secret practices and one's outward public behavior. Saving face by following the rule of purity lies not so much in a person's inner moral compass, but in the extent to which the person is able to present an image of

goodness to the outside world. In Dara's case, the pursuit of a better life for his family forced him to "go down the wrong path." While believing himself to be "truthful," Dara—as we saw in chapter 2—hid his wrong-doings from those around him, fearful that a revelation of the truth would sacrifice everything he had worked so hard for. Because Dara had been able to do the "wrong thing" without getting caught, because his identity had become "two-sided," he knew that those around him would not slander him, but talk about his "good qualities" even though he believed that his inner, "bad" qualities outweighed his "good" ones.

In the face game, being perceived as truthful and honest is even more important than actually being truthful and honest at all times. Lying is the price that one sometimes has to pay in order to accumulate moral capital. This is why Dara was not willing to have anyone in his own social networks find out about his moral transgressions, but readily admitted them to outsiders, including myself. Preserving face by following norms of good behavior in one's interactions transforms into a symbolic re-source that is then used to preserve one's reputation and that of one's family. A good reputation, in turn, translates to greater opportunities in the form of job prospects, networks, marriage mobility, and social sup-port. In Dara's case, his reputation led to marriage mobility, enabling him to marry a young woman from a relatively well-off family. Dara would do the wrong thing, but strove to keep it a secret so that he could obtain the moral capital required for exchange into friendship, marriage, and even closer family ties: "I don't know about your secrets, and you don't know about mine. I don't know the secrets of my mother, father, brother, or sis-ter, but if I found out, we would all run away from each other." For youth like Dara, keeping secrets regarding indiscretions—keeping their "moral badness"[1] from social punishment—becomes a tool for self-preservation. Keeping secrets offers the prospect of another world,[2] whereby the young person can reinvent himself, presenting himself as a dignified, virtuous individual who abides by social conventions. Secrets, then, become the means by which the face-saver forms the personage he is expected to assume. Secrets, like masks, both conceal and expose.[3] They define face-savers' social roles or the roles in which they are assigned, but they also obscure discordant realities about them.[4]

In the face game, the emphasis on an outward presentation of moral purity is a reflection of the dualism present in everyday life. As emphasized in chapter 1, this dualism is not unique to Iran, but can be found in other cultures and societies as well. However, cultural, social, and political considerations differentiate the content of this dualism in Iran from that found in other countries. The Iranian Sufistic tradition of dualism, which in turn derives from Manichaeism, can today be found in Iranian Shi'ism, where it is reflected in the opposition between "undesirable external physical desires and needs and internal spiritual needs."[5] Stemming from Manichaeism's emphasis on the duality between the inner soul and the physical, material world, Iranian culture, throughout the centuries, has been shaped by the dichotomy between the external, manipulated self (*zaher*) and the inner world of one's feelings and desires (*baten*). In its current Islamic iteration, this duality further appropriates elements of ancient Arabian culture, from which the multifaceted concept of hijab (modesty, shyness, cover) is derived, and which holds that there are private and public components to every person. Protecting the secrets and sanctity of one's *baten* through social dissimulation by way of the *zaher* that one presents to the outside world becomes the means by which one can navigate this dualism. It is through the *zaher* that one preserves face in the community and preempts threats to one's social standing.

The tension between one's inner desires and one's actual public behavior presents the question of whether self-disclosure can ever occur. I knew face-savers like Dara who revealed their "true" selves among strangers like myself, people whom they knew they would not see again. By confiding in people whom they are not close to rather than their colleagues, both Dara and Parisa, the accessories vendor we met in chapter 2, avoid being "subject to [incompatible] institutional expectations about appropriate behavior."[6] According to Mario Small, people are aware that their roles as colleagues, sons, daughters, or spouses carry certain expectations. However, it is when someone's role as a confidant also overlaps with her role as "evaluator, competitor, provider or some role other than listener or supporter that creates the potential for conflict" and that leads the individual to turn to weak ties out of "fear of incompatible expectations."[7] These weak ties tend to have less competing roles than their strong counterparts. Indeed, face-savers like Dara who confided their secrets in me felt that because of my role as listener (rather than as potential work competitor), I would be less likely to divulge their *baten* to others. In these cases, face-savers felt no perceptible threat to their reputation, and as such, used the conversation as a cathartic outlet to express their inner feelings and thoughts. Even if outsiders like myself revealed their secrets, no loss of face would occur since the outsider's circle of acquaintances and friends did not overlap with that of the face-saver.

Other face-savers were intimate with close family members and friends, particularly family members and friends who they knew would not reveal their secrets and who they felt could understand them.[8] Family gatherings that Yas had with some of her closest cousins are particularly illustrative of instances where the walls of the formal *zaher* break down and allow a person to more closely align her inner and outer selves. I was privy to one particular gathering, which took place in her uncle's home. Yas and her cousins sat in her cousin's small sewing studio with the door closed so that other family members could not overhear their conversations. Topics revolved around certain "taboo" subjects, including premarital relationships. One cousin, Sheyda, started to describe her boyfriend, who was going to school abroad. Eventually, Sheyda revealed that she had multiple boyfriends. The conversation later turned to me and whether I had any boyfriends, and whether they were Iranian or *khareji*.

While this encounter reveals how there is a "deep curiosity about the *bāten* of others,"[9] it also discloses how the extent to which one can expose the contents of one's inner self—and by extension, the extent to which one feels that shaming will occur—is also highly contingent on one's perceptions of others' empathy, regardless of the strength or weakness of the tie. Nina, for instance, confided in me that a young male neighbor had asked her for a hug. As the neighbor was not Nina's *mahram* (a family member one is not permitted to marry because of close kinship),[10] it would have been considered *haram* (forbidden by Islamic law) for Nina and the neighbor to touch. Nina kept this encounter a secret from her sister. "If I tell Baharan, she'll say that I made him rude." Given her older sister's "multiplex"[11] role as both confidant and evaluator, Nina felt that Baharan would not be able to lend the empathetic ear that she needed to recover from the situation, negatively judging her for her misdeed instead. Confirming social theory that belies the import of strong ties in secret-sharing practices,[12] Nina confided a potentially risky, shame-inducing piece of information to someone she was not as close to, believing that the benefit of understanding, in this case, would outweigh any cost. By the same token, Sheyda divulged her secret not only to her strong ties (her close cousins), but also to a weak tie (myself), believing that I (as opposed to distant family members) would understand her situation given my foreign background.

Despite these examples of inner release, the importance of presenting an image of moral uprightness is the focus of face-savers' day-to-day public activities. Without being perceived as morally upstanding by their communities, youth like Nina, Dara, and Sheyda have an infinitely harder time making the "right" friends, gaining marriage mobility, or being recommended for a well-paying job. Neighbors and acquaintances come to see them, according to Dara, as "polluted." To understand why being considered morally pure is such an imperative component of day-to-day life, we must first understand how the concept of purity itself has been given shape in Iranian history.

## Purity versus Pollution in Iran

The Persian national epic, the *Shahnameh*, or the Book of Kings by Ferdowsi, composed in the eleventh century, relates the history of Iran from its fabled past up until the downfall of the Sasanian Empire and the Islamic conquest of Iran in the seventh century. A central text in the literary repertoire of Iran, the *Shahnameh* has come to be the symbol, par excellence, of Iranian ethno-national identity.

Dominant in the *Shahnameh* is the fight of good against evil. This tension is reified not only in the epic's praise of the Iranian nation as superior to all other nations, thus creating an ethno-territorial identity that separates Iran from other regions.[13] It is also visible in the *Shahnameh*'s various moral exaltations of justice, order, and virtue instead of cruelty, greed, and evil, and in the epic's exploration of the consummate internal struggle that men face between their "better and lesser selves."[14] The following passage is from a scene where the mythical king Fereydun, reigning during Iran's pre-Zoroastrian age, addresses two of his sons, Salm and Tur. The two sons had threatened Fereydun with war for allocating the best part of his kingdom, Iran, to his third and favored son, Iraj. According to Salm and Tur, war could be averted only if Fereydun "takes the crown off [Iraj's] worthless head so that the world is freed from him" and "gives him a corner of the world where he can sit and be out of [Fereydun's] sight like [they] are."[15]

I will tell you a story if you will listen:
You will reap the same evil you sow . . .
This world is not our permanent home . . .
If greed replaces wisdom in you
The devil becomes your accomplice . . .
I am on my out of this world
This is not the time for strife . . .
When hearts are empty of greed
Both dust and the thrones of kings seem the same
One who sells his brother for dust
Will never be considered of pure origin
This world that has seen and will see many people like you
Will not be tamed by you
However close you become with God today
It will lead to your salvation on Judgment Day.[16]

Later, in an effort to reconcile tensions between his father and his brothers, even at the expense of giving up his own throne, Iraj goes to Salm and Tur, only to be murdered by them. Iraj's son, Manuchehr, ultimately avenges his father's murder by killing the two brothers.

In the end, it is Iraj who becomes the final hero of this legend; it is his name, rather than those of Salm and Tur, that lives on in Iranian historical memory.[17] Iraj and what he stood for—the ability to travel the path that leads to God, to be free from greed, jealousy, and evil—have become the iconic symbol of those killed in defense of good.[18] To be similarly judged as "pure," to preempt being knocked down by the world, people believe that one has to be mindful of God and travel down the right path in life in order to reap rewards. Time and time again, I heard face-savers highlight how a person must do her work in the "right" way, to act in a way that is "appropriate" in the eyes of society, and to be "remembered as good." The importance that face-savers attach to goodness is not necessarily reflective of their internalization of the lessons of the *Shahnameh* (I suspect many did not know the story), but of the way that the *Shahnameh*'s concept of purity has been historically appropriated into Iran's socio-religious fabric.

Indeed, the epic's emphasis on the temporality of life and the necessity to spend one's fleeting days in divinely sanctioned purity, free from greed, further finds resonance in both Iran's pre-Islamic Zoroastrian past and its Shi'a Islamic present. In the battle between Ahura Mazda (the God of Wisdom) and Ahriman (the Destructive Spirit) in Zoroastrian texts, Iranians are "naturally perceived as being on the side of the good."[19] The concept of Iran as both geographically superior to all other nations (embodied in Iran being the "best" part of Fereydun's kingdom in the *Shahnameh*) and morally dominant (embodied in Zoroastrianism's association of Iranians with Ahura Mazda) implies that Iranians have a "kinship camaraderie based on [their] ethnic purity."[20] As such, according to these texts, Iranians have to be hyper-vigilant against moral pollutions that can jeopardize their ritual purity.

Shi'a Islamic jurisprudence in Iran appropriated this dichotomization of purity and pollution to emphasize all those *nejasat*, or impurities, that could contaminate the bodies of believers in Iran. These impurities ranged from certain activities, such as drinking and gambling, to other humans, particularly those who were considered adulterated and who were located both inside and outside the Shi'a community.[21] The emphasis on ritual purity, on moral goodness, ultimately came to define Shi'a self-identity in Iran and later, the identity of Iran's Islamic regime. In Shi'a Islamic mysticism, the human struggle for virtue, manifested in the struggle against one's *nafs*, or carnal desires and passions, comprises a person's spiritual development.[22] This belief came to represent a component of Iranian revolutionary discourse and to largely define the identity of Iran's Islamic regime.[23]

Unique about the founding of Iran's Islamic Republic was that it encoded the concept of purity onto public space. As mentioned in chapter 1, individual virtue was largely ensured through the act of veiling: after the revolution, women were legally required to wear the hijab in public and to cover their bodies either by donning the *chador* (preferred) or wearing a *manto* and headscarf. Men, too, were no longer allowed to wear shorts or short-sleeved shirts (though the latter, today, is largely permissible). Attracting attention through pretentious acts such as having a fashionable hairstyle or wearing makeup and swanky clothing was looked down upon and subject to policing. Gender segregation, a form of veiling that was seen to safeguard the "moral values of society from corruption,"[24] was enforced in many public spaces, including schools, buses, and beaches. Billboards and posters that emphasized the importance of ritual purity for Iranian identity dotted city landscapes. All of these constituted ways that the Islamic Republic endeavored to fight moral pollution and to create the model, virtuous Islamic citizen.[25]

Today, one continues to see the emphasis on "goodness" in public, albeit in a less obvious way. Many male TV news anchors, for instance, sport a more au courant *hezbollahi* look,[26] the full beards and simple hairstyles of the early revolutionary years replaced with designer stubble and lightly gelled hairstyles with clean side parts. The dark-colored headscarves and bare faces of female news anchors have largely been replaced with colorful hijab and light makeup. As the government views outward appearance as an indication of one's morality and commitment to the revolution's ideals, these small shifts in aesthetics signal a more discreet campaign to promote morality.

Nevertheless, morality monitoring continues to persist underneath the radar, with its enjoinments constituting moral calling cards that distinguish the "good" from the "bad." Mary Douglas argues that distinguishing the "dirty" elements of society from the "pure" elements is ultimately a quest to make society "conform to an idea"[27] and to "condemn[] any object or idea likely to confuse or contradict cherished classifications."[28] To be a citizen in Iran, to be someone who preserves the social order, means to be a morally upright, unpolluted, *pak* (pure) Islamic citizen, manifested through one's appropriate outward appearance and behavior. To not follow the regime's rules of purity means not only to lose face, but also to face legal censure. Thus, the consequence of being labeled dirty is to be subject to ritual cleaning through condemnation.

In Iran today, the emphasis on pure behavior has become institutionalized through the office of Setad-e Amr beh Ma'ruf va Nahy az Monkar (see chapter 3). Manifested institutionally as a branch of the country's police forces, the office has led to self-censorship of the "bad."[29] Setad's emphasis on enjoining good further implies that ensuring purity is not only the individual's responsibility, but the responsibility of society as a whole: it is each citizen's duty to safeguard the virtue of the community. The watchful eye of the state thus becomes reflected in the watchful eye of the community itself, imposing a particular normative vision of purity onto society. This leads censorship to become "an internal impulse, a component of one's habitus, proper socialization, and personal ethics."[30]

In this context, inappropriate public self-revelation such as displaying affection toward the opposite sex, dressing indecently, or getting caught using substances leads not only to a loss of face, but also to intimations of immorality by those in one's own community.

There is a tendency to view this post-revolutionary imposition of morality and self-censorship in Iran as wholly negative. In this understanding, imposition, by definition, implies the repression of the *baten*, of one's "true" self. As such, it is argued, Iranians have had to live a double, almost schizophrenic life, acting one way in private while another way entirely in public. Anthropologist Roxanne Varzi argues that an "ideological public sphere"[31] in Iran has led to the bifurcation of the self. When the inner world of youth and the outer world of the Islamic Republic "are morally diametrically opposed, to the degree that what is condoned in one world is forbidden in the other (and vice versa), shame comes into play. And with this shame is a denial or split of self in order to survive."[32] However, as discussed earlier, this view of an inside/outside dichotomy in Iran overlooks the fact that the practice of presenting one face in public while another, perhaps a completely different one, in private, is not unique to the Islamic Republic, but can be found in all cultures and throughout history.[33] It is the particular elements that constitute a proper *zaher* and the specific consequences of not abiding by the inside/outside division that differ among societies.

Further still, even in the same society, as Mahmood emphasizes, presupposing that public behavior is always at odds with one's inner desires assumes "that there is a natural disjuncture between a person's 'true' desires and those that are socially prescribed."[34] However, we must consider the possibility that ostensibly imposed models of behavior may be aligned with some people's real desires and may be seen as constitutive of the "conditions for the emergence of the self."[35] As Donya, a thirty-one-year-old seamstress, stated emphatically, "I was raised in a family that was this way [concerned about *aberu*]. I don't feel forced. I like living by the rules." Even those who are forced to scrupulously alter their behavior in public may do so willingly because they believe that the benefits that may come from observing social norms of behavior may outweigh any perceived costs. In these instances, the gap between one's private behavior and public ideals of morality is not seen as leading to an identity crisis, but as a means by which one can "prove" his inner virtuosity and more closely align his *baten* with his *zaher*, a point that I will detail below. In this view, practice makes perfect.[36]

Here we may question what the effect of dominant ideas of purity has been on the youth in this study. To what extent have moral discourses surrounding "proper," "virtuous" conduct been co-opted by face-savers and their communities? What are the contours of moral purity in these low-income settings? Rather than assume *a priori* that enforced performances of purity necessarily create negative consequences for youth, my main concern is to understand both the logic behind these performative displays of goodness and the repercussions—good and bad—that may stem from these youths' struggles for validation.

## Moral Purity among Face-Savers

The Islamic Republic brought out onto the surface and codified into law notions of proper Islamic conduct and morality. However, Islam was the dominant religion in Iran long before the Islamic regime took hold and as such, "Islam was and is bound to be a major component of an Iranian's identity, regardless of whether or not there was ever an Islamic republic."[37] The Islamic Republic's enforced commitment to visible acts of moral purity is simply an extension of this history.

For the youth I came to know, being Muslim "does not just mean that they believe in and practice Islam but that they live in a Muslim culture that weaves religion into the textures of daily life in ways that make the divine continuously present."[38] As in other Muslim contexts, most expressions that face-savers use—from farewells (*khoda hafez*—may God keep you safe) to wishes (*agar khoda bekhad*—if God wills it) to references to the future (*inshallah*—God willing)—all invoke the divine in some manner so that "daily conversation rarely carries on long without invocations of God."[39] However, while as in other contexts there are different degrees of routine religious practice among face-savers—for instance, not all of these youth pray—Islam permeates their everyday lives in ways that set face-savers apart from their counterparts in other Muslim-majority countries.

Living in an Islamic Republic means that public spaces in Iran are imbued with reminders of the governing ideology.[40] Reminders not only include the daily *azan*, or call to prayer, that is broadcast from neighborhood mosques, fasting during the month of Ramadan, or rituals associated with funerals. They also include practices and reminders that are more or less unique to Iran:[41] images of Imam Khomeini plastered on billboards and walls, mural paintings of martyrs who lost their lives during the Sacred Defense (in reference to the Iran-Iraq War), and religious performances and processions during Ashura. At school, students stand in line to listen to Qur'anic recitations by classmates; mandatory prayers and religious education courses are other instances by which young men and women are surrounded with objects, images and sounds that are reminders of Islamic values.[42] This everyday inculcation of Islam, in turn, shapes face-savers' own desires for purity.[43] Consider the following, written by fifteen-year-old Mohammad Karimi, a high school student:[44]

> Satellite television pollutes the pure souls of youth like me. Why should a young person pollute his eyes with sin? The religion of Islam doesn't accept this. A young person who doesn't want others to play with his *aberu* can control his actions at this age. After he's grown up, he can't control his actions.

Satellite dishes, forbidden by the Islamic Republic for being a pollutant that promotes anti-Islamic, indecent behavior and practices, have nevertheless become ubiquitous in Iran (see chapter 3). Households have come up with elaborate strategies to hide their dishes from the authorities, including draping a piece of cloth over satellite dishes and positioning them in an inconspicuous corner of their roofs.[45] Nevertheless, Mohammad Karimi and his family espouse public moral discourses that view satellite television as a pollutant, especially among youth, that will jeopardize one's purity and threaten one's face. Here, the quest for purity counterbalances the negative experience of pollution.[46] The notion that Islam directs a person to "control" his actions through propriety and the avoidance of pollutants provides Mohammad Karimi with an instructional guide that simultaneously functions to maintain his *aberu*.

Face-savers believe in themselves as capable of being virtuous and see acts of moral uprightness as an opportunity to prove their self-worth even when they have failed to follow the other rules of the face game. Recall Farbod, the student we met in chapter 2 who had failed his classes and was struggling academically, garnering ill fame in the process. Farbod knew that high marks for good behavior would help him save face by partially compensating for his substandard academic record and proving to his teachers that he was not "bad." As he told me, "In my first year of high school, I wanted my discipline grade to be high so that my teachers would know that I wasn't a bad person. I ended up getting a 20!"

Face-savers' belief in the importance of being morally pure often takes on a dogmatic character, whereby they use other people's degree of virtuosity as a yardstick to either judge their worthiness as potential friends or to decide whether to remain their friends. The following exchange with Maryam, a fifteen-year-old high school student in south Tehran, is indicative:

MARYAM: I have both good and bad friends.
MANATA: How are they bad?
MARYAM: It's not proper for me to say. Some of them have boyfriends. One of them ran away with her boyfriend because her family found out [that she had a boyfriend]. But she has come back since then. Another one, I saw her smoking in the park, surrounded by some guys.
MANATA: Are you still friends with them?
MARYAM: No.

In other instances, the weight attached to moral goodness takes on the form of teachable moments, whereby face-savers will "teach" others how they should behave, as the following excerpt from my field notes illustrates:

Sari. February 7, 2011. Our English lesson is over and Karim and the boys have walked me to the corner, where we stand around waiting for my cab to come. Karim's friend, Farshid, starts to harass Bijan, Karim's younger brother who has Down's Syndrome. Farshid then proceeds to swipe Bijan's baseball hat off his head. At first, Karim doesn't notice, but once he realizes what has happened, he starts hitting Farshid and pulls off one of Farshid's shoes and throws it in the dumpster located near us. Seeing this, another friend, Sohrab, picks Farshid up and starts carrying him to the dumpster, threatening to throw him in. [The next day]: When I mention the incident to them during our lesson, Karim states calmly: "Farshid made a moral error."

Farshid's "moral error" was harassing someone who did not have the ability to defend himself. In doing so, Farshid became the subject of a lesson, whereby he was "taught" not to morally falter again. In cases like this, where the moral infraction is considered to be relatively small, it is often resolved through a "lesson." However, some moral violations are considered beyond teachable and necessitate cutting off ties, as in the case of Maryam's "bad" friends who smoked and had relations with the opposite sex.

Among face-savers, then, norms of purity that often derive from religious traditions are reinforced through certain embodied moral practices.[47] These practices, as I will demonstrate below, primarily manifest themselves in one's sexual cleanliness, (non)use of substances, and fraternization with the "proper" people. These public practices are seen by community members as indicators of the face-saver's morality and signal his inner goodness in a way that a commitment to hard work, self-sufficiency, and aesthetic labor do not.

## Sexual Cleanliness

As the above example of Maryam indicates, a face-saver's *shakhsiyat*, and particularly that of a young woman, is intertwined with judgments of her sexual cleanliness. To be viewed as morally *kasif* (ritually unclean) rather than *najib* (decent) inflicts a blow not only to the young woman's face, but also to that of her family, since her family's reputation largely lies in securing her modesty. Intimations of moral uncleanliness most clearly manifest themselves when young women are seen using too much makeup, wearing too revealing or tight-fitting clothing, or, most importantly, interacting with non-*mahram* males. Consider the following statement:

> [Manata], it's good that even though you're coming from America, you don't wear a lot of makeup. Your eyebrows look like a girl's and not like those of a grown married woman's. If anyone sees you, they would think

you're a normal, unmarried girl. Have you seen Mina, Yas's sister? She looks like a married woman [with her makeup and overshaped eyebrows]. (*Niousha, Yas's cousin*)

While Mina was able to save face among her upper-class friends by embodying a particular look (see chapter 3), she lost face among those in her family's inner circle because she did not take precautions in translating the look favored by her friends to that expected by her own community of family and neighbors. The look—a full face of heavy makeup, overly plucked eyebrows, and tight-fitting clothes—that allowed her to fit in with one public was seen as a marker of moral uncleanliness by another. In the eyes of this latter public, the way Mina dressed and looked was connotative of a girl who practiced a certain sexual freedom and was not *najib*. Indeed, predominant among the communities I observed was the belief that "good women must have good *hejāb*."[48] The more covered a female face-saver was in terms of dress, the better she would be judged. Young women who wore heavy makeup and dressed in what was perceived to be a gaudy manner were often the subject of ridicule and scorn among those in their neighborhood.[49] Baharan, for instance, recalled how a young woman seated next to her on a neighborhood bus wearing heavy makeup became the subject of ridicule by the other female passengers.

Thus, as long as young women like Mina did not embody the moral code of purity through their appearance, they could not hope to gain the socioeconomic incentives from this secondary public that others, including their own family members, could accumulate:

Manata, I'm going to tell you something and you're going to be shocked. Mina and Hooman called it quits because their ways of thinking didn't match. He proposed marriage to me a week later and now we're going to get engaged in six months. Mina doesn't care; she told our mom, "Why not Yas and Hooman?" Mina has like a hundred boyfriends and he wasn't like that [someone who dates around]. And when Hooman found this out about Mina through a mutual friend, he really started to dislike her. When his parents initially found out that he was dating an Akbari sister, they thought it was me! But when they found out that it was Mina, they weren't happy. (*Yas*)

Yas's pending engagement to Hooman, someone whom she considered "good" because of his demonstrable self-sufficiency (see chapter 2) came as a result of her perceived moral cleanliness relative to her sister. Not only did Yas adopt careful calculations to present divergent fronts to the two publics to which she was regularly exposed (i.e., her extended family and the outside community), she was also never seen associating with non-*mahram* men, whereas Mina violated these rules time and time again.

As it turns out, Yas not only judged other girls like her sister for their dating behavior, but, akin to other community members, evaluated young men as well for not being morally strong enough to resist temptation. From my fieldnotes:

> Green Park, Sari. May 16, 2010. Yas and I sat down on a bench to people watch. We noticed a group of four school girls sitting around and laughing. "They're here to get guys," said Yas. "There's no reason for girls to leave school to come to the park in the middle of this hot weather. See the way they're giggling, they're trying to attract the attention of those guys over there." Yas pointed to two young men sitting across from the girls. Eventually, the girls got up and two of them sat on a bench next to another guy and immediately struck up a conversation with him. The other two girls sat behind them. "Look how rude they are, how easily they went and are talking to him. Those other boys had character, they didn't like girls like that."

Young men are, therefore, not immune to insinuations of sexual impropriety. Nonetheless, there is certainly a double standard. Given the gendered nature of morality monitoring, young men are given more latitude to hang out with the opposite sex than are young women. However, as Yas's comments reveal, self-restraint and a strong character are also prized traits for men and are indicative of their inner virtuosity. To be seen flirting, picking up girls, and going on dates slowly chips away at this morality.

Nevertheless, because young men do not suffer extensive damage to their *aberu* and marriage prospects for engaging with the opposite sex—indeed, these young men are often still able to marry "good" girls—families focus their energies on their daughters. Due to the consequences to their daughters' marriage mobility, many of the families of the female face-savers I came to know largely restricted the movements of their daughters in public spaces for fear that their daughters would be evaluated as "loose" women by others. If a daughter lost face by appearing to be unclean, one response was to marry her off as soon as possible so that she could recultivate her virtue and be able to regain some of the face that she had lost.

Consider Layla's story. A young lower-class woman who lived in Sakineh's neighborhood, Layla had been shamed by her neighbors for committing the double taboo of having a boyfriend and running off with him. As Sakineh recounted, "Layla had run off with him for two years. She wasn't a good girl." When Layla returned to the neighborhood, she agreed to enter into an arranged marriage with another young man whom her parents deemed acceptable. "Layla regretted what she had done and now she's back on track," Sakineh stated emphatically. In her new role as a devout wife, Layla salvaged her good name; neighbors like Sakineh deemed her to have become "good" again. By demonstrating a renewed adherence to "keeping with dominant ideas about appropriate moral behavior"[50] within the purity rule, Layla was able to reclaim the admiration of those who once berated her.

However, there are instances when female face-savers are unable to regain the community ties and social support that once permeated their lives. Divorce is one such instance. Normative understandings of divorce shape the judgments that friends and kin make in regard to the divorcée. Drawing on the popular notion that "a woman who has gone to the house of fortune (i.e., her husband's house) in a white dress (i.e., wedding dress) must also come out of the house of fortune in a white dress" (i.e., the *kafan*, a white cloth that enshrouds the deceased Muslim),[51] some community members tend to withdraw social support from a woman who has undergone divorce. Jamileh, a thirty-year-old who had initiated and managed to secure a divorce from her husband, a drug addict, by giving up her *mahr* (dowry), explained what happened to her:[52]

> When I got married, I had a lot of friends. But now that everyone's heard that I'm divorced, no one says, "What are you doing?" No one asks how I am. Everyone runs away from me. When a woman gets a husband, everyone looks at her and pays attention to her. But if she's not successful

in her marriage and wants to get a divorce, God help her because she no longer has a place, neither among her family nor among the community.

To be able to acquire a job or maintain respect in their current ones, some divorcées, like Ariana, the lingerie vendor we met in chapter 2, hide their divorce from their colleagues and bosses so that they will not be socially ostracized. While women like Jamileh and Ariana can regain moral capital among their communities through a second marriage, the stigma of divorce often remains with women and renders the prospect of a second marriage that much more difficult.

While recovering one's face from divorce is difficult, being found out as a prostitute makes the likelihood of regaining one's dignity and reputation next to impossible. To be perceived as a prostitute is deemed antithetical to purity and results not just in damage to one's moral capital, but in "negative moral capital,"[53] whereby one's moral worth is destroyed in its entirety. Regardless of how much a person needs aid, once her moral capital is destroyed, social disdain becomes a substitute for benevolence, as the following excerpt from my fieldnotes indicates:

Sari. July 1, 2010. I met sixteen-year-old Ava outside the gate of one of Sari's cemeteries this afternoon. Ava was sitting with a group of older women begging for money. "This is my *shoghl* [job]," Ava responded when I offered her money and asked her if she had any other job. "I'm married. My husband plays around with girls. I don't care what he does, he can do whatever he wants. The girls give it up easy." After I left Ava to enter the cemetery, the cemetery guard approached me. "Why were you talking to her? This is what these women do. I know that girl. She was just in a guy's house. They make 40–50,000 *tomans* a day [doing what they do]."

The guard's censure of my interaction with Ava reflects how Ava's strategy to deal with her poverty and her husband's infidelity has negative repercussions for her "quality of life and chances for eventually escaping poverty."[54] When a woman like Ava is known as a *zan-e kharab* (ruined woman), she has to endure not just stigmatization and disgrace, but also contempt, which denies her access to community goods. The guard's comments made it clear that given Ava's line of work, my attempt to form a connection with and to provide aid to Ava was unwelcome. It is highly unlikely that even if Ava changes her lifestyle, she will be able to secure a respectable standing within the community, as her work history has left a permanent scar in her life.[55]

## Drug Use

Drug addiction is dangerous for the country's present and future.
—President Hassan Rouhani[56]

For the past two decades, the threat of drugs as a pollutant to the moral and social order has become of central concern among policy makers in Iran. In a meeting at the drug control headquarters on July 30, 2019, President Rouhani insisted that the fight against drugs is the responsibility of all institutions in the country. It is, as he emphasized, a national responsibility to rescue society and youth from the problem of addiction.[57] The recent increasing rise of substance abuse in Iran, with some one and a half million Iranians officially classified as drug-dependent, has propelled much of this discourse.[58] The relentless flow of narcotics into Iran from neighboring Afghanistan and Pakistan, coupled with the increasing accessibility and decreasing price of opium, along with the availability of cheap crystal meth (known locally as *shisheh*), has largely contributed to the growing number of users in the country.[59] Drug use is often deemed to be a problem among Iran's disenfranchised youth population, and social analysts point out that "with the lack of jobs, entertainment, and social outlets, a restless and hopeless Iranian youth will continue to look to drugs for solace and escape from the realities of a restrictive life."[60]

Correlation, however, is not causation. Indeed, the presence of youth who avoid any asociation with drugs challenges the perceived causal relationship between youth marginalization and substance abuse. Among face-savers, drug use is considered an egregious—if not the most egregious—moral transgression. No one I spoke with admitted to using or trying drugs (although, certainly, this may not have been an accurate indication of their experiences). Indeed, drug use and dealing are all highly stigmatized among face-savers and considered to be the downfall of a person's reputation and his subsequent ability to accrue moral capital. As a result, face-savers who want to have a competing chance to gain upward mobility try to stay as far away as possible from even the smallest insinuation of using drugs, considered the quintessential moral pollutant. However, poverty may act as an ancillary stimulus impelling substance abuse: a failure to compete in the face game and the subsequent loss of moral capital may influence one's decision to turn to drugs. Not having anything to lose becomes an incentive to disengage altogether.

To compete for moral validation and avoid losing the game, face-savers take pains to prevent themselves from being stigmatized as a user. An afternoon I spent with Yas provides a useful example. That particular afternoon, Yas accompanied me on one of my field excursions to one of the poorer neighborhoods in Sari, where, according to Yas, "everyone was a drug dealer and addict." While both of us were wearing the mandatory hijab required of women in public, I noticed that Yas had pulled the ends of her headscarf over her face as soon as we entered the neighborhood, exposing only her eyes. "Someone might recognize me. I don't want them to think that I hang out here," she explained. In a similar vein, Karim often avoided playing football or fraternizing with friends near the railway tracks located near his neighborhood, knowing that it was where, according to Karim, all the "drug addicts hung out."

While drug use is highly stigmatized in these communities, drugs constitute a large part of some of these face-savers' lives. These youth have immediate family members, often fathers, brothers, or husbands, who have gone down the "wrong" path.[61] However, these young men and women take pains to distinguish themselves from their drug-using brothers, husbands, or fathers. Nina, the freelance artist, and her sister, Baharan, for instance, had a brother, Khalil, a drug user, who was in and out of jail during the time I knew them. Rarely did they mention Khalil to me or anyone in their circle of friends unless someone inquired about his health. In these latter instances, the sisters would often frown and express their disapproval of his life choices. Other young women whose husbands are users often hide this fact from friends and colleagues, as Parisa, the accessories vendor, did in order to avoid being branded as "bad" people. For these youth, the necessity of compensating for their family member's unfavorable behavior prompts their own quest to be seen as morally upright and good.

Of course, not all face-savers are successful in their pursuits. In the time I knew him, Farbod, the young man who struggled academically, but partially compensated with his good behavior scores, eventually came to gain a reputation among community members as a "bad" person. Farbod's father was an unemployed drug user while his mother was a domestic worker who occasionally received cash and in-kind gifts from her employers. Two years after my English lessons with Farbod had ended, one of his mother's former employers, Zohreh, related how Farbod's mother was having an affair and lamented how Farbod had most likely gone down the same path as his father, "hanging out with the bad kids in town." In Zohreh's eyes, Farbod's youthful laziness had turned into depravity. Among the few of his mother's former employers whom I knew, not only were none of them willing to hire her again due to her perceived moral degeneration, but they were also reluctant to extend a helping hand to Farbod himself.

To avert the shame and ostracization that accompany even the slightest insinuation of drug use (as in Farbod's case), face-savers like Maryam, whom we met earlier, are wary in their interactions with others, taking precautions such as cutting off ties in order to ensure that those whom they hang out with are clean. However, unless friends are caught in the act, as in Maryam's case, making sure that one's friends and acquaintances are not users is more difficult than it appears. There is a certain moral ambiguity that surrounds others.[62] According to Aria, the twenty-six-year-old clothing vendor we met in chapter 1, "You can't trust anyone. Your friends shouldn't smoke, they shouldn't do opium. [But] you have to be careful. Youth now are looking to look good. . . . [With] drug addicts, you can't tell they're drug addicts anymore." When face-savers are not careful about whom they hang out with because they cannot "tell" whether the person is a "drug addict," family members often step in, as was the case with Shiva, a twenty-year-old lingerie vendor in Bazaar Markazi:

> I knew this guy [Nader] in high school, and he eventually asked for my hand in marriage.[63] My parents asked around after him, and found out that he wasn't a good person. People told them that he was an addict. But he would always clean up before seeing me, so I could never guess. My family disapproved of the marriage and I couldn't say anything above my

family's word. I held out for a while. Nader would come to school and start harassing me. I told my father and my father took me out of school for a year [so that Nader couldn't bother me]. When I look back at this whole experience, I think to myself how God helped me.

So important was averting an association with drugs that Shiva's parents were willing to sacrifice Shiva's education in order to preserve her reputation. In preempting the possibility of marital dissolution by breaking up a high-risk union before it begins, parents like Shiva's are able to avoid the community stigmatization that comes with possible nuptial discord and divorce.

Shiva herself agreed with her parents' strategy, knowing that marrying a drug user would have ultimately led to her own downfall and the subsequent shaming of herself and her family. Considering herself divinely blessed that her parents were able to peel back Nader's performance and expose his reality, Shiva believed that other youth who were not willing to sacrifice love for preserving their face would meet ruin. Recalling the story of a colleague, Mahtab, Shiva stated, "Mahtab has a boyfriend who everyone says is a drug addict, but she won't listen and says that she's going to marry him anyway. She needs to fall before she comes back." In this view, a "fall" or loss of face is the only way that some people can realize their mistakes and attempt to make up for them. When it becomes impossible to avert a likely downfall, sometimes the only way a person can ultimately win the face game is to lose.

## The "Right" Crowd

As purity is a manifestation of one's inner goodness, family members often discipline youth to be hyper-cautious in their behavior, specifically in their interactions with others. Sakineh was perhaps the exemplar of setting strict parameters of behavior to regulate her children's contacts. In particular, as we saw in chapter 2, Sakineh did not allow her younger school-aged son, Mohammad, to spend much time hanging out with his friends outside of school hours. She worried constantly that too much leisure time spent with other boys would expose Mohammad to polluting ideas, get him "caught up in the wrong crowd," and lead him down a path of crime. Sakineh was so successful in her efforts to control

Mohammad's behavior that his classmates referred to him as a *bachcheh mosbat* (someone who does everything he is supposed to; a goody two-shoes). "Mohammad has the imprint of a *turbah* stuck to his forehead," his friends would say in an effort to explain to me why he would not hang around with them.[64] As they saw it, Mohammad was too preoccupied spending his downtime praying on the *turbah* and doing what he was told than consorting with them.

Despite their teasing, Mohammad's friends, too, knew that it was important to associate with admired others and avoid the unrighteous. The best way to do this was to keep oneself engaged. As we have seen, Mohammad's neighbor, Karim, spent the down time he had mingling with others in Mr. B's grocery store. Like Karim, face-savers often keep themselves occupied with schoolwork, extracurricular activities, or jobs. While motivations to become self-sufficient, to appear hardworking, and to make money are important propellers, these youth are also driven by the belief that too much leisure time can lead a person to toxic friends. "Some people aren't really in favor with others in the community," said twenty-eight-year-old Ibrahim, a worker in a mechanic's shop. "If you're friends with those people, then others will start to think the same way about you that they do about them." To avoid getting caught up with these "problematic" people and with any potential *khulaf kari* (wrongdoings) that can ensue by engaging with them, many face-savers believe that keeping busy is the best antidote to being lured down the wrong path. Work, in this sense, is a means to keep one's virtue and reputation. Elaborating on the importance of work, twenty-year-old Mazdak, another worker in a mechanic's shop, said:

> It's not good to just waste time. When you're unemployed, people will say that he's either wasting away at home or on the street. It's nothing special. But when you're working, they're not worried, they say he's doing something, he's going after his future.

Of course, a sustained focus on being evaluated as morally good by avoiding social situations with the slightest risk of moral lapse can also prevent face-savers like Mohammad from developing more extensive collective networks of social ties, an outcome that can prove essential for fostering future socioeconomic growth. Indeed, as we saw in chapter

2, Sakineh's hyper-vigilance that prevented Mohammad from "wasting time" in the neighborhood also inhibited him from gaining access to influential others, people who could have helped him attend college. As Goffman notes, "Fear over possible loss of face often prevents the person from initiating contacts in which important information can be transmitted."[65] This, however, does not take away from the fact that the strategies that youth like Mohammad and their families deploy to present virtuous fronts can simultaneously represent a "potent resource in exercising power"[66] in the face of socioeconomic degradation.

## *Asliyat* (Origins)

Avoiding drugs, being sexually modest, and associating with the virtuous are all means that facilitate proper ethical conduct by restraining behavior. Without embracing these embodied practices, or at least giving the appearance that they embrace them, youth cannot hope to be judged as respectable, honest, and all-around good, regardless of how hard they work or how well they dress. The customary character judgments that community members and youth made of others during my time in the field indicate that a person's embodied goodness is his most highly valued trait.

This was accentuated through the emphasis that people placed on a person's integrity when advising me on whom I should talk to for my research or what home I should enter for my English lessons. "The father has a roving eye," Karim told me when I inquired about tutoring his neighbor's daughter. Arash, another young man, advised me not to help a family because they would "spend it on cigarettes." Often statements concerning who was "good" were couched in language about the uprightness of the person's family. As in other contexts in the Middle East, the purity of the family unit, the purity of one's *asliyat*, or origins, is seen to reflect on the purity of the individual.[67] As such, coming from an upright and respectable family helps in securing a connection, job, or social opportunity.

Kian, a sixteen-year-old who ended up becoming an apprentice at the bookstore where Naghmeh and Fereshteh worked (see chapter 3), was hired because of his father's reputation. The bookstore proprietors had hired Kian's father, Jamal, a carpenter, on a contractual basis to remodel the store. In the eyes of the proprietors, Jamal had a "pure hand." "Kian's family was a good family, they were *aberumand*," Zohreh, one of the proprietors, recounted to me. While Kian later proved to be an honest, hardworking, and clever apprentice, he had not established his worthiness before he was hired. Nevertheless, Kian was given a chance because of his father's perceived positive moral fiber. But what of those face-savers who come from "disreputable" families, those whose parents, siblings, or husbands are known to have engaged in moral transgressions?

Among face-savers, there are many like Nina, Parisa, and Baharan, who must either cope with drug or alcohol abuse in their families and/or have parents, like Farbod does, who have gained a reputation for being sexually licentious. In these instances when their family name can be associated with disrepute, youth have a starting disadvantage regardless of how closely they abide by the face rules themselves. These young men and women have to work that much harder to prove themselves worthy of the friendship, job, or social opportunity. Proving themselves often means hiding their family's storied pasts from their employers and friends, as Parisa did. Alternatively, if the family is "found out" and the family name has been discredited, youth have to compensate for their family's behavior by going the extra mile, as Nina and Baharan did. Being exceptionally restrained in one's outward behavior, studying diligently enough to get into college or engaging in demanding work from a young age, and being hyper-vigilant in one's appearance are all strategies that can help disassociate a face-saver's own integrity from that of her family. In these instances, the face-saver's personal agency is the most important factor in determining the social and economic rewards that she receives, while the role of external factors such as family or background becomes secondary.[68]

## An Ethical Conundrum

"I try not to go down the wrong path, but it's not possible. Even if you try to be good, people force you to go down the wrong path. This place is really bad," Aria, the young man we met in chapter 1, explained as he told me about his efforts to stay on the right track while hustling in Bazaar Markazi to make ends meet.[69] At twenty-six years of age, Aria had received a diploma in city planning. But, as he would tell me, he used to be a *sheytun* (a devil, that is, he "horsed around" a lot) and because of this, ended up working in the bazaar, where he makes little money despite working long hours. These days, Aria hopes to rent a store located far away from "bad" Bazaar Markazi, somewhere he can make enough money to finally have some spare time.

Given that youth like Aria adhere to a moral code that emphasizes both material merits (physical appearance, connections, money) and non-material merits (purity), they are presented with a potential ethical paradox. On the one hand, their aspirations for jobs, good grades, wealth, connections, and trends both preserve their face and strengthen their position within their communities. On the other hand, youth recognize that their struggles to advance in these realms can involve moral transgressions, which can also inflict a blow to their face if they are caught. In order to make more money, for instance, some shop apprentices face the option of stealing from the shop coffers when their bosses are not looking. Others, like Dara, have to make the choice between making an honest sale and a profitable one where they intentionally quote customers exorbitantly high prices. How do youth make these trade-offs? We know that in the face game, the performative aspect of the rules takes center stage and that secrecy becomes the price one has to pay to gain moral confirmation. But how do face-savers justify, to themselves, potential lapses in the moral rule of purity in order to get ahead? How do they themselves feel about putting up a façade?

For some face-savers, wrongdoing reflects their belief that everyone lapses at one point or another and that indiscretion is even sanctioned by certain authority figures like teachers. In this view, transgression is a prerequisite to achieving certain ends. This outlook makes youth feel that they are exempt from moral restrictions on mobility-oriented actions. Consider the following conversation I had with Karim:

KARIM: Everyone cheats! If you don't cheat, there's something wrong.
MANATA: In what way?
KARIM: Because then you won't get good grades.
MAJID (KARIM'S FRIEND): One of my teachers was saying that if you can get away with cheating in his class, then we would all get a 20. And everyone cheated! We all ended up acing the class!

Other youth justify their moral offenses by relying on the notion of determinism. According to this perspective, there is always a possibility for humans to commit moral wrongdoings. When attempting to gain some measure of economic success, this is seen as a form of reprieve from the occasional moral hiccup. Dara used the notion of divine determinism to rationalize why his transgressions sometimes failed to bring about his desired economic ends. In this outlook, the will of the divine ultimately determines whether or not his decision to give priority to economic advancement over moral purity will, in fact, allow him to secure a particular financial objective:

> I believe in both God and in prayer, but I still commit offenses. They [those who commit indiscretions] say people are *ja'ez al-khata* [Arabic quote that states that human beings are capable of sin]. I say human beings may sin, [but] should not sin [*here, Dara means that a person should strive for virtue*]. Isn't that right? Me, myself, I go down the wrong path most of the time. I regretted it. I was never proud of it. I regretted it the moment I did it. I would say, God, why did I do that? But it wasn't in my hands, it was out of my control. I [also] say human beings can commit wrongdoing. But that doesn't mean they can do anything they want. Me, myself, I commit wrongdoing most of the time. I was supposed to take a motorcycle up north, and the price I quoted the customer was way too high. . . . He told me that we would go at ten in the morning. He agreed to it. If it were my destiny, that money would have been my *ruzi* [*loosely, an earning deemed to be from God*] for today. But because it wasn't my destiny, the guy didn't come today, and he might not come tomorrow either. (*Dara*)

By justifying his secret violations of the purity rule as something that is not unique, as something that is even widely acknowledged, Dara highlights his own respectability while disassociating himself from the undignified, who "do anything they want." Dara sees both his public performance and his private actions as right, if not ideal.[70] In Dara's view, his indiscretions are predicted and thus, out of his hands. In committing wrongdoings that enable him to gain some economic advantage, Dara considers his lapses as more acceptable than the offenses of those who simply violate the moral rule of purity at whim. Ultimately, it is divine will that decides one's fate. This belief operates to absolve Dara of the consequence of his actions: missing out on his *ruzi*.

In determining who is worthy of the rewards that come with being "good," what communities consider most important is the way that a person presents himself to an audience. For the individual himself, being secure in the knowledge that any private violations of the purity rule reflect his God-given humanity provides little solace when he is caught in the act. When a face-saver is completely sincere, that is, when his inner world catches up with his outward presentation, the consequence can be either rejection by his community or embrace, depending on how closely the resulting alignment of his *baten* and *zaher* matches community norms.

But until the time when a person's *baten* and *zaher* become one and the same, judgments of character based on performance are an illusion. This illusion, in turn, is created and reinforced by community members' complicity in the face game.[71] Confidence in the face game means that community members keep it going, despite the fact that winning the game can sometimes be an "ambiguous achievement."[72] Indeed, the game may reveal little more than the face-saver's ability to stage-manage a certain guise, a certain moral superiority that can then be used to gain increased social and economic capital. In these instances, the game reveals little to nothing about the contingencies involved in determining who has a better chance of winning the game and who does not. Gone unnoticed is the role of structural constraints such as one's family background. In the face game, sometimes those who are most in need of help, like Farbod, fall by the wayside despite their every intention to be a good person. So, too, do youth who want to find a job or receive good grades, but cannot because there are no available jobs or because they are responsible for taking care of their siblings and earning money for the household in the wake of a parent's death and, consequently, have little time left to study.

Why does the game attract, then, despite being an imperfect measure of one's morality? Among youth who lack the initial social and economic means to distinguish themselves from each other, playing the game allows them to gain the dignity, prestige, and distinction that they feel are often lost to them in the course of their everyday lives. Moral boundaries that dictate how one should act become a form of moral capital that, all else being equal, incentivizes proper decorum and separates the deserving from the undeserving poor.[73]

Twenty-eight-year-old Fahima, for example, was considered by her neighbors to be exceedingly good and pure. As a result, they constantly asked her to undergo religious fasts in their stead in return for a sum of money. Fahima made enough money by carrying out these fasts that she considered this her job. For Fahima and those like her, being and doing good provides meaning to their lives and renders their lives manageable in a way that few other actions may. Ultimately, in practicing virtue, face-savers create moral boundaries. These boundaries, however, are not necessarily and always born of a desire to exclude others in order to simply maintain dignity. The appeal that these boundaries have extends far beyond simply reaffirming face-savers' own self-worth to encompass the rewards that come from living a life true to their values. Boundaries serve not simply as a means to exclude, but also as a means to scale up.

5

## Moral Conformism and Its Contents

And as much as I'd like to believe there's a truth beyond
illusion, I've come to believe that there's no truth beyond
illusion. Because, between "reality" on the one hand, and
the point where the mind strikes reality, there's a middle
zone, a rainbow edge where beauty comes into being, where
two very different surfaces mingle and blur to provide what
life does not: and this is the space where all art exists, and
all magic.
—Donna Tartt, *The Goldfinch*, 2005

As I write this, many of the youth I knew have moved on with their lives.
Karim, the football player, attends a relatively prestigious university in
Iran. Nina, the freelance artist, married her fiancé, a store owner, and
has a one-year-old son. She is attending university and continues her
artistic productions, this time making small handmade figurines. Her
sister, Baharan, was able to get into a doctoral program at a prestigious
university and earns relatively decent pay providing social science con-
sultative services to various organizations and individuals. Fereshteh,
the bookstore apprentice, married a young man from a well-to-do family and now runs her own store in Tehran.

While these youth have been able to play the face game and play it
well, their success is underscored by the fact that they have not been
derailed. Indeed, many other youth have failed to effectively protect
the veil of *aberu* that covers them: stories of drug addiction, of young
women engaged in premarital sexual relations, of young men who sit
idly at home without work, and of fathers who cannot provide for their
families abound in daily gossip. What all of these stories illustrate is
that the face game has created a micro-system of stratification within
poverty, whereby those who win are granted certain concessions and
benefits while those who lose simply lag behind. Though this has repro-

duced cycles of inequality within communities, it has also created new pathways for upward mobility in status. This drive for status has been such that we cannot readily discern some young people's class status in Iran through the image that they project. Poverty is not always seen. Rather, it is felt and actively fought against. What does this mean for our understanding of Iranian society at the present moment?

> In the eighties, we had a lot of problems. There was the [Iran-Iraq] war, and then after the war, we, *daheh-ye shasti-ha* [youth born circa the 1980s], really suffered in every way. Families had a lot more problems and worries. The hits we *shasti-ha* suffered were really a lot. After the war, we couldn't continue our education and the job situation was such that those of us who wanted to work couldn't go into government jobs and had to work in *kar-e azad*. . . . We brought ourselves up from really difficult conditions. (*Behzad, twenty-nine-year-old laborer in a car shop in Sari*)

The Islamic Republic today is a postwar society with a newly aspirational youth cohort. The mere existence of pathways enabling some of these youth to become part of the globalized world of fashion and trends, to gain a higher education, or to become entrepreneurs was much more constrained for the majority of young Iranians in the 1980s, during Iran's eight-year-long war with Iraq. For *daheh-ye shasti* youth like Behzad, who were born during this period of wartime, memories of the socioeconomic hardships that their parents and they themselves endured have served as push factors, impelling them to cling ever more tightly to the moral code enshrined in the face game. To these youth, hard work is the means by which they can "bring themselves up." "I haven't reached all my goals," said Behzad, "but I try. I make an effort to reach those things I want. I work for it." Similarly, twenty-eight-year-old Ladan, a relatively successful seamstress in Sari, stated, "I want both my husband and I to work hard so that our children can have the sort of life that we never had growing up. I don't want my children to suffer the same economic hardships that I did as a child."

The relative normalization of social structural patterning that we can observe in Iran today is testament to both the Islamic Republic's fast-changing postwar milieu and the lengths that people will go within this setting when faced with unequal life chances. An economic boom, increasing oil revenues, and the lifting of some international sanctions—all events that happened in the past two decades—have opened spaces for young Iranians from all walks of life to become participants in the country's broader socioeconomic fabric, albeit in varying degrees. For the youth whose stories I shared in the pages of this book, this participation is predicated on how well they can, according to Behzad, "submit to the will of society." To submit to what society wants, to ensure that they don't become "bad" in the eyes of others, means that they must protect their face. "The most important thing I can pass down to my children," said Donya, "is for them to protect their *aberu*."

The consequence of protecting one's *aberu*, of gaining the favor of others, and of subsequently becoming a socioeconomic participant in society is the incremental rise in the face-saver's standing in the community. Small gains create status distinctions within the social worlds of youth like Behzad, Ladan, and Donya. Indeed, face-savers use interpersonal evaluations of self-sufficiency, hard work, purity, and appearance to judge where peers stand on the socioeconomic hierarchy. Other community members, too, evaluate youth on the basis of these dimensions. Those young men and women who are able to project an admired front and use the opportunities subsequently afforded to them are able to reap the benefits of being favorably evaluated. As such, rather than resist or reject the internal moral code of conduct through which their practices are collectively gauged, the youth in this book attempt to adhere to it as best they can, secure in the knowledge that through facework, they have a chance at improving their station in life.

However, there are face-savers who ultimately lose the game because they are unable to present themselves in a carefully calculated manner and get caught. Reasons for their loss are both culturally defined and structurally determined. Some are endowed with relatively lower levels of street smarts in their social interactions due to the hyper-vigilance of elders in policing the time they spend in the public sphere. Others are less likely to take financial risks—risks that can play a significant role in determining the outcome of the game. Still others have to deal with the aftermath of a divorce and the social stigma that ensues.

Nevertheless, losing face does not mean that these youth will not be able to climb up the proverbial ladder later on in life. In certain instances, as in the case of Layla, demonstrating a renewed adherence to the face rules enables youth to recapture community admiration. Face is thus not always an either/or scenario: youth are not labeled as either those with face or those without. Violations of the rules governing face behavior often result in a decrease—rather than a total loss—of the amount of one's face.[1] Many times, the young person can still acquire value, admiration, and social standing by later embodying the moral status distinctions of facework.

As the numerous examples in this book have shown, face-savers position themselves to win status points that can facilitate their ability to attain elements of mobility within poverty. In so doing, these youth reaffirm the collectively sanctioned fields of social practice within the face system such as being well-dressed, responsible, and independent. While other groups in other contexts may value similar virtues, what makes the face system for the youth in this study especially noteworthy is the implications that it carries for these youths' "small-scale . . . silent strivings"[2] to become fully integrated into society.

The experience of poverty among face-savers certainly brings them measures of frustration and disillusionment. As one sixteen-year-old street vendor, Babak, remarked:

> I wanted to get my bachelor's degree and have a job where I sat behind a desk, but I had to drop out of the ninth grade in order to meet my family's expenses. There are no hopes when you have a job like this. Hopes are for those who have reached the top. People like us don't have hopes.

However, when I spent enough time to look at the unspoken vernacular contexts in which their lives and stories unfolded, I found that these very youth undertake dozens of silent movements that reaffirmed the importance of face and the "nuances of social interaction."[3] As Babak explained to me as our acquaintanceship grew, "My hope is to become successful, to not be dependent on others. I'm saving up to buy my own store."

In attempting to "not be dependent on others" and to safeguard their face, the young people I observed, like Babak, created small windows of opportunity that often became their ticket to adult life. Their actions not only belie the standard story of marginalized youth in Iran and in the broader Middle East as a generation in wait. They also contradict studies that argue that "long periods of waiting are not spent in building human capital, saving for a home, or other activities that signal hope."[4] Rather than live in an "undignified liminal state of pre-adulthood,"[5] many youth engage in cultural practices that can, and do, interact with structural constraints to create spaces where they can be integrated into the social networks and local economies of the communities in which they live. Accentuated conformism facilitates small leaps of mobility that enable some youth to get a better job or to find love and to get married.

The context-specific rules governing face behavior exemplify the way in which the desire to maintain dignity can serve as a powerful driver to move ahead in life, however small the advances may be. Rather than adopt a fatalistic and generalist perspective, then, we should take a more nuanced approach to the study of these young people's everyday lives and be attentive to the existence of cultural practices—in this case, facework—that not only limit but also facilitate motivation and action.[6] To focus solely on the marginalization, hopelessness, and exclusion of poor youth overlooks how daily practices create moral hierarchies that in turn affect the distribution of material and social goods within a community. Despite their verbal assertions of not being able to escape their conditions, face-savers use the face system to their advantage to take part in the broader life of the community in which they live and to assert their autonomy. As Jay MacLeod has noted, "Individuals are not passive receivers of structural forces; rather they interpret and respond to those forces in creative ways."[7] Face-savers similarly demonstrate their agency in the face of socioeconomic hardship. However, they do this through their appropriation, rather than their rejection or creative re-articulation, of prevailing social norms.

This is a significant point. For the past four decades, ethnographic studies and journalistic accounts of Iranian youth have overwhelmingly focused on the Islamic Republic's restrictive governmental system and on the subsequent social, economic, and political exclusion of the country's youth. As such, Iranian young people's everyday practices—practices that range from the clothes they wear to the music they listen to—are often interpreted as evidence of their resistance and rebellion against dominant and constrictive state norms. Resistance has become the theoretical model par excellence used to explain the complexity of behavior found among youth in Iran today.[8]

Throughout this book, I have challenged this rather myopic view of youth culture by exploring how a group of young men and women not typically included in studies of youth culture in Iran—that is, those who are from the lower classes and not predominately from the capital city—attempt to move forward within the context of their lives. What I found were youth who possess an ever-present moral economy revolving around facework that guides their deliberate actions and use of limited material resources. It is their aspirations for a dignified life, rather than their defiance or resistance, that shape their attitudes and practices.

These face-savers, rather than being hopeless, frustrated walking rebels, are bounded and situated agents who attempt to secure their livelihoods through a collectively embedded and contextually strategic moral code that allows them to save face in front of those who are in their social networks. This code serves as an evaluative benchmark that builds these youths' moral capital and enables them to distinguish themselves from those who have not been able to embody the code's set of values. By adjusting their behavior to fit normative expectations, youth are able to exchange this moral capital for the social and economic opportunities they need to incrementally improve their lot in life. Subjective measures of worth can thus provide objective wins that facilitate poor young people's struggles to transform their lives.

## Performance versus Reality?

In understanding youths' efforts to improve their lives in this way, can we come to the conclusion that face-savers are simply calculating agents who put on a performative front to get what they want? How can one distinguish between deception and truth when the stakes for revealing one's "true" self are so costly? If face-savers are continuously concerned with putting up a misleading appearance, then are they not themselves "walking contradictions, bundles of tension ready to snap?"[9]

> I try to protect my *aberu* as much as I can. It's a goal that everyone has. *Aberu* is the social character that others see of you, so it has to be posi-

tive and it has to be protected. I try not to be in people's judgments. Before I do something, I think to myself whether it's bad for me or not in other people's eyes. Take smoking cigarettes, for example. If others see me smoking cigarettes, what will they think of me? I try not to do this so that when other people see me, they don't judge me and say this guy is a *sigari* [smoker]. There are certain values that have to be protected. Everyone builds his own character. A person makes his own *aberu*. A saying from old times says that others don't ruin your *aberu*, you yourself do. So, above all, I have to be true to myself, to evaluate my own behavior so that then others can judge me. When I think something is okay in my eyes, but it's not appropriate in the eyes of society, I try not to do it to the extent I can. I try to live in a good way. If people remember you as good, this is reason to be proud: to have people say that this person was a good person, that nobody disliked them. This means that their *aberu* was protected. (*Ibrahim, twenty-eight-year-old laborer in an automotive shop in Sari*)

What is particularly revealing about Ibrahim's comments is that he does not experience the tension that is typically assumed youth in Iran suffer through as a result of the social front that they feel compelled to present to society. Because Ibrahim tries to "live in a good way," he attempts to embrace, as best he can, the values that society believes are appropriate and good. For Ibrahim, constant scrutiny of his own behavior further enables him to be "true to [himself]." He has thus become "emotionally attached to the image [he] present[s] to the world."[10] In their struggles to advance, face-savers come to believe in the value of the image they produce.[11]

To be well-liked, to be remembered as good, and to be judged positively all reveal how face-savers like Ibrahim navigate between their public and private selves as they construct their identities. Yes, this navigation involves a strategic performative element and a certain self-editing. However, face-savers view this hyper-vigilance in self-editing their behavior as beneficial: it is a means toward the end goal of protecting *aberu*. Without this self-editing, without negotiating between his *zaher* and his *baten*, a person has no one to blame but himself when his "social character" falls into ruin. The destruction of one's character, as we have seen, is ultimately the destruction of one's prospects for a better future.

The figurative split between the *zaher* and the *baten*, while useful as an analytical tool to understand the process of facework, has also unfortunately become a trope that is often used to highlight a unique post-revolution mentality that has seeped into Iranian youth, one characterized especially by confusion stemming from a (seemingly) oppositional duality between the public and the private selves. Viewing the inner and outer selves as diametrically opposed in this way mirrors how the word "face" has come to develop a "strong negative connotation" in the West, implying a "false social appearance covering an unseemly inner reality."[12] However, as Adelkhah, Setrag Manoukian, and Olszewska have all pointed out, this process of self-editing is not unique to Iran.[13] Rather, cultural systems the world over encourage their citizens to conform to socially acceptable norms that may or may not coincide with what citizens would have chosen for themselves. People's actions subsequently become a way to straddle their public and private lives, thereby creating continuity—rather than opposition—between the two realms.[14]

Therefore, rather than always positing a difference between the *zaher* and the *baten*, it may be useful to also look at the spaces of overlap between these two aspects of the self. Indeed, as social norms may coincide with a person's own inner motivations, there is also a certain internalization of publicly sanctioned codes of conduct. For instance, we saw in chapter 4 how Donya underscored that she liked "living by the rules." Said twenty-nine-year-old Farhad, a laborer in an automotive shop, "I wear what I want, but according to the values of my family." As they were raised in families that espoused the face system, Donya and Farhad co-opted and saw as "natural ethical behavior" the conduct and mannerisms condoned by the face game.[15] For face-savers, then, living a life they value means living by the rules. While they may not always agree with the rules, they keep to them as best they can so that they can gain the approval of others and cement their position as good people in the community.

Going beyond viewing youth culture as a monolith and understanding the various cultures that comprise what is often singularly referred to as youth culture necessitate understanding how people may view state- or community-imposed norms as completely legitimate. In the process of playing by the rules of the game, face-savers do not view the rules or the game itself as taxing or questionable, but rather as completely normal and self-evident. For face-savers, it is a process by which they become themselves. The presence of these youth within the broader social milieu of Iran belies essentializations about a uniform youth culture in Iran—and elsewhere—characterized by its members' countercultural tactics.

Rather, the strategies face-savers pursue are representative of certain motivations for action that are less emphasized in studies of youth culture: those of consumption, competition, and, particularly, aspirations for a better life.[16] The donning of chic yet modest clothing, for instance, is as indicative of some of these youths' religiosities as it is symptomatic of their desires to fit in and to compete with their peers for greater recognition and social standing. Their purchase of smartphones is suggestive of not only their desires to be in touch with friends and keep abreast of the latest news and trends through social media, but also their desires to be part of the global marketplace of consumer technology. As such, to fully understand what it means to be young today means to understand the different subjectivities that various young people espouse.

What face-savers' motivations further reveal is that we must move beyond viewing seemingly authoritarian state policies as necessarily oppressive to individual freedoms.[17] To be sure, in Iran, state policies, as Olszewska notes, have not been the only drivers of social change and subject formation; rural-urban migration, demographic shifts since the Iran-Iraq War, a young urban population, greater education among all segments of Iran's youth, and the inevitable arrival of new media and satellite in Iran have all contributed to the slow but very real embourgeoisement of Iranian society beyond the middle classes.[18]

The Islamic Republic's role in all of this, of course, has not been nominal: the regime has been, after all, at the heart of Iran's "developmental drive."[19] The state has made large investments in education, in cultural activities and buildings, including art houses and language, technology, poetry, and music classes in lower-income areas. It has also conferred material benefits and incentives to those who espouse its ideology, including members of the lower classes, students, and families of martyrs. In all of these populist efforts, the Islamic Republic has simultaneously contributed to empowering the lower classes and raising their aspirations. Desires to gain status in one's community, to ingratiate oneself among the middle classes, and to be part of a globalized marketplace can thus be read as by-products of the state's active attempts at inclusion.

## Poverty, Status, and Mobility

What insights does the face system give us about what it means to be young, poor, and aspirational in the current global moment? The stories of the youth in this book crystallize an important feature of social mobility: both subjective evaluations and objective resources matter in determining life outcomes.[20] Community perceptions of youth confer status, which can subsequently result in marginal but meaningful objective gains such as jobs, gifts, better marriage prospects, or social connections. It is in this context that I would like to place a discussion of poverty and mobility with respect to Iran and in reference to theoretical approaches in the study of social stratification more generally.

Within stratification studies, scholars have traditionally examined individual social mobility as a process of generationally transitioning from one occupational category to another. In this vein, some studies have placed concentrated effort on identifying how valuable resources, such as income, education, and social networks, are allocated across various occupational categories in the division of labor.[21] From this vantage point, institutional arrangements and practices that are not conducive to enabling occupational status and prestige and allowing the poor to break through their class origins are justification for the perpetuation of poverty cycles. In this perspective, one has moved up, especially in comparison to the parental generation, when one has been able to accrue the resources (e.g., education) needed to transition to a job higher in status. Analysts contend that in Iran, formal labor market rigidity and a lack of adequate new jobs to absorb the large numbers of young workers contribute to the inability of youth to acquire stable, high-status, formal sector employment that can enable them to engage in the consumption patterns that define middle-class status.[22] Patterns of labor force movement thus become a proxy for individual success and well-being in the Islamic Republic.

There have also been scholars who have utilized the language of *intra-class* mobility to argue that social mobility also occurs among occupations located within the boundaries of a particular class.[23] However, in this viewpoint, frequent horizontal mobility between a number of closely related blue-collar occupations, for instance, is not emblematic of upward mobility per se, but of the highly class-bound nature of the actors involved[24] or the proletarianization of certain jobs.[25] Thus, in attempting to integrate intra-class movements into analyses of life chances, studies succumb to the idea that upward social mobility largely occurs when people are able to move out of their own social class of origin. In this view, those Iranian youth who are successful in horizontally transitioning to a similar but slightly better-paying job would be considered to have "moved *on* in their lives . . . but not *up*."[26] The perceptions and experiences of the youth themselves are often not considered indicators of their higher levels of well-being, despite recent research that has shown the significance of the "agency and experiences of the poor" in determining whether social mobility has taken place.[27]

Without denying that the face-savers in this book may not achieve large leaps in social mobility as long as they do not break through their own class, I argue that they are able to achieve meaningful short-distance upward shifts—what I have defined in the introduction as *incremental mobility*—in their economic resources and social connections that are germane for understanding their chances of ultimately escaping poverty.[28] These shifts result from these young people's status as *aberumand* individuals and operate to confer further marginal but meaningful gains in standing that can help them overcome social stigmatization. When these youth perceive that they are doing better relative to others in their own socioeconomic group as a result of their conformism to social norms, whether it is securing a better-paying job in the informal labor market, purchasing brand-name outfits, or gaining acceptance into community networks, they gain both status and inner satisfaction. Indeed, as Wilensky notes, "There is no reason to believe that an individual's subjective mobility orientation is a weaker source of social integration than his objective mobility experience."[29] From the perspective of incremental mobility, then, moving up is not always solely defined by the distance of a person's movements in the occupational realm, but also by notions of relative gratification, as the following statements reveal:

> A lot of people say to themselves that they want to be the boss, and a lot of workers around here say that they want to open up their own poultry farming business, but I think that's stupid. As a laborer, I have my own money and I don't have to deal with making profits or selling or stuff like that. (*Davud*)

I've been working here for the past year from morning until night. I make 110,000 *tomans* a month. That's good pay! I used to work in a beauty supply store and the lady only gave me 60,000 *tomans* a month. (*Nazgol*)

As the chapters in this book have shown, face-savers like Nazgol and Davud undertake more modest social and economic shifts in their lives that they perceive and experience as meaningful and as indicative of their personal success,[30] despite the fact that these movements may never lead to large-scale structural mobility. These incremental gains, as we have seen, also have the potential to exert some independent influence on the structure of opportunities available to these youth later on in their lives. As such, incremental mobility enables us to capture the potential richness of the experience of mobility among youth in Iran and address the efforts that they are making to socially advance, to integrate themselves within Iranian society at large, and to find meaning in their lives.[31] By shifting our focus to how face-savers accrue incremental resource gains, we can further elaborate on our notion of mobility in Iran to incorporate that of intra-group upward mobility. In so doing, we can use as a metric for well-being not the extent to which the pursuits of the poor lead to class mobility per se, but rather the extent to which their activities provide accumulative advances *within* their socioeconomic group. Thus, what observers and analysts may construe as the seeming persistence of poverty among youth in Iran may in fact be rationalized by these young actors to constitute a slow and tedious but upward march so long as they achieve outcomes that are valuable to them. Poverty thus becomes a "way station[] to something better."[32]

Indeed, many of these youth create a sub-stratification system *within* conditions of poverty that enables them to improve their lot in life in ways that traditional perspectives of mobility cannot account for. The ethical code face-savers espouse serves not only as a means by which they differentiate themselves from others, but also as a mechanism by which their incremental mobility is constituted. Among these youth, being hardworking and honest in one's line of work, not engaging in drug use, hanging out with the right crowd, and keeping up-to-date on the latest fashions and trends all serve to raise their status and recognition. This recognition, in turn, can lead to small yet meaningful advances in their networks and economic fortunes. Thus, individual and community perceptions of what constitute high status when "acted and lived without being stated . . . become norms and values explicitly recognized."[33] Beliefs in what signifies a reputable, *aberumand* person come to comprise objective benchmarks of social standing. These benchmarks or rules of the game subsequently serve as powerful drivers that exert some autonomous influence on these young people's behavior, life outcomes, and ultimately, their perceptions of the "good life."

What these findings do not mean, however, is that the small leaps of mobility brought on by following the rules of the face game are necessarily enough to reverse conditions of socioeconomic hardship. As we have seen, the face game did not provide most of the youth in this study with the ability to escape poverty by leaps and bounds. Many of the youth I knew are still concerned with making ends meet, though they have married up. Many still budget excessively, and many are worried about losing their jobs, making rent, paying the bills, or buying a house. While these young men and women have certainly distinguished themselves as *aberumand* and successful people within the communities in which they live, they still struggle to achieve the middle-class lifestyle they aspire to.

Following the rules of the game can also operate to constrain choice and hinder action as much as it can facilitate it. Take, for example, the comment of Arash, whom we met in chapter 4, who told me, "I know a family who's in need, but it's better not to help them because they'll spend all the help that they can get on cigarettes and bad things like that." As Arash's comment illustrates, a focus on morality and saving face can hurt those who are most in need, often depicting individuals who have failed to follow the face rules as undeserving of help. This process of conferring certain incremental benefits to some who have saved face while not others also works to intensify the segmentation of people within the same socioeconomic class, which leads to a durable micro-system of stratification within poverty. This, in turn, can reproduce cycles of poverty within communities.

Further still, an emphasis on following the face rules—for instance, on becoming economically self-sufficient as quickly as possible—can also constrain the capacity of some to pursue social goods, like a college education, that can prove essential for bringing about more lasting changes in the young person's life.[34] Jobs in the informal economy, while vital in providing face-savers with a good, quick source of cash income and autonomy, can also inhibit them from pursuing more sustainable but slower career paths in the formal economy. However, given their existential constraints, face-savers follow the paths by which they believe they have the best chance of saving face and getting ahead. This calculation of chance is very much related to the importance that morality, as encompassed by the face system, has in their lives. For instance, youth who have a family to support will calculate their chances of quickly becoming financially independent through work in the informal sector as a better option than going to college and putting off making money. As Gretchen Purser describes, these calculations reveal just how constrained the poor's choices are, but how vital it is for their ability to maintain their sense of worth to be able to make a choice.[35] The life that comes as a result of a constant abidance by social norms is not a life untethered by economic hardship, but a life that provides conformists with a sense of agency and purpose.

## The Moral Self

Social norms also serve to create a moral self. While this book has emphasized how morality—as embodied through the practice of saving face—is intimately linked to the acquisition of status,[36] it should not go unsaid that being a good, moral person was not itself an important end goal for the youth I met. Indeed, the practices of the youth in this book reveal that not all human conduct is motivated out of what Bourdieu argues is a desire to reproduce social standing and prestige.[37]

The importance that face-savers attach to being remembered as "good people," to not doing anything that others will deem "inappropriate," to being, as one young man stated, "truthful to oneself" all relate a profound need to espouse the moral sensibilities of the face system for its own sake rather than simply "as [a] form[] of capital to accrue power and distinction in the social world."[38] Abtin, an eighteen-year-old high school student, recounted how working the land to help his grandfather led him to be seen as *aberumand* in the eyes of his neighbors:

> Some time ago, my grandfather was farming the land. I saw that he was alone and I went to help him since I knew he had a heart ailment. Some people saw us: neighbors and passersby. My goal was to do my grandfa-

ther's work and for my grandfather to not get more sick. [The people who saw us said] I was *aberumand*. [It was more important to me] to make my grandfather happy, it wasn't important what they would think of me.

Here we have a case where the pursuit of morality trumps the quest for status. Abtin presented himself as a morally upstanding person in the community by engaging in hard work to help another. However, he did not do this in an effort to impress others and win face points, but in a genuine attempt to assist his ailing grandfather. In Abtin's view, the presence of his neighbors did not matter; he would have helped regardless of whether anyone was there to see—and judge—his good deed.

The rules of the face game—those socially constructed norms of behavior that define what is good and right for a person to do—create a blueprint for material success, but they also serve as moral guideposts, directing those who play the game as to the "right" way to live. The more one plays the game, the better one gets at embodying the "good." The better one gets at embodying the good, the more one differentiates oneself from the "bad." Practice makes perfect. Practice creates the moral self. According to Talal Asad and Saba Mahmood, human beings develop moral selves—that is, they become virtuous—through repeated, religious practices.[39] In this view, it is cultural practice, rather than some preexisting moral identity, that begets goodness. Practice not only reinforces but mutually constitutes moral subjectivities.[40] The embodied practices of face, such as engaging in physical labor, studying diligently, wearing smart clothes, and hanging out with the right people, create the moral dispositions associated with being a "good" and *aberumand* person—dispositions such as purity, *kelas*, self-sufficiency, and diligence. As Donya recounted:

I used to think about people's opinions before; I didn't want people to think that I dressed badly [for example]. I don't think that way anymore. I suffered for thinking of what other people thought all the time. I think everything of mine is my *aberu*. I'm a well-mannered, good-looking girl. I really try to pay attention to protecting my *aberu*. I do it for myself. My purity, my morality, my behavior—all of this is my *aberu*.

Donya's comment directs attention to the way outlooks regarding face can change over time. Initially, Donya attempted to save face solely to please others. Over time, the everyday practice of saving face became so engrained in her, so "woven . . . into the very fibers and bones of [her] body,"[41] that she now does it reflexively for herself: no longer does she consciously worry about whether her actions will lead others to think she is "bad," for she knows that she has finally come to fully embody what it means to be an *aberumand* person. She deems "everything" of hers to now constitute her *aberu*: her mannerisms, style of dress, morality, and wholesomeness. While today Donya saves face for her own sense of self-worth, there are unintended rewards to her practice: over the past few years, Donya has been so successful in cultivating this good, moral self that she has been able to attract an extensive clientele, which, in turn, has enabled her to open—and keep open—her own sewing shop in Sari.

What the stories of Donya and the other face-savers in this book ultimately highlight is a struggle not just to manage everyday life when faced with conditions of hardship, but to also be a good person and to lead a good life according to a set of socially constructed rules about what is moral and worthwhile "to be and to do."[42] That abiding by the rules can lead, as in Donya's case, to status, prestige, and relative material success does not detract from the fact that by playing the game, by embodying its prescriptive claims day in and day out, one becomes transformed by the game itself. The game serves as a tool that shapes and shifts a person's moral subjectivities through ongoing, repeated practice.[43] That youth like Dara have to sometimes engage in a performance of "goodness" in order to play by the rules simply means that "goodness" is a process of becoming. It is when the external and internal selves align that one has reached the pinnacle of sincerity and that the moral self has been established.[44] The navigation between the performative aspects of one's self and one's inner realities defines one's subjective existence.

As others have found in different contexts, in playing the face game, the young people in this book exercise a form of individuality that is both public and private.[45] These youth are very much dependent on community evaluations of their worthiness in constructing their public selves—as such, their selves are formed through their relations with others; simultaneously, they also have their own private realities, desires, and aspirations.[46] The face game, through its emphasis on the creation of a certain kind of public self, becomes a route to realizing these personal dreams. The caveat, of course, is that if private realities do not align with the virtues of the face system, then they must be hidden in order to achieve this success.[47] Thus, with modifications, face-savers' public lives become the mechanism by which they can bring their private hopes and dreams to fruition.

In following an ethical code that derives from cultural norms and traditions, face-savers are in large part practicing the moral prescriptions propagated by the custodians of the Islamic Republic. Indeed, the virtues promoted by the face system—respectability through self-sufficiency and one's work, moral and sexual cleanliness, and a well-kempt appearance—are all moral directives that are actively encouraged by the state itself, visible in its public debates, billboards, television programs, and official speeches. While demonstrative of the Islamic state's hegemonic influence, the adoption of the face system is nevertheless also indicative of face-savers' own individual agency. By using the face system to pursue their dreams and to attempt to better their lives, face-savers carve a space for themselves within the hegemony of the state, a space where they can garner recognition and esteem, and, in turn, exert some independent influence on the social and economic trajectory of the country. Power is thus not concentrated in the hands of any one actor. It further, as Foucault reminds us, need not be negative, repressive, or exclusive.[48] It can be a force that "produces reality [and] domains of objects and rituals of truth."[49] Power both influences subjects and is, in turn, influenced by subjects themselves:[50] power both constitutes and is constitutive of the self. The very existence of the face game is symptomatic not just of the power of the state, but also of the youth themselves. In the face game, power—whether exercised by the state or the individual—is not an intrinsically oppressive force, but one that can lead to positive change.

* * *

How long it will take to realize this change is uncertain. Face-savers, by virtue of their material poverty, do not have the same extent of social ties, opportunities, and resources that come naturally to their elite counterparts. Face-savers live in a world where shifting welfare policies, lack of jobs, inflation, and the looming threat of even more sanctions serve to jeopardize their livelihoods at any given moment. Anxiety about the future is their constant bedfellow. It is no surprise then that the face game holds the sway that it does among these youth. The game assures its winners freedom from constant adversity. It assures love, friendship, refinement, and money. It assures a life better than one's own.[51]

But this assurance is not a guarantee. Like all games, for every winner, there has to be a loser. What determines the outcome of the game is not always skill, strategy, and manipulation, but also sheer luck. Those who are dealt a better hand—such as those who are born in a "good" family, those who have supportive spouses, and those who have the opportunity to cultivate their street smarts—have a much better shot of playing by the rules and winning the game than those who are not. Many who lose re-enter the game, but depending on the magnitude of their initial loss, they may never be able to recover and end up walking away.

Winning the game also depends on structural forces that are beyond the control of the players themselves. The function of the state in creating stable jobs, in providing economic security to street vendors like Shahpur, and in delivering crucial support for sustainable social goods like higher education and skills-training to low-income communities cannot be underestimated.[52] Thus, while power is everywhere, it is distributed unevenly.[53] Indeed, the state holds a disproportionate concentration of power, and this serves to render it a major determining force in the life outcomes of these youth. As such, the state must be attuned to the everyday concerns of the poor, to the various cultural contingencies that shape their behavior, and to the myriad ways in which they respond to challenges. Recognizing these is the first step in creating policies and sustainable reforms that can ultimately enable poor young men and women to live the sort of "good" life that they envision for themselves. Of course, until this happens, these youth will continue to advance their cause quietly.[54] For some, like the face-savers in this book, this struggle will take the form of simply attempting to play by the rules.

This book began by describing the deceptive nature of appearances. Adversity takes many forms, some less visible than others. In practicing an accentuated form of moral conformism, face-savers attempt to divert attention away from their economic disadvantage to their ambitions for a life better than their own. In placing an external cover on their sufferings, face-savers delude, but this delusion permits them the chance to prevail over the hand they have been dealt. They struggle to fit in in order to stand out and recast themselves as successful citizens.

In the end, in playing the game, face-savers embody a way of being in this world. The game facilitates their claim to respect. It is a force that serves not only to create social order and hierarchization, but also to catalyze these young people's membership in a broader cultural milieu. With all the challenges that face Iran at the present moment, the fact that small, often overlooked everyday practices have the power to imbue some with greater presence and dignity points to the opportunities that lie within the specter of uncertainty.

# ACKNOWLEDGMENTS

This book—in its various forms—has constituted a formative part of my life. The journey leading to its completion has been filled with the most extraordinary people, individuals who have touched my life in ways too innumerable to mention here. The following is my attempt to acknowledge the enormous debt of gratitude that I have for them, although it will always fall short of the generosity and kindness that they have imparted.

I am forever grateful to the communities, families, and individuals who let me into their lives in Iran and taught me what it means to be brave and to have courage in the face of seemingly insurmountable odds. While I cannot name them here, without them, neither this book nor the wonderful trajectories of my own life would have been possible.

I am indebted to the kindness and generosity of my mentor and friend Martín Sánchez-Jankowski. Martín's unwavering support throughout this whole project, his reading and re-reading of multiple drafts, hours of conversations, and infinite kindness helped me navigate the often difficult terrain of fieldwork, analysis, and write-up. His steadfast belief in me and my work from my very first days at Berkeley helped see this project through to its completion, and for that I cannot thank him enough. Mike Hout's endless compassion, guidance, and mentorship have been crucial in the development of this book and my own trajectory as a scholar. His insights and readings helped see me through some of the most difficult moments of the project, enabling me to refine and rework many of my ideas. I am forever grateful. Cihan Tuğal served as an inspiration throughout this whole process, patiently guiding me through the gaps. His own incisive, ethnographic inquiries on the Middle East have inspired my own and have made me a better ethnographer, and I am eternally grateful. At Berkeley, I also benefitted tremendously from the insights of Peter Evans, Ilene Bloemraad, Laura Enriquez, Raka Ray, and Christine Trost, all of whom helped me refine my theories and methods. Members of the Center for Ethnographic Research writing group, Corey Abramson, Phillip Fucella, Silvia Pasquetti, and Katie Marker not only read multiple early drafts of this project and provided feedback that was crucial in shaping it, but their support and friendship were invaluable during my graduate career. Nabilah Siddiquee, Teresa Gonzales, Angela Fillingim, and Maia Sieverding are indomitable spirits whose friendship grounded me. The kindness and friendship of Stacy Du, Alexandre Poirier, Victoria Lee, and Omar Nayeem sustained me throughout my time at Berkeley. Shideh Dashti and Shawhin Roudbari have been with me from the start, always helping me see the bigger picture and critically think through my findings. I am grateful for their more than sixteen years of friendship.

My love for the sociological study of Iran and the Middle East was born at Cornell University at my academic home in the Near Eastern Studies Department. Michelle Campos encouraged my passion for social inquiry by introducing me to the academic nexus between sociology and Iranian studies. Her unwavering support over the years led me to follow in her footsteps and enter the world of academia. Ross Brann nurtured my curiosity for the Middle East, patiently guiding me through my own critical inquiry and serving as an exemplar of the teacher-scholar. Shawkat Toorawa, Munther Younes, and David Owen mentored me throughout, unweary in their infinite support and kindness. My confidantes Fatima Iqbal, Maria Khan, Scilla Michelluci, and Michelle Pavlis were my staunch allies. At Harvard University, Arlene Dallalfar guided me through the process of developing my own sociological imagination, teaching me how to think critically about the juncture of poverty and youth studies. Fereydoun Safizadeh introduced me to youth scenes in Iran and further nurtured my love for ethnographic inquiry. I was incredibly fortunate to learn from Shahla Haeri, who mentored me during my earliest fieldwork phases, teaching me the importance of understanding the lived experiences of marginalized groups, and setting an example for scholarly excellence. Susan Kahn helped steer me through my data and provided invaluable mentorship in navigating academic life—one that I hope to pass down to my own students. At Harvard, I also had the immense privilege to learn from Roy Mottahedeh, Wheeler Thackston, and Sunil Sharma, to all of whom I owe my grounding in the history, culture, and language of Iranian society. Inspiring conversations with friends including Nabilah Siddiquee, Neil Aggarwal, Julia Buchmann, Martin Nguyen, Joseph Shamis, Abigail Krasner Balbale, and Zeba Khan helped me make sense of my fieldwork.

My chance meeting with Negar Razavi in Tehran in the summer of 2006 has led to more than a decade of friendship and rich conversations.

I owe this book to the insights, feedback, and support of countless wonderful scholars, colleagues, and friends. The brilliant Afshin Marashi graciously read through drafts of this manuscript and helped see me through my own roadblocks. My colleagues Noah Theriault, Erika Robb Larkins, Mitchell Smith, Aqil Shah, Bushra Asif, Miriam Gross, Amel Khalfaoui, and Gershon Lewental helped clarify my own thinking during the writing process, and I am so grateful. Alexander Jabbari's incredible support and astute insights, suggestions, and feedback have been instrumental to this book. Shir Alon has generously supported this project with her unwavering kindness. Kaveh Ehsani and Norma Claire Moruzzi commented and provided invaluable feedback on various aspects of this project with their characteristic kindness and modesty. I owe an incredible debt to Asef Bayat, whose work motivated this project all those years ago and who encouraged me from the outset, offering critical insights that were vital in shaping the book. I am eternally thankful to the brilliant David Smilde, whose support and compassionate critiques of earlier drafts of this study shaped it into its present form. In Qatar, Mehran Kamrava welcomed me into the Center for International and Regional Studies at Georgetown University in Qatar and kindly read through drafts of the manuscript, providing invaluable direction. Zahra Babar and Suzi Mirgani encouraged me, providing priceless support for this project. I am indebted to Ross Brann and Michelle Campos, who have critically read various early incarnations of this book, sharpening the final product through their incisive comments. Kathleen Kelly has been truly exceptional, providing endless encouragement and support throughout the whole publication process. Teresa Gonzales has provided more feedback than anyone, her invaluable support making the process of writing less solitary. I am thankful beyond words.

In the greater academic domain, conversations with amazing scholars and friends have greatly influenced me while conducting the research and writing for this project. I thank in particular Minoo Moallem, Mounira Charrad, Houchang Chehabi, Diane Singerman, Ted Swedenburg, Malgorzata Kurjanska, Lior Sternfeld, Nazanin Shahrokni, Shirin Saeidi, Ayça Alemdaroğlu, Florence Muwana, Negar Ghobadi, Rania Sweis, and Nosheen Ali. I owe a debt of appreciation to my students, who motivate me every day with their perceptive insights. I thank Stanford's Abbasi Program in Islamic Studies for inviting me and providing critical feedback on earlier versions of this project.

This book would not have come into existence if it were not for the masterful support of the best editor one could ask for, Ilene Kalish. Ilene has provided unwavering encouragement throughout the whole process, her feedback and insights critical to improving my work. I am thankful to Amy Best, Lorena Garcia, Jessica Taft, and the editorial board at New York University Press for their enthusiastic support for this project from the very beginning. I owe a debt of gratitude to Sonia Tsuruoka, Rosalie Morales Kearns, Alexia Traganas, and the production team, who carefully guided this book to publication. This project has benefitted tremendously from the comments and suggestions of the anonymous reviewers, and I am truly grateful.

Funding for the research and publication of this book was made possible by the the Andrew Mellon Foundation, the Center for Ethnographic Research at UC Berkeley, the Center for Middle Eastern Studies at UC Berkeley, the Center for International and Regional Studies at Georgetown University in Qatar, the Department of International and Area Studies at the University of Oklahoma, the Office of the Vice President for Research, and the Office of the Provost at the University of Oklahoma.

My deepest gratitude goes to my inner circle. Fatima Iqbal, Maria Khan, and Teresa Gonzales have been constantly by my side for almost two decades, nourishing my soul with joy. My incredible brother-in-law, Farzin Mahmoudzadeh, has been my stalwart supporter and source of creative inspiration. My *shir zan* mother-in-law, Shahrzad Moeini, and my brilliant father-in-law, the poet and author extraordinaire Reza Mahmoudzadeh, have been angels on this earth, their love and faith sustaining me through some of my most challenging times. My grandparents, whose memory I sustain in my heart, have been my moral compasses.

I owe everything I am to my parents, who immigrated to this country more than three decades ago and passionately fought to build the good life for their only child; to my father, whose relentless compassion, integrity, and drive have molded me, and to my mother, whose strength, resilience, and love have served as my life's touchstone. And to Farzan, my hero, the love of my life, the fortuitious encounter that has led to all that is magical and good.

# NOTES

## INTRODUCTION

1 This quote is inspired by Saʻdi, who wrote in his magnum opus, *Gulistan*, "The rich man is not a stranger, neither in the mountain nor in the deserts; wherever he goes he pitches his tent and takes up his quarters; whilst he who possesses not the comforts of life, but is destitute of the means of supporting himself, is a stranger, and unknown in his native country" (243).

2 In Shiʻa Islam, Imam refers to a descendant of the Prophet Mohammad and the leader of the Muslim community.

3 Misleading visual symbols of destitution are not unique to Iran. See, for instance, Singerman's (1995) discussion of residential buildings in central Cairo.

4 For some examples of these studies, see Abrahamian (1993); Afary (2009); Kazemi (1980); Keddie (2006); Khosravi (2008, 2017); Kinzer (2008); Mahdavi (2008); Nooshin (2005); and Varzi (2006).

5 Olszewska (2013).

6 See, for instance, Dhillon and Youssef's (2009) as well as Salehi-Isfahani and Dhillon's (2008) studies on waithood in the Middle East.

7 Asef Bayat's (1997) seminal work, *Street Politics*, approaches the question of how Iran's marginalized groups cope with uncertain structural conditions by examining the everyday struggles of ordinary people in pre- and post-revolutionary Iran. Bayat stresses the central role that cultural beliefs about *aberu* (face) and the desire to maintain dignity play in shaping how Iran's lower class goes about obtaining public goods and improving their lot in life. What is not addressed, however, are the specific, everyday cultural practices associated with *aberu* wherein Iran's poor attempt to attain a better life. There have also been a select number of ethnographic studies of Iran that have studied the experiences of ordinary Iranians and move beyond the resistance paradigm. Among these are studies of low-income working women in Tehran (Bahramitash and Olmsted 2014); participants in the metaphysical scene (Doostdar 2018); the Boir Ahmadi tribal group in Lorestan province (Friedl 2014); the religious beliefs among men in an Iranian village (Loeffler 1988); the subjectivities of young Afghan poets in the Pearl of Dari Cultural Institute (Olszewska 2015); urban women in Tehran's civil courts (Osanloo 2006); the spiritual and materialist desires of female Hezbollah activists (Saeidi 2018); and the beliefs and ritual pratices of Basiiji men (Thurfjell 2006). Shahabi's (2006) study of youth culture in Iran takes into account "conformist" and "radical" youth who either conform to or actively

promote the values of the Islamic regime, respectively, while Arghavan (2013) argues that even nonconformist youth are motivated by factors that stem not from political rebellion, but from desires to be fashionable and to enjoy life. Behrouzan's (2016) study of the integration of medical discourse into everyday life in Iran contends that popular psychiatric discourses provide a means for youth to navigate their positions in Iran today. Atwood's (2015) study of contemporary Persian literature, though not an ethnography, is novel in that it provides a textual analysis of the spatial practices of youth, practices that reveal young people's economic and social-sexual concerns, rather than their political resistance. Adelkhah's (2000) notable study of modernity in post-revolutionary Iran challenges the assumed dichotomy between a despotic government and a freedom-loving civil society by showing the deep interlinkages between state and society and how each is shaped and modified in response to the other.

8  I use the terms "low-income," "lower-class," and "poor" interchangeably in this study to capture these youths' relative socioeconomic standing in relation to their middle- and upper-class counterparts. As Iran does not have an official national poverty line, I rely on minimum wage guidelines and perceptions of inequality to assess young people's standing in the socioeconomic hierarchy.

9  Goffman (1967, 5).

10  Adelkhah (2000).

11  Ibid., 70.

12  In Foucault's conceptualization, this is the contradiction inherent in subjectivation. See Foucault (1980; 1982).

13  Mahmood (2005).

14  My conceptualization of agency is largely informed by Mahmood's (2005) analysis of poststructuralist feminist theory and agency, particularly her critique of Butler's (1993) discussion of agency. Both Mahmood (2005) and Butler (1993) examine the role of performativity of social norms in individual subject formation. However, for the latter, agency is located primarily in the subversion or questioning of these social norms, whereas for the former, agency lies not necessarily in resistance to social norms, but in the very embodiment of and compliance to social norms that, in turn, "endow[] the self with certain kinds of capacities that provide the substance from which the world is acted upon" (Mahmood 2005: 27).

15  I use Sherman's (2009) conceptualization of moral capital as one's perceived moral worth.

16  See Scott (1985).

17  For an overview of the sociological and anthropological literature on youth cultures and youth cultural practices, see Bucholtz (2002).

18  For examples of these studies, see Becker (1963); Bourgois (2003); Cohen (1955); Hebdige (1979); MacLeod (2008); Matza and Sykes (1961); Sánchez-Jankowski (1991); Smilde (2007); Whyte (1955); and Willis (1977).

19  Alternatively, drawing from observations and interviews with Black and Latino boys in Oakland, CA, Rios (2011) argues that acts of youth resistance do not

simply stem from a desire to gain respect, but also emerge as a conscious attempt to transform the unjust system of oppression that punishes and stigmatizes them.

20  See, for example, Lamont (2000); Newman (1999); Purser (2009); Sherman (2009); and S. Smith (2007).

21  See Hewitt and Stokes (1975, 2). Hewitt and Stokes argue that when people feel that their desired identities are going to be jeopardized by a behavior, they will use prospective "disclaimers"—e.g., "I know this sounds stupid, but . . ."—to "ward off and defeat in advance doubts and negative typifications" (3). Mills's (1940) conception of "motives" (the answers people provide to unquestioned explanations of social conduct), Scott and Lyman's (1968) model of "accounts" (excuses people provide), and Hall and Hewitt's (1970; 1973) conceptualization of "quasi-theories" (explanations people give for sticky social interactions) provide retrospective definitions of past events. All are similar in that they offer strategies for people to repair their social image. In the few instances when I noticed that it occurred, face-savers largely used "accounts" to justify their deviations from the face rules (see chapter 1 in this book).

22  See Olszewska (2013). Beeman (1986) also notes the importance of status and hierarchy in Iran.

23  Olszewska (2013, 10).

24  Harris (2012).

25  See Bayat (1997; 2013) and Kazemi (1980).

26  Bayat (1997; 2013).

27  Bayat (1997).

28  Since the onset of the Iranian Revolution, all Iranian women have been required to wear either a chador (a long piece of fabric, worn wrapped around the head and upper and lower body, leaving only the face and hands exposed) or a manto and headscarf in public. A manto is an outer garment frequently comprised of either a cotton shirtdress (worn in the warmer months) or a trenchcoat/peacoat (worn in cooler months), both of which must reach to at least mid-thigh, although trends in recent years have favored an open, unbuttoned look. Mantos can be any color of one's choosing, although dark colors are the norm. Frequently worn either tight or open today by more fashion-forward segments of the population, mantos are considered to be one of the most important articles of dress in a woman's wardrobe since they are the most visible item of clothing. Headscarves have similarly followed changing fashion trends over the years, with loosely wrapped headscarves exposing the maximum amount of hair one can get away with becoming the present-day norm among the more trendsetting segments of the population. During Ashura, the tenth day of the month of Muharram (the first month of the Islamic calendar), devout Iranians mourn the death of Imam Hussein, the grandson of the Prophet, who was killed in the Battle of Karbala by the forces of the Umayyad caliph Yazid on October 10, 680. Mourning rituals commerating the martyrdom of Imam Hussein, including processions and passion plays, are common during the month of Muharram. For an overview of Muharram in contemporary Iran, see Shams (2015).

29  Olszewska (2013, 3).

30  Statistical Center of Iran (2016).

31  See also Bayat (2018). Contrary to popular assumptions, as Harris (2017) argues, it was rising expectations as a result of the 1979 Revolution, rather than pronatalist policies, that led to increased marriage rates and birthrates in the immediate aftermath of the revolution. On reasons behind the increase and eventual decline of birthrates in Iran in the 1980s, see Harris (2017).

32  *Financial Tribune* (2017). According to figures released by the Statistical Center of Iran, this number stood at 24.4 percent in the summer of 2016. Statistical Center of Iran (2016).

33  See Bayat (1997) and Vakil (2011).

34  In 2016, under the Iran Nuclear Deal, the United States and European nations lifted sanctions that were imposed on Iran over its nuclear program in return for Iran's agreement to curtail its nuclear activities. However, in May 2018, under the presidency of Donald Trump, the United States withdrew from the nuclear deal, reimposing sanctions on the country and exacerbating Iran's already precarious economy.

35  See Kazemi (1980) and Bayat (1997).

36  For an excellent analysis of the causes and consequences of the Land Reform Program, see Hooglund (1982).

37  Ibid., 48, 50.

38  Kazemi (1980); see also Hooglund (1982).

39  Abrahamian (2008, 142).

40  Ibid. See also Kazemi (1980).

41  Kazemi (1980); Hooglund (1982).

42  Hooglund (1982, 97). For more on the consequences of the land reform law on landholders, sharecroppers, and agricultural laborers, see also Abrahamian (2008).

43  For a discussion of the various push factors for relocation, see Amirahmadi and Kiafar (1987). For a discussion of the pull factors leading to rural-urban migration during this time period, see Bayat (1997). See also Cleveland (1999) for consequences of migration for this new population of urban poor. According to Mottahedeh (1985), many of these new urban poor were young men between the ages of twenty and twenty-four and women between the ages of thirty-four and thirty-nine.

44  Kazemi (1980).

45  Ibid.

46  Madanipour (1998).

47  Bayat (1997) coined the term "quiet encroachment" to refer to the silent ways that the poor advance onto the spaces of the rich and powerful in order to live a life of dignity.

48  Mottahedeh (1985).

49  Ibid. For a comprehensive overview of the early history of radio, see Sreberny-Mohammadi and Mohammadi (1994, 43–58). The Shah exiled Ayatollah Khomeini in 1964 for his opposition to elements of his White Revolution, including his plans to reduce clerics' property rights.

50  Abrahamian (2008).

51  Ibid., 148.

52  Ibid.

53  See, for instance, Mottahedeh (1985).

54  See Bayat (1997).

55  For an overview of the poor's politics during the revolutionary period, see Bayat (1997).

56  Ibid.

57  Ehsani (1994). According to Ehsani (1994), by 1990, the official inflation rate was more than 20 percent.

58  Schirazi (1993).

59  Abrahamian (2008).

60  Ehsani (2006a) and Loeffler (1986). For an overview of the Construction Jihad and mobilization efforts during and after the Iran-Iraq War, see Lob (2017).

61  For a comprehensive overview of the establishment and functioning of the IKRC, see Harris (2017).

62  Ehsani (2006b, 89).

63  For a more detailed discussion of the social changes that occurred in rural areas in Iran as a consequence of the regime's developmentalist inclinations, see Ehsani (2006b)

64  Ehsani (1994).

65  See Ehsani (1994) and Harris (2017).

66  The price of basic goods, however, was kept low. For a comprehensive overview of postwar social protections, including health insurance schemes and price subsidies, see Harris (2017).

67  Ghamari-Tabrizi (2009).

68  Moslem (2002, 144).

69  See also Harris (2017).

70  Ehsani (1994).

71  Ibid.

72  Ibid. See Ehsani (1994) for a detailed overview of the state's economic performance during the second period (beginning in 1991) of the reconstruction era.

73  See also Bahramitash (2003b).

74  Khatami adopted the phrase "dialogue among civilizations" as a counterargument to Samuel Huntington's "clash of civilizations" thesis. Khatami elaborated on his concept at the 2000 United Nations Conference of the Dialogue among Civilizations.

75  See Abrahamian (2008) for a summary of reform-era social changes in Iran.

76 See Harris (2017) for how social justice was seen as the driver for welfare reforms during the Khatami era; using the poverty rate of $5/day, Harris (2017) and Salehi-Isfahani (2016) show a decline in the absolute poverty rate from approximately 30 percent in 1997 to approximately 9 percent in 2005. According to Harris (2017), the decline in the absolute poverty rate continued despite the barrel price of oil hitting a record low of $10 in 1999.

77 Harris (2017).

78 Ibid. See also Salehi-Esfahani (2005).

79 Amuzegar (2005); Maloney (2015).

80 Amuzegar (2005).

81 Ehsani (2006a).

82 See Ehsani (2009) and Maloney (2015).

83 Axworthy (2015).

84 Maloney (2015).

85 See also Harris (2017).

86 Fars News Agency (2012).

87 Ibid.

88 Harris (2017).

89 *Toman* refers to the superunit of currency in Iran. While the rial is the official currency, most Iranians use the term *toman* in their everyday transactions. Therefore, I also use the term *toman* in this book when referring to Iranian currency. 1 *toman* = 10 *rial*s.

90 Salehi-Isfahani and Mostafavi-Dehzooei (2017).

91 The Joint Comprehensive Plan of Action (JCPOA), commonly known as the Iran Nuclear Deal, was a 2015 agreement reached between Iran and the P5+1 (the United States, the United Kingdom, France, China, Russia, and Germany) whereby Iran agreed to curtail its nuclear production activities for a period of ten years in exchange for the lifting of all UN Security Council sanctions as well as nuclear-related multilateral and national sanctions. See U.S. Department of State (2015).

92 See Erdbrink (2018).

93 World Bank (2018).

94 A series of economic protests spread across provincial cities in Iran from December 28, 2017, to January 7, 2018, as a result of a proposed budget bill that aimed to increase the price of oil and food staples.

95 I use Goffman's (1955) definition of facework as the work that actors have to undertake in order to present a certain image of themselves and to protect their face.

96 Wilensky (1966, 110–11).

97 Wilensky (2002, 51).

98 Rather than assert the independence of life's various mobility ladders, Blau and Duncan (1967) and subsequent multivariate work demonstrate how variables such as education, community of origin, race, and marriage interact to influence

economic outcomes. However, these latter studies' emphasis on occupational hierarchies as the basis of social stratification, while crucial, does also limit analysis of other criteria communities use for social differentiation, a shortcoming that Blau and Duncan (1967) themselves highlight. I thank Mike Hout for helping me think through this.

99 See Germani (1966) and Weber ([1922] 1978).

100 Germani (1966, 379).

101 Ibid.

102 For studies in this vein, see, for example, Abu-Lughod (1986); Bayat (1997); Hashemi (2015); Hoodfar (1997); and Singerman (1995).

103 The concept of moral code is similar to Deeb and Harb's (2013) conceptualization of "moral rubric," which they define as a "categorical guide or source of guidance" that is constituted by a set of generally accepted "ideals and values that are revealed as well as produced through discourses and actions." (19).

104 Fischer (1982, 35).

105 Deeb and Harb (2013) similarly note how some youth in south Beirut are obsessed with living the "right way." However, for the youth in their study, the "right way" does not simply constitute adhering to moral rubrics, but negotiating them in their attempts to define themselves.

106 Sayer (2004).

107 Sherman (2009, 66).

108 Lamont (2000, 279, n2). Lamont (2000) similarly found that the social worlds of workers revolve around their moral worldviews.

109 See Bourdieu (1984; 1986) and Sherman (2009, 8).

110 Gries (2004, 26).

111 Harris (2012).

112 Cf. Sánchez-Jankowski (2008).

113 A few young people I knew were thirty years old, and one was thirteen years old. I include some of their narratives in the pages that follow, as they are especially poignant representations of broader patterns in the fieldwork.

114 This reflects the dollar value in April 2019.

115 I define the informal economy as the portion of the market economy that is untaxed, unregulated, and characterized by the small scale of its operations (ten or fewer workers). Furthermore, the informal sector is distinguished from the illicit sector. The informal sector constitutes jobs that are not explicitly criminalized, unlike, for example, prostitution and drug trafficking.

116 Cf. Dohan (2003).

117 Bourdieu (1984); Sánchez-Jankowski (2008).

118 Dohan (2003, 242).

119 Ibid.

120 Cf. Olszewska's (2015) discussion of her unease in taking the headscarf off in front of men as she became more familiar with the norms of modesty dominant in the Afghan households of Iran she observed.

121 Olszewska (2015) similarly found that her reserved attitude fit well with cultural norms that expect women to be *sangin* (solemn, heavy) rather than *sabok* (light, foolish).

122 Cf. Olszewska (2015), who notes how being a researcher from a major Western institution served as a marker of prestige in the community she studied.

123 Sánchez-Jankowski (2002).

124 See, however, Kazembeyki (2003) and Islami (1372/1993). See also Pourshariati (2008) for detailed information on the region of Tabarestan during the time of the Arab conquest of Iran. For an analysis of early, local historiographies of Tabarestan, see Melville (2000). For detailed information on Tehran and its city fabric, see Madanipour (1998).

125 According to the website of the Management and Planning Organization of Mazandaran, in 2017 Sari was home to 504,298 people. See https://mazandaran.mporg.ir.

126 Madelung (1975); see also Pourshariati (2008).

127 Madelung (1975).

128 Madelung (1993).

129 Ibid.

130 Hambly (2008); Perry (1984). See also Amanat (2017) for a comphrehensive overview of Agha Mohammad Khan's reign.

131 Fraser (1826); Kazembeyki (2003).

132 Kazembeyki (2003).

133 Ibid.

134 Ibid.

135 Abrahamian (1982).

136 Ibid.

137 Other *payin-e shahr* neighborhoods that I observed included those located near Sari's city belt and those in the outer perimeters of the city, near Sari International Airport.

138 Kazemi (1980) similarly found that the migrant poor in pre-revolutionary Tehran maintained ties with their villages of origin. Others have also found that rural-urban migrants in other contexts and places, including Mexico (Butterworth 1970), Turkey (Karpat 1976), Lebanon (Deeb and Harb 2013), India (Mishra 2016), Botswana (Lesetedi 2011), and sub-Saharan Africa (Gugler 1996), similarly retain strong relations with relatives in their villages of origin.

139 The term Saravi refers to a resident of Sari. Similarly, Tehrani refers to a resident of Tehran.

140 See Ho (1976, 871).

141 Kheirabadi (1991, 81).

142 See Keivani, Mattingly, and Majedi (2005). In 1982 the Islamic Republic enacted the Urban Land Law, which enabled the newly established Urban Land Organization to possess farms in cities that had housing and land issues as well as to possess land that had previously been developed (Azizi 2002). While the Urban

Land Law facilitated the poor's access to urban land, it also led to rapid urban expansion, leading to the development of shantytowns (Azizi 2002).

143 Borjian (2005).

144 Farzanegan (2014).

145 Ibid.

146 See Keivani, Mattingly, and Majedi (2005).

147 See also Olszewska (2013).

148 See Bourdieu (1977); Sherman (2009); and Veblen ([1899] 1953). Sherman's (2009) study of moral capital in a low-income rural community in the United States similarly found that outward displays of "goodness" or moral worth— particularly those that were manifestations of one's independence, self-sufficiency, hard work, and family values—conferred socioeconomic opportunities, thereby becoming a form of "tradeable symbolic capital" (185). In her study of low-income, young Black men and women from Michigan, S. Smith (2007) too found that a strong work history and work ethic are decisive factors in determining whether or not community members provide job placement assistance to young people.

## CHAPTER 1. SAVING FACE

1 For more on the gendered dynamics of veiling in Iran, see Khosravi (2008).

2 Ibid.

3 Ibid.

4 For more on the contrast between the *zaher* and the *baten*, see Beeman's (1986) seminal study on power relations and cultural norms in Iran; the Sasanian Empire later exiled the founder of the religion, Mani, as the new religion was considered to threaten Zoroastrianism's hold as Iran's dominant religion.

5 Khatami (1393/2014).

6 Ibid.

7 Ibid.

8 Ibid.

9 Beeman (1986, 69–70).

10 Ibid., 72.

11 Ibid., 11.

12 Throughout the rest of the book, per Haim's (2002) definition, I will use the term *aberu* as "face" to refer to a person's reputation even though its literal definition is "water of the face"; in a 2005 survey of the political culture of 4,879 individuals led by Mohammad Fazeli in Iran, 75 percent of respondents said they disagreed with the statement "The *zaher* and *baten* of the majority of people are one," indicating that respondents believed that people put on a public appearance that is not a reflection of their inner selves. See Hajiani (1393/2014).

13 Lange (2007, 435).

14 Zaborowska (2014).

15 Ibid., 120.

16  Ossowska (1980, 53).

17  Ibid., 54. These values differ by culture and context; in the context of the Iranian youth I knew, these values revolved around hard work and self-sufficiency, purity, and taking care of physical appearance. See chapters 2–4 in this book.

18  In this particular instance, the young woman regained the *aberu* she had lost by ultimately repaying the loan and gaining the community's trust through her actions and demeanor. As I will demonstrate in later chapters, there are various degrees of *aberurizi*, and a partial removal of *aberu* does not lead to the complete loss of one's face.

19  Zaborowska (2014, 123).

20  Ibid.

21  Ibid.

22  Ossowska (1980, 53).

23  Goffman (1972).

24  Ibid., 13.

25  Goffman (1956, 69).

26  Pitt-Rivers (1965).

27  Wikan (1984) has also shown that shaming precludes public denunciations in Iran and Oman.

28  For more on how ordinary practices can become imbued with power, see Abramson and Modzewelski's (2011) study on how participation in cage fighting serves to organize participants' lives and the ways they approach their everyday activities.

29  The term *taqiyyeh* comes from the Arabic root w-q-y, which connotes protecting, guarding, or preserving.

30  Momen (1985).

31  For more on alternative views of success revolving around morality rather than economic standing, see Lamont (2000).

32  Lamont and Molnár (2002, 168).

33  Bayat (1997, 13).

34  See also Lamont and Molnár (2002, 168).

35  Following Bourdieu (1986), I refer to social capital as the combination of actual or virtual resources linked to a person's network of connections. I refer to economic capital as money or resources that can be immediately converted into money (Bourdieu 1984).

36  Goffman (1967, 5).

37  Salehi-Isfahani and Egel (2007).

38  See Ray's (2003) discussion on the aspirations gap as well as Hashemi (2017).

39  See Hashemi (2017).

40  Sánchez-Jankowski (1999).

41  Ray (2003).

42  Abrahamian (1993, 32).

43  Ibid., 133. In their seminal study on "class reshuffling" after the 1979 Revolution, Behdad and Nomani (2009) argue that the growing middle class in Iran has en-

joyed increasing job opportunities, the majority of which are concentrated in state employment.

44  Abrahamian (1993).

45  Ibid., 140.

46  Statement made by Khameini in his 1997 Iranian New Year's speech. *Keyhan*, 16.1.1376 (1997) as cited by Adelkhah (2000, 173).

47  The regime is also aware that the future well-being of the Islamic Republic is directly contingent on the support of the youth population, particularly youth in the lower and lower-middle classes, who comprise the majority of youth in Iran and who will ultimately comprise the future torchbearers of the Republic. To this end, moderate-minded policies, relaxation in social norms, and tacit support for aspirations to middle-class lifestyles have also been ways for the regime to preempt losing popular youth support. See also Chehabi (2006).

48  See Abrahamian (1993) for a detailed account of the regime's "ideological adaptability" and "intellectual flexibility" in its efforts to adapt to the modern era (2).

49  Ehsani (2009).

50  Ibid. According to Ehsani (2009), in the aftermath of the Iran-Iraq War, this alliance took place in the privatization of urban land, with the state imposing taxes and fees on urban developers in return for providing them with protection from political pressures and zoning laws. Later on, privatization centered on industrial and financial institutions.

51  Kian-Thiébaut (1999).

52  Ibid.

53  Ibid. See also Olszewska (2013).

54  Adelkhah (2000).

55  Website of the Imam Khomeini Relief Committee: https://portal.emdad.ir.

56  Adelkhah (2000, 6, 5). See also my discussion in the introduction.

57  Abrahamian (2009). The IKRC, for example, also provides welfare support to the poor residing in other countries, including Palestine, Afghanistan, Iraq, Syria, and Lebanon.

58  See Ehsani (1999).

59  Website of the Bahman Farhangsara: https://bahman.farhangsara.ir.

60  Amir Ebrahimi (1995).

61  Ehsani (1999).

62  Amir Ebrahimi (2001).

63  Ibid.

64  Ehsani (1999, 25–26).

65  By positing these youth as "backward" because of their seeming initial lack of aspirations (or their lack of the "right"—i.e., middle-class—aspirations), some NGO workers like the one quoted here justify the NGO's raison d'être.

66  Compare to Germani's (1966) discussion of how new modes of consumption have led to the embourgeoisement of the working class in industrial societies.

67  *Ta'arof* can be loosely defined as extremely polite language and compliments that infiltrate everyday life in Iran (see also Beeman 1986). While *ta'arof* can

sometimes be insincere, it can also be an expression of fondness (Beeman 1986). A number of studies have analyzed *ta'arof* in Iran. In addition to Beeman (1986; 1976), see, for instance, Assadi (1980); Behnam and Amizadeh (2011); Hillman (1981); Loeb (1978); and Majd (2008). For an excellent analysis of how the performance of the rituals of *ta'arof* are used to affirm ethno-national identity and belonging among second-generation Iranian youth in the diaspora, see Maghbouleh (2013).

68  Hewitt and Stokes (1975, 10).

69  Yas stated this when members of her paternal family expressed shock at seeing her in a local park with a friend (myself). See chapter 3.

70  Barkow (1975).

71  Ibid., 558.

72  Comment made by a sixteen-year-old in Sari to justify his low grades in school.

73  Stated by a young female salon apprentice in Sari.

74  Comment made by a seventeen-year-old informal laborer in Sari.

75  Bloch (1989); Khosravi (2008).

76  Mahmood (2005, 149).

77  Ibid., 139. As Mahmood (2005) argues, this definition of habitus differs from Bourdieu's conceptualization of the term: for the latter, habitus is the product of the "unconscious imbibing" (139) of structured dispositions that comes from an individual's class background without regard to the "pedagogical process by which a habitus is learned" (139).

78  "Mechanisms" refer to the pathways that connect a cause to an effect (Hedström and Swedborg 1998). In this sense, mechanisms can be seen as the "cogs and wheels" that link two events (Elster 1989). For more on the mechanism-based approach to social theory, see Hedström and Swedberg (1998).

79  Sánchez-Jankowski (2008, 345–46).

80  Ibid.

81  See also Sánchez-Jankowski (2008); Sherman (2009); and Vaisey (2009).

82  Sherman (2009).

83  The term "cultural toolkit" was first developed by Swidler (1986); Sherman (2009) similarly notes how her informants drew from various moral understandings that comprised their cultural toolkit to make their lives meaningful.

84  Ismail (2006, 77).

85  See also Sherman (2009), who found that her informants drew moral distinctions between "deserving" and "undeserving" poor.

86  Ibid., 98.

87  O. Lewis (1959).

88  I define "poverty trap" as the "mechanisms that could cause poverty to persist" (Bowles, Durlauff, and Hoff 2006:2).

CHAPTER 2. ALL IN A DAY'S WORK

1  *Financial Tribune* (2017b).

2  Salehi-Isfahani (2010b, 5).

3 The popular phrase *kar jowhar-e mard ast* (working is a man's essence) attests to the societal importance attached to labor as the embodiment of manhood.

4 Kia (2015, 146).

5 Ibid., 151. See also Schayegh (2009) for an analysis of how science became used as a means by which Iranian modernists attempted to institute reforms in Iran.

6 Khamenei (2018).

7 Kia (2015, 160).

8 Bayat (1997); Kazemi (1980).

9 World Bank (2017).

10 This number is according to Iran's Ministry of Economic Affairs and Finance. See *Financial Tribune* (2017).

11 See also International Labor Office (1972). "Employment, Incomes and Equity: A Strategy for Increasing Productive Employment in Kenya" (International Labor Office 1972) was significant, as it demonstrated that unlike popular pre-conceptions of the time, the informal sector was far from being marginal and economically inefficient. According to the report, rather than constituting jobs located on the periphery of towns or the economic realm, the informal sector is intimately tied to the formal economy in many ways. It is simply characterized by its informal method of doing things and by its "(a) ease of entry; (b) reliance on indigenous resources; (c) family ownership of enterprises; (d) small scale of operation; (e) labour-intensive and adapted technology; (f) skills acquired outside the formal school system; and (g) unregulated and competitive markets" (ILO 1972: 6).

12 Ibid.

13 Rather than pay a monthly rent, Amir Hossein used the *rahn* system. In this system, "the tenant pays the landlord a lump sum of money, roughly one-fifth of the total value of the property, and moves in. At the end of the rental term, the landlord returns the same amount to the tenant, who only moves out upon receipt of the money" (Koutlaki 2010: 18). The *rahn* system is often profitable for land-lords, as they can acquire a large profit on the lump sum due to the substantial bank interest that can accrue on the sum (Koutlaki 2010). During the time of my fieldwork in south Tehran, this interest rate was as high as 28 percent. If the *rahn* is high enough, then there is no need for the tenant to pay a monthly rent. It was not clear whether Amir Hossein paid a monthly rent on top of the 150,000-toman *rahn* he gave to the landlord.

14 See also Hoodfar (1997).

15 Cf. Dohan (2003).

16 Ibid.

17 That face-savers do not suffer from starvation does not mean that nutrition is not a problem. The shortage of micronutrients that comes from not being able to af-ford certain healthful food items is an issue among some of the families I knew.

18 For more on the functioning of reciprocity networks, see Bienen (1984); Denouex (1993); Lomnitz (1977); Nelson (1979); Norton (2001); and Waterbury (1970).

19 See Singerman (1995, 69).

20 Mauss ([1925] 1990); Sahlins (1972).

21 Cf. Hoodfar (1997).

22 Sahlins (1972).

23 Dohan (2003).

24 See Gregg (2005, 30–33) for an overview of (mis)perceptions of fatalism in Middle Eastern societies. Scholars who have subscribed to this view of Islamic fatalism include Ayrout (1963); Fukuyama (1992); Huntington (1993; 1996); B. Lewis (1990); and Patai (1973). For a comprehensive critical analysis of perceptions of Islamic fatalism, see Acevedo (2008).

25 Gregg (2005, 30).

26 These views find resonance in Weber's various theses on Islam, which assert that certain Islamic values (e.g., irrational fatalism) that arose as a result of patrimonial socioeconomic structures hampered development and modern capitalism in the Middle East (Turner 1974; Acevedo 2008). For an excellent overview of Weber's theses on Islam, see Turner (1974).

27 See Gregg (2005) and Patai (1973).

28 Gregg (2005, 33). Gregg's finding is based on his observations of the Imeghrane of Morocco's High Atlas.

29 Regarding this, Gregg (2005) argues that the "opening of opportunity breeds a kind of achievement-oriented, 'Muslim-ethicist' religiosity; the closing of opportunity breeds resignation in the solace of religious fatalism" (33). To this end, he argues "'fatalism' plays no larger role in Islam than it does in Hinduism, Buddhism, Confucianism, or Christianity" (33).

30 See also Elder (1966, 229).

31 Ibid. Using the 2002 Gallup Poll of the Islamic World, Acevedo (2008) empirically tested Elder's two-dimensional view of fatalism in Turkey, Lebanon, Iran, Indonesia, and Saudi Arabia and found that Iranians tend to be more theologically than empirically fatalistic.

32 Acevedo (2008).

33 Friedl (2014).

34 Cf. Hoodfar (1997).

35 Bahramitash and Salehi-Esfahani (2009); Karimi (2011). Some scholars attribute the decline in female employment during this time to the job dismissal of many women who did not wear the mandatory head covering (see Nomani and Behdad 2006). Nevertheless, it is unclear how much this would have actually impacted total female unemployment rates, as this process simply made room for women who were loyal to the Islamic establishment to replace them (see Bahramitash and Salehi-Esfahani 2009).

36 Bahramitash (2004; 2007); Bahramitash and Salehi-Esfahani (2009).

37 See Bahramitash and Salehi-Esfahani (2009).

38 See Bahramitash (2003a).

39 Bahramitash and Olmstead (2014).

40 Harris (2012).

41 For a comprehensive ethnographic study of some of the employment experiences of lower-income women, see also Bahramitash and Olmsted (2014).

42 Salehi-Isfahani (2010a). This process renders the jobs of older workers more or less permanent, thereby placing younger workers—especially young female workers—at an employment disadvantage; for instance, the unemployment rate of urban young women between the ages of twenty and twenty-nine was 54.7 percent in 2008, as compared to 26.1 percent for urban young men between the ages of twenty and twenty-nine (Salehi-Isfahani 2010a). Further complicating matters according to Salehi-Isfahani (2010a) is that current labor laws allow employers to offer short-term contracts (less than one year) to younger workers, thereby raising turnover rates among youth and further reinforcing the position of older workers.

43 Bahramitash (2013) similarly found that among low-income working women in Tehran, their husbands' income volatility was often a main reason why women took up work in the first place.

44 See also Lamont (2000). For an analysis of how the working poor in Iran draw on the virtues of hard work to differentiate themselves from the non-working poor and claim dignity, see Hashemi (2018).

45 See also Bayat (1997).

46 Dohan (2003).

47 Ibid., 65.

48 See also Bahramitash (2013).

49 See also Molyneux (2002, 186). As I will later argue, this process of conferring social capital on some but not others can also work to reproduce inequalities within communities. In this vein, see also Bourdieu (1977) and Portes and Sensenbrenner (1993).

50 Sánchez-Jankowski (1991) similarly found that low-income individuals in the United States believe that it is who a person knows, rather than what they know, that will help him get ahead in life. Lending further support to this notion, in a 2003 survey conducted among college-educated people in Iran, it was found that 81 percent of the informants believed that not having money or connections would lead to the loss of one's individual rights (Daftar-e Tarh-ha-ye Melli 1382/2003).

51 In Iran, as in other countries in the Middle East, consanguineous marriages are both lawful and common, especially marriage to a patrilineal cousin. The saying *dokhtar 'ammu, pesar 'ammu, 'aqd-eshan tu aseman-ha basteh shodeh* (the marriage of patrilineal cousins is recorded in heaven) is illustrative of how some families even view this type of marriage as ideal. These marriages are seen to strengthen the solidarity of the larger family unit, particularly solidarity with the paternal lineage. Kin marriages in the Middle East have been widely documented (see, for instance, Abbasi-Shavazi, McDonald, and Hosseini-Chavoshi 2008; Harkness and Khaled 2014; Holy 1989; Hoodfar 1997; Khuri 1970; Shah 2004; Singerman 1995; and Rugh 1984). Thank you to Alexander Jabbari for helping with the translation of the saying.

52 In his study of the Mexican American barrio, Dohan (2003) similarly found that a set of cultural norms and rules existed in the community that when integrated into people's "everyday public persona[s] meant an easier time during daily rounds and a greater sense of physical and emotional security" (264, n12).

53 There were a few instances when young women in their late twenties recalled their fathers' disapproval of their education. The young womens' fathers believed there was no reason for their daughters to go to school, since their primary responsibility was to take care of their current and future households. Many of these young women, however, were able to receive their high school diplomas before they settled down as wives and mothers.

54 Sherman (2009).

55 See Dohan (2003, 142–47) on street smarts.

56 Friedl (2014, 204).

57 Ibid.

58 Ibid., 197.

59 See also Dohan (2003).

60 Ibid., 147.

61 Zohreh knew Omid since he was a young boy and recounted the details of his story to me.

62 The ability to undertake moderate risks—as opposed to low or high risks—was also a key factor determining the socioeconomic success of gang members in the United States (see Sánchez-Jankowski 1991).

63 Sherman (2009, 6).

64 Friedl (2014).

65 See also discussion in Friedl (2014, 120).

66 Ibid. Views of hard work as a prerequisite to divine favor can further be found in Islamic scriptures. According to Ali and Al-Owaihan (2008), the "Quran instructs Muslims to persistently work whenever and wherever it is available" (7), as evidence by the following Qur'anic verse: "Disperse through the land and seek the bounty of God" (Qur'an 62:10). Similarly, the Prophet Mohammad preached hard work and the importance of divine reward: "No one eats better food than that which he eats out of his work" and "God bless the worker who learns and perfects his profession" (Ikhwan-us-Safa 1999: 290 as cited by Ali and Al-Owaihan 2008:10).

## CHAPTER 3. DRESS FOR SUCCESS

1 Bourdieu (1984).

2 See also Adelkhah (2000).

3 Beeman (1986).

4 Finkelstein (1991).

5 Ibid.

6 Goffman (1963).

7 Mazandarani is a regional language belonging to the Iranian language family (related to, though distinct from, Persian). The common language among face-savers

in Mazandaran province, Mazandarani is often popularly connoted with being *dehati* and low-status, whereas the form of Persian spoken in the capital, Tehran, is connoted with high status and class.

8  See, for example, Hoodfar (1997); Ismail (2006); and Singerman (1995).

9  Hoodfar (1997) has likewise indicated the importance of these types of networks in Egypt for facilitating social and economic life among the poor.

10  In this particular seaside resort, one had to pay fees (approximately 7 USD at the time) in order to go to the beach or to rent out bikes.

11  See Featherstone (1991). As Featherstone (1991) argues, "knowledge of new goods, their social and cultural value, and how to use them appropriately" is particularly relevant for "aspiring groups" like face-savers who "adopt a learning mode towards consumption and the cultivation of a lifestyle" (19).

12  Sherman (2009).

13  Khosravi (2008) similarly found that youth in Tehran's upper-class neighborhood of Shahrak-e Gharb regularly differentiated between themselves and the *javad*s or "'traditional, backward, poor, village-minded, southern Tehranis'" who lived in the southern parts of the city (70).

14  Bauer (1985) found a similar pattern in her study of migrant women in south Tehran.

15  Ibid.

16  Finkelstein (1991).

17  Goffman (1956).

18  Hammermesh and Biddle (1994); Hammermesh (2011).

19  Hammermesh (2011).

20  See Hashemi (2019) for an analysis of how the poor's attempts to fit in lead to elite backlash in Iran.

21  Olszewska (2015, 19).

22  See also Klaufus (2012, 700), who found that some members of the urban elite in Ecuador perpetuated the urban myth that their low-income counterparts had "bigger and nicer homes" than they did; as Klaufus notes, this can also be read as indicative of the upward mobility of some members of the lower classes.

23  See, for instance, Hammermesh and Biddle (1994); Hammermesh (2011); and Mears (2011).

24  Likewise, Sherman (2009) found that in the rural United States, communities place strong pressure on men to work and become the breadwinners of the family.

25  Marashi (2008, 6); Hedayat (2017). See also discussion in Hashemi (2018).

26  Amin (2004).

27  We can see this equation of American fashions with "class" in other contexts as well. For instance, Deeb and Harb (2013) have shown that in Beirut, the United States has become the cultural benchmark for elites and upwardly mobile aspirants who desire to communicate their transnational connectedness.

28  Amin (2004). Unveiling did not occur overnight, but was implemented gradually over the course of Reza Shah's reign (Sedghi 2007). It became official policy in

1936, following Reza Shah's address at Tehran Teachers College on January 7, subsequently referred to as Women's Emancipation Day. Unveiling served to transfer "some patriarchal power from the clergy to the state" (Sedghi 2007: 89), which ultimately angered the former; following the abdication of Reza Shah Pahlavi in 1941, his son, Mohammad Reza Shah, lifted the ban on the veil.

29  Amin (2004).

30  Ibid.

31  Ibid.

32  As told to *Chelcheragh*, a youth magazine in Iran. Dehghan (2013).

33  Deeb (2006).

34  Ibid.

35  *Khareji* brands are also coveted because, as Khosravi (2008) notes, they are connotative of high quality and standards in Iran. Among the upper-class young men and women he interviewed, it was important to have the original brands rather than the knockoffs that were popular among my face-savers. For more on the perceived superiority of *khareji* versus domestic goods, see Khosravi (2008, 102–10).

36  As Mears (2011) notes, aesthetic labor refers to the style labor that employees of the service sector undertake in order to embody the "right" look—that is, the one that can bring the most profit. For more on the early concept of aesthetic labor, see Nickson et al. (2001); Warhurst et al. (2000); and Witz, Warhurst, and Nickson (2003).

37  See also Alikhah (2015).

38  Ibid.

39  See Mofrad (2014).

40  Zeydabadi-Nejad (2010); see also Mofrad (2014).

41  Mofrad (2014).

42  Ibid.

43  For examples of a few such social media accounts on Instagram, currently the most popular platform for fashion influencers, see Bahar (@fashionsandwichbybahar), Niloofar Alipoor (@nilooxstylebook), and Anita Moshkelgosha (@anitamoshkelgosha).

44  For reference, see www.thesartorialist.com.

45  For reference, see therichkidsoftehran (@therichkidsoftehran) as well as their website, www.theRKOT.com. There is debate as to whether many of these pictures are actually taken in Iran and whether the young men and women portrayed are in point of fact wealthy or upwardly mobile aspirants (see Shahrabi 2014).

46  Olszewska (2013).

47  Khosravi (2008, 120).

48  While youth did not use the terms *farangi(-ma'ab)*—"Western wannabes" (Elling and Rezakhani 2015)—or *fokoli* (an Iranian dandy who embraces Western styles and forms of dress), this equation of trendy men's fashion with femininity is similar to the criticism Khosravi (2008) details that was leveled by intellectuals in Iran in the 1960s and 1970s against *fokolis* or *farangi (-ma'ab*s) for being

Westernized, alienated from their own culture, and having a low degree of manliness as opposed to the manly, honorable *jahel* (ignorant person) who could often be found in the downtown areas of the city.

49 Sánchez-Jankowski (2008), in his seminal study of the poor in the United States, similarly found that the poor presented different aspects of their selves among members of their primary public and among those in the secondary public.

50 Khosravi (2008, 120).

51 Mears (2011, 119).

52 Simmel (1957); see also Mears (2011).

53 Mears (2011) likewise shows how supermodels in the United States increase their chances of success by actively molding their bodies and personalities in order to acquire the winning look (88).

54 Wacquant (1995, 66). Wacquant argues that pugilists service, mold, and purposely manipulate their bodies to convert them into "recognition, titles and income streams" (Wacquant 1995: 67). The body thus becomes an asset, a form of bodily capital that, if molded correctly, becomes a source of socioeconomic mobility. See also Wacquant (2004) and Mears (2011).

55 See Mears (2011, 98–103).

56 Ibid.

57 Ibid.

58 Foucault ([1978] 1995, 184).

59 Olszewska (2015, 209).

60 Finkelstein (1991); Morgenthau and Person (1978).

61 Singerman (1995, 7).

62 In this way, I move beyond traditional understandings of politics that focus, among other acts, on "participating in the electoral process [or] making claims on the state" (Mahmood 2005: 35). Rather, as Mahmood highlights, the political is also inscribed onto everyday, transformative practices that can unintentionally challenge the normative order of things.

63 Singerman (1995, 7).

64 Likewise, Mears (2011) argues that it is the possibility—rather than the probability—of "achieving greatness" that spurs fashion models in the United States to "continue working against vague and punishing aesthetic ideals" (119).

## CHAPTER 4. BE GOOD, DO GOOD

1 Simmel (1906, 463).

2 Ibid.

3 Beidelman (1993). Significantly, the original Latin definition of the word "person" was "mask" (Mauss 1979).

4 Beidelman (1993).

5 Beeman (1986, 69).

6  Small (2017, 159).

7  Ibid., 163.

8  Olszewska (2015) found a similar pattern among the Afghan community she observed in Mashhad, Iran, where close friends practiced greater intimacy among themselves than they did when they were with people whom they did not know well.

9  Olszewska (2015, 193).

10  A *mahram* would include one's parents, grandparents, siblings, children, aunts, and uncles.

11  Small (2017).

12  See Simmel (1950) and Small (2017).

13  Amanat (2012).

14  Farahani (2010).

15  Ferdowsi (1988, 111).

16  Ibid., 114.

17  Shahbazi (2004).

18  Ibid. Siavash is another mythical hero in the *Shahnameh* who is remembered for his purity and goodness of heart. His stepmother, Sudabeh, falls in love with him, and when Siavash refuses her advances, she accuses him of raping her. To prove his innocence, the king, Kay Kavus, Siavash's father, forces Siavash to ride through a large, blazing fire; if Siavash can come out unscathed, he will be proven innocent of the crime. Siavash rides through the fire on his horse unharmed, thereby proving his virtue. Siavash is ultimately killed at the hands of Afrasiab, the emperor of the region of Turan in Central Asia. According to legend, with every drop of blood that dripped from Siavash, a plant grew in the same spot. Iranians today use the plant, later named siyavashan, as a cure-all for a variety of illnesses, thus indicative of its perceived virtuous properties.

19  Amanat (2012, 11).

20  Ibid.

21  Ibid. See Amanat (2012) for a comprehensive analysis of the political implications of the differentiation between ritual purity and pollution.

22  Thurfjell (2006); Schimmel (1975).

23  Thurfjell (2006).

24  Khosravi (2008, 46).

25  Hagiographies of pious men admired for their self-discipline—men known as "friends of God"—have become increasingly popular in Iran over the past two decades and represent another means by which the state has attempted to cultivate moral virtue and spiritual development among youth. For a comprehensive analysis, see Doostdar (2018, 175–230).

26  *Hezbollahi* refers to someone who is "of God's Party" and indicative of those who are ideological followers of the Islamic regime (Elling and Rezakhani 2015: 9). The *hezbollahi* look, in turn, emphasizes "a simple appearance, and unpretentiousness," and is "an aestheticization of poverty" (Khosravi 2008: 37).

27 Douglas [1966] 2002, 2.

28 Ibid., 45.

29 See also Olszewska (2015).

30 Ibid., 189.

31 Varzi (2006, 12).

32 Ibid., 157.

33 See also Manoukian (2012).

34 Mahmood (2005, 149).

35 Ibid.

36 In a similar vein, Deeb's (2006) ethnography of a southern suburb of Beirut discusses how certain women in the community believe that a gap between one's personal beliefs and public ideals of piety is, in fact, good. The gap implies a process of "becoming." That is, the more one practices approved social norms of public piety, the "better" one gets at cultivating her faith and the more one's *baten* and *zaher* will align.

37 Varzi (2006, 138).

38 Gregg (2005, 112).

39 Ibid.

40 Thurfjell (2006, 86–87).

41 Shi'a contexts in the Middle East, such as the southern suburbs of Beirut, Lebanon, where the 1979 Revolution in Iran is regarded as a source of inspiration for "battles against oppression and injustice" (Deeb 2006: 201) among the marginalized Shi'a community, are other areas where similar public symbols of Shi'ism are present.

42 Thurfjell (2006, 87).

43 See Gregg (2005).

44 Mohammad handed this to me when I asked him to write down what advice he would give to youth his age.

45 These practices today are not as widespread as they were in the past, largely due to fewer crackdowns by the authorities.

46 See also Gregg (2005).

47 Deeb (2006) also describes how certain Lebanese Shi'a women use both embodied and discursive practices of piety as visible markers of their morality.

48 Thurfjell (2006, 72).

49 Thurfjell (2006), too, found that among low-income communities in the city of Isfahan, Iranian women (and, to a lesser extent, men) were judged by their appearance.

50 Deeb and Harb (2013, 209).

51 This was a popular phrase among the communities I studied.

52 To force a reluctant husband to come to the bargaining table, women looking for a divorce often give up their dowry in exchange for the right to divorce (see Osanloo 2006).

53 Sherman (2009).

54 Ibid., 66.

55 The institution of temporary marriage, or *sigheh*, in Iran, which is viewed in a negative light by many Iranians, enables those women who desire it to enter into a marriage for a specified period of time (which can be as short as one hour). Since Ava was already married, she could not be part of a temporary marriage with another man. For an excellent, detailed examination of the perception and practice of the institution of temporary marriage in Iran, see Haeri (1989).

56 Tasnim News Agency (2019).

57 Ibid.

58 See Ghiabi (2018a). For a detailed ethnographic analysis of the everyday lives of drug users in Tehran, see Ghiabi (2018b).

59 See Nikpour (2018).

60 Afkhami (2009, 208).

61 While drug use certainly exists among women in Iran, I did not encounter instances where face-savers acknowledged female relatives as users. This may be reflective of the relatively lower rate of female drug use as compared to male drug use in Iran. See Ghaderi et al. (2017).

62 Doostdar (2018) similarly found that his interlocutors in Iran complained of the difficulty of distinguishing morally good people from bad ones in present-day Iran.

63 While having boyfriends was a route to losing face in the community, many female face-savers did have such relations. However, they took pains to hide these relationships from others, employing tactics including using pseudonyms for these friends in their cell phones or arranging to meet them in places where no one they knew could see them.

64 A *turbah* is a small clay tablet that the Shi'a place their foreheads on during prostration in prayer.

65 Goffman (1972, 39).

66 Trouille (2013, 14).

67 Abu-Lughod (1986) similarly found that the Awlad 'Ali Bedouins of the Western Desert of Egypt draw their honor from their *asl* (orgin/ancestry/nobility). Among the Awlad 'Ali, their bloodline becomes the basis of moral differentiation between themselves and other tribes. In this view, those who cannot trace their genealogical connection to the "pure Arab tribes who were the first followers of the Prophet Muhammad" are of lesser moral worth (44).

68 See also Sherman (2009).

69 Unlike Dara, who told me how he would swindle customers, Aria never revealed to me what "wrong" things he felt forced to do. As I spoke with him in his place of work, it was most likely that Aria did not want colleagues overhearing and finding out about his transgressions.

70 See also Pamuk (2015). According to Koutlaki (2010) when one's *zaher* and *baten* correspond the "believer reaches the point of utmost sincerity or unity of thought and action that ultimately leads to a union with God" (193).

71 Cf. Mears's (2011) discussion of how the "magic" produced by the editorial game is an illusion upheld by producers "committed to the production of the 'edgy' look" (69).

72 Ibid.

73 Sherman (2009).

## CHAPTER 5. MORAL CONFORMISM AND ITS CONTENTS

1 Contrast this to Peristiany's (1965) claim that honor "divides social beings into two fundamental categories, those endowed with honour and those deprived of it" (10).

2 Bayat (1997, 157).

3 Ho (1976, 874).

4 Salehi-Isfahani (2010, 7).

5 Mulderig (2011, 1).

6 Bourdieu (1984); Swidler (2000).

7 MacLeod (2008, 152).

8 Atwood (2015).

9 Olszewska (2015, 210).

10 Gries (2004, 24).

11 Cf. Mears (2011).

12 Gries (2004, 22).

13 See Adelkhah (2000); Manoukian (2012); and Olzewska (2015).

14 Adelkhah (2000).

15 Olszewska (2015, 189).

16 See Atwood (2015); Olszewska (2015); and Razavi (2014).

17 Adelkhah (2000); Olszewska (2013; 2015).

18 Olszewska (2015).

19 Harris (2017).

20 See Wilensky (1966).

21 For classic examples of studies in this vein, see Blau and Duncan (1967); Featherman and Hauser (1976); Goldthorpe and Hope (1972); and Goldthorpe and Marshall (1992).

22 According to Salehi-Isfahani (2010a), formal labor market rigidity in Iran gives preference to older, already employed workers, in effect forcing youth to "wait their turn." For those without means, these periods of waiting, in turn, lead young people to "leave school earlier to take up temporary jobs that neither provide stepping stones to future careers nor improve their chances of marriage and family formation" (7).

23 See, for example, Aminzade and Hodson (1982) and K. Smith (2007).

24 K. Smith (2007).

25 Aminzade and Hodson (1982). Aminzade and Hodson (1982) draw on marriage records from 1830 to 1872 in the city of Toulouse to argue that the "proletarianization of certain trades resulting from the development of industrial capital-

ism" led to mobility "across the skilled/unskilled line" (453). They argue that to determine whether upward mobility has occurred within a class, researchers must "analyze the changing historical content of occupational titles" (453). Occupational movement is thus still privileged over other measures of upward mobility.

26  K. Smith (2007, 100–101).

27  Klaufus (2012, 693).

28  Ibid.

29  Wilensky (1966, 131).

30  See also Germani (1966).

31  See also Venkatesh (1994).

32  Aminzade and Hodson (1982, 455).

33  Bourdieu (1977, 232).

34  See also Bayat (1997; 2013).

35  Purser (2009).

36  Bourdieu (1977; 1990).

37  Bourdieu (1977; 1990). See also Calhoun (1993); Lamont (1992); and Winchester (2008).

38  Winchester (2008, 1759).

39  Asad (1993); Mahmood (2005). Compare this to Deeb's (2006) and Deeb and Harb's (2013) finding among some members of Lebanon's Shi'a community who asserted that one should first learn about the reasoning behind a particular belief or practice before one commits to it.

40  See Winchester (2008).

41  Levin (1985, 215).

42  Winchester (2008, 1754). Compare to Deeb and Harb (2013), who find that in Lebanon, Shi'a youth view fulfilling social obligations as vital to being "good" people.

43  Winchester (2008).

44  See Koutlaki (2010).

45  Here I draw from Olszewska's (2015) argument that "individuality has a public and private face" (20). While the Afghan refugees she interviewed gained a "public reputation and biography" through their relations with others, they were also recognized for their individual education and achievements (20). Thus, the self is dependent on others and on the individual for its construction.

46  Ibid.

47  This finding resonates with Olszewska's (2015) argument that a contradiction between a person's public reputation and his private face leads him to keep "personal interests" a "secret, known only to a few confidantes" (21).

48  Foucault ([1978] 1995; 1982; 1998).

49  Foucault ([1978] 1995, 194).

50  Bourdieu (1993); Butler (1990); Mahmood (2005).

51 Describing an altogether different context, but one similarly predicated on appearance, Mears (2011) argues that the world of fashion promises its participants "a life of being extraordinary" (261). Like the assurance of the face game, this promise is "sustained by a handful of success stories but predicated on a thousand invisible failures" (261).

52 See also Bayat (1997; 2013).

53 Bayat (1997).

54 Cf. Bayat (1997).

# BIBLIOGRAPHY

Abbasi-Shavazi, Jalal, Peter McDonald, and Meimanat Hosseini-Chavoshi. 2008. "Modernization or Cultural Maintenance: The Practice of Consanguineous Marriage in Iran." *Journal of Biosocial Science* 40 (6): 911–33.

Abrahamian, Ervand. 1982. *Iran between Two Revolutions*. Princeton, NJ: Princeton University Press.

———. 1993. *Khomeinism: Essays on the Islamic Republic*. Berkeley: University of California Press.

———. 2008. *A History of Modern Iran*. Cambridge: Cambridge University Press.

———. 2009. "Why the Islamic Republic Has Survived." *Middle East Research and Information Project* 39 (250).

Abramson, Corey, and Darren Modzelewski. 2011. "Caged Morality: Moral Worlds, Subculture, and Stratification among Middle Class Cage-Fighters." *Qualitative Sociology* 34: 143–75.

Abu-Lughod, Lila. 1986. *Veiled Sentiments: Honor and Poetry in a Bedouin Society*. Berkeley: University of California Press.

Acevedo, Gabriel. 2008. "Islamic Fatalism and the Clash of Civilizations: An Appraisal of a Contentious and Dubious Theory." *Social Forces* 86 (4): 1711–52.

Adelkhah, Fariba. 2000. *Being Modern in Iran*. Translated by Jonathan Derrick. New York: Columbia University Press.

Afary, Janet. 2009. *Sexual Politics in Modern Iran*. Cambridge: Cambridge University Press.

Afkhami, Amir Arsalan. 2009. "From Punishment to Harm Reduction: Resecularization of Addiction in Contemporary Iran." In *Contemporary Iran: Economy, Society, Politics*, ed. Ali Gheissari, 194–211. Oxford: Oxford University Press.

Ali, Abbas, and Abdullah Al-Owaihan. 2008. "Islamic Work Ethic: A Critical Review." *Cross Cultural Management: An International Journal* 15 (1): 5–19.

Alikhah, Fardin. 2015. "Artifacts: The Satellite Dish." Ajam Media Collective, September 3. https://ajammc.com.

Amanat, Abbas. 2017. *Iran: A Modern History*. New Haven: Yale University Press.

Amanat, Abbas. 2012. "Introduction: Iranian Identity Boundaries: A Historical Overview." In *Iran Facing Others: Identity Boundaries in a Historical Perspective*. ed. Abbas Amanat and Farzin Vejdani, 1–39. New York: Palgrave Macmillan.

Amin, Camron. 2004. "Importing 'Beauty Culture' into Iran in the 1920s and 1930s: Mass Marketing Individualism in an Age of Anti-Imperialist Sacrifice." *Comparative Studies of South Asia, Africa and the Middle East* 24 (1): 79–95.

Aminzade, Ronald, and Randy Hodson. 1982. "Social Mobility in a Nineteenth Century French City." *American Sociological Review* 47: 441–57.

Amirahmadi, Hooshang, and Ali Kiafar. 1987. "Tehran: Growth and Contradictions." *Journal of Planning Education and Research* 6 (3): 167–77.

Amir Ebrahimi, Masserat. 1995. "Ta'sir-e Farhangsara-ye Bahman bar Zendegi-ye Ejtema'i va Farhangi-ye Zanan va Javanan-e Tehran" [The effect of the Bahman Cultural Center on the social and cultural life of the women and youth of Tehran]. *Goftogu* 9: 17–25.

———. 2001. Interview in "Tehran: Fragmented and Feminized." *Bad Jens*, February. www.badjens.com.

Amuzegar, Jahangir. 2005. "Iran's Third Development Plan: An Appraisal." *Middle East Policy* 12 (3): 46–63.

Arghavan, Mahmoud. 2013. "Tehrani Cultural Bricolage: Local Traditions and Global Styles of Tehran's Non-Conformist Youth." In *Cultural Revolution in Iran: Contemporary Popular Culture in the Islamic Republic*, ed. Annabelle Sreberny and Massoumeh Torfeh, 27–43. New York: I.B. Tauris.

Asad, Talal. 1993. *Genealogies of Religion: Discipline and Reasons of Power in Christianity and Islam*. Baltimore: Johns Hopkins University Press.

Assadi, Reza. 1980. "Deference: Persian Style." *Anthropological Linguistics* 22 (5): 221–24.

Atwood, Blake. 2015. "Tehran's Textual Topography: Mapping Youth Culture in Contemporary Persian Literature." *ALIF: Journal of Comparative Poetics* 35: 123–51.

Axworthy, Michael. 2015. *Revolutionary Iran: A History of the Islamic Republic*. Oxford: Oxford University Press.

Ayrout, Henry. 1963. *The Egyptian Peasant*. Boston: Beacon.

Azizi, Mohammad Mehdi. 2002. "Evaluation of Urban Land Supply Policy in Iran." *International Journal of Urban and Regional Research* 22 (1): 94–105.

Bahar, Mohammad-Taqi. 1989. *Divan-e Ash'ar*. 2 vols. Preface by Mehrdad Bahar. Tehran: Tus.

Bahman Farhangsara. https://bahman.farhangsara.ir.

Bahramitash, Roksana. 2003a. "Islamic Fundamentalism and Women's Employment in Iran." *International Journal of Politics, Culture, and Society* 16 (4): 551–68.

———. 2003b. "Revolution, Islamization, and Women's Employment in Iran." *Brown Journal of World Affairs* 9 (2): 229–41.

———. 2004. "Market Fundamentalism versus Religous Fundamentalism." *Critique: Journal of Middle Eastern Studies* 13 (1): 33–46.

———. 2007. "Female Employment and Globalization during Iran's Reform Era (1997–2005)." *Journal of Middle East Women's Studies* 3 (2): 56–86.

———. 2013. *Gender and Entrepreneurship in Iran: Microenterprise and the Informal Sector*. New York: Palgrave Macmillan.

Bahramitash, Roksana, and Jennifer Olmstead. 2014. "Choice and Constraint in Paid Work: Women from Low-Income Households in Tehran." *Feminist Economics* 20 (4): 260–80.

Bahramitash, Roksana, and Hadi Salehi-Esfahani. 2009. "Nimble Fingers No Longer! Women's Employment in Iran." In *Contemporary Iran*, ed. Ali Gheissari, 77–125. Oxford: Oxford University Press.

Barkow, Jerome. 1975. "Prestige and Culture: A Biosocial Interpretation." *Current Anthropology* 16 (4): 553–72.

Bateson, Mary Catherine, J. Clinton, J. Kassarjian, H. Safavi, and M. Soraya. 1977. "Safa-yi Batin: A Study of the Interrelations of a Set of Iranian Ideal Character Types." In *Psychological Dimensions of Near Eastern Studies*, ed. L. Carl Brown and Norman Itzkowitz, 257–74. Princeton, NJ: Darwin Press.

Bauer, Janet. 1985. "Demographic Change, Women, and the Family in a Migrant Neighborhood of Tehran." In *Women and the Family in Iran*, ed. Asghar Fathi, 158–87. Leiden: Brill.

Bayat, Asef. 1997. *Street Politics: Poor People's Movements in Iran.* New York: Columbia University Press.

———. 2007. *Making Islam Democratic: Social Movements and the Post-Islamist Turn.* Stanford: Stanford University Press.

———. 2013. *Life as Politics: How Ordinary People Change the Middle East.* Stanford: Stanford University Press.

———. 2018. "The Fire That Fueled the Iran Protests." *Atlantic*, January 27. www.the-atlantic.com.

Becker, Howard. 1963. *Outsiders: Studies in the Sociology of Deviance.* New York: Free Press.

Beeman, William. 1976. "Status, Style and Strategy in Iranian Interaction." *Anthropological Linguistics* 18 (7): 305–22.

———. 1986. *Language, Status, and Power in Iran.* Bloomington: Indiana University Press.

Behdad, Sohrab, and Farhad Nomani. 2009. "What a Revolution! Thirty Years of Social Class Reshuffling in Iran." *Comparative Studies of South Asia, Africa and the Middle East* 29 (1): 84–104.

Behnam, Biook, and Niloufar Amizadeh. 2011. "A Comparative Study of the Compliments and Compliment Responses between English and Persian TV Interviews." *Language, Linguistics and Literature: The Southeast Asian Journal of English Language Studies* 17 (1): 65–78.

Behrouzan, Orkideh. 2016. *Prozak Diaries: Psychiatry and Generational Memory in Iran.* Stanford: Stanford University Press.

Beidelman, T. O. 1993. "Secrecy and Society: The Paradox of Knowing and the Knowing of Paradox." In *Secrecy: African Art That Conceals and Reveals*, ed. Mary H. Nooter, 41–52. New York: Museum for African Art.

Bienan, Henry. 1984. "Urbanization and Third World Stability." *World Development* 12 (7): 661–91.

Blau, Peter, and Otis Dudley Duncan. 1967. *The American Occupational Structure.* New York: John Wiley and Sons.

Bloch, Maurice. 1989. *Ritual, History, and Power: Selected Papers in Anthropology.* London: Athlone.

Borjian, Maryam. 2005. "Bilingualism in Mazandaran: Peaceful Coexistence with Persian." *Languages, Communities, and Education* 65: 65–73.

Bourdieu, Pierre. 1965. "The Sentiment of Honour in Kabyle Society." *In Honor and Shame: The Values of Mediterranean Society*, ed. Jean G. Peristiany, 191–243. London: Weidenfeld and Nicolson.

———. 1977. *Outline of a Theory of Practice*. Cambridge: Cambridge University Press.

———. 1984. *Distinction: A Social Critique of the Judgment of Taste*. Cambridge: Harvard University Press.

———. 1986. "The Forms of Capital." In *Handbook of Theory and Research for the Sociology of Education*, ed. J. G. Richardson, 241–58. New York: Greenwood.

———. 1990. *The Logic of Practice*. Stanford: Stanford University Press.

———. 1993. *The Field of Cultural Production*. New York: Columbia University Press.

Bourgois, Philippe. 2003. *In Search of Respect: Selling Crack in El Barrio*. Cambridge: Cambridge University Press.

Bowles, Samuel, Steven N. Durlauf, and Karla Hoff. 2006. "Introduction." In *Poverty Traps*, ed. Samuel Bowles, Steven N. Durlauf, and Karla Hoff, 1–13. Princeton: Princeton University Press.

Bucholtz, Mary. 2002. "Youth and Cultural Practice." *Annual Review of Anthropology* 31: 525–52.

Butler, Judith. 1990. *Gender Trouble: Feminism and the Subversion of Identity*. New York: Routledge.

———. 1993. *Bodies That Matter: On the Discursive Limits of "Sex."* London: Routledge.

Butterworth, Douglas. 1970. "From Royalty to Poverty: The Decline of a Rural Mexican Community." *Human Organization* 29 (1): 5–11.

Calhoun, Craig. 1993. "Habitus, Field, and Capital: The Question of Historical Specificity." In *Bourdieu: Critical Perspectives*, ed. Craig Calhoun, Edward LiPuma, and Moishe Postone, 61–88. Chicago: University of Chicago Press.

Chehabi, Houchang. 2006. "The Politics of Football in Iran." *Soccer and Society* 7 (2–3): 233–61.

Cleveland, William. 1999. *A History of the Modern Middle East*. Boulder: Westview.

Cohen, Albert. 1955. *Delinquent Boys: The Culture of the Gang*. New York: Free Press.

Daftar-e Tarh-ha-ye Melli. 1382/2003. *Arzesh-ha va Negaresh-ha-ye Iraniyan* [Values and worldviews of Iranians]. Tehran: Vezarat-e Farhang va Ershad-e Eslami.

Datta, Amira. 2016. "Migration from Contemporary Bihar." In *Internal Migration in Contemporary India*, ed. Deepak Mishra, 204–221. New Delhi: Sage.

Deeb, Lara. 2006. *An Enchanted Modern: Gender and Public Piety in Shi'i Lebanon*. Princeton, NJ: Princeton University Press.

Deeb, Lara, and Mona Harb. 2013. *Leisurely Islam: Negotiating Geography and Morality in Shi'ite South Beirut*. Princeton, NJ: Princeton University Press.

Dehghan, Saeed Kamali. 2013. "Iran's President Signals Softer Line on Web Censorship and Islamic Dress Code." *Guardian*, July 2. www.theguardian.com.

Denoeux, Guilain. 1993. *Urban Unrest in the Middle East: A Comparative Study of Informal Networks in Egypt, Iran and Lebanon*. Albany: State University of New York Press.

Dhillon, Navtej, and Tarik Yousef. 2009. *Generation in Waiting: The Unfulfilled Promise of Young People in the Middle East*. Washington, D.C.: Brookings Institution.

Dohan, Daniel. 2003. *The Price of Poverty: Money, Work and Culture in the Mexican American Barrio*. Berkeley: University of California Press.

Doostdar, Alireza. 2018. *The Iranian Metaphysicals: Explorations in Science, Islam, and the Uncanny*. Princeton, NJ: Princeton University Press.

Douglas, Mary. [1966] 2002. *Purity and Danger: An Analysis of the Concepts of Pollution and Taboo*. London: Routledge.

Ehsani, Kaveh. 1994. "'Tilt but Don't Spill': Iran's Development and Reconstruction Dilemma." *Middle East Report* 191: 16–21.

———. 1999. "Municipal Matters: The Urbanization of Consciousness and Political Change in Tehran." *Middle East Report* 212: 22–27.

———. 2006a. "Rural Society and Agricultural Development in Post-Revolution Iran: The First Two Decades." *Critique: Critical Middle Eastern Studies* 15 (1): 79–96.

———. 2006b. "Iran: The Populist Threat to Democracy." *Middle East Report* 241: 4–9.

———. 2009. "Survival through Dispossession: Privatization of Public Goods in the Islamic Republic." *Middle East Report* 250.

Elder, Joseph. 1966. "Fatalism in India: A Comparison between Hindus and Muslims." *Anthropological Quarterly* 39 (3): 227–43.

Elling, Rasmus Christian, and Khodadad Rezakhani. 2015. "Talking Class in Tehroon." *Middle East Report* 277.

Elster, Jon. 1989. "Social Norms and Economic Theory." *Journal of Economic Perspectives* 3 (4): 99–117.

Erdbrink, Thomas. 2018. "Steep Slide in Currency Threatens Iran's Economy." *New York Times*, April 11. www.nytimes.com.

Farahani, Dana. 2010. "'Shahnameh' and Iran: Epic Tales for Epic Times." *Tehran Bureau*, June 21. www.pbs.org.

Fars News Agency. 2012. "Ahmadinejad Praises Iran's Subsidy Reforms Plan." *Payvand*, May 10. www.payvand.com.

Farzanegan, Mohammad. 2014. "Civil Society and Natural Resource Management in Iran." NUPI-MSCE Seminar Paper 10–2014, Oslo.

Featherman, David, and Robert Hauser. 1976. "Prestige or Socioeconomic Scales in the Study of Occupational Achievement?" *Sociological Methods and Research* 4 (4): 403–22.

Featherstone, Mike. 1991. *Consumer Culture and Postmodernism*. London: Sage.

Ferdowsi, Abu'l Qasem. 1366/1988. *Shahnameh*. Vol. 1. Edited by Jalal Khaleqi Motlaq. New York: Bibliotheca Persica.

*Financial Tribune*. 2017b. "Spring Unemployment at 12.6%." July 5. https://financialtribune.com.

——. 2017a. "High Cost of Employment Boosting Informal Economy." October 17. https://financialtribune.com.

Finkelstein, Joanne. 1991. *The Fashioned Self*. Philadelphia: Temple University Press.

Fischer, Claude. 1982. *To Dwell among Friends: Personal Networks in Town and City*. Chicago: University of Chicago Press.

Foucault, Michel. [1978] 1995. *Discipline and Punish: The Birth of the Prison*. Trans. Alan Sheridan. 2nd Vintage ed. New York: Vintage.

——. 1980. "Truth and Power." In *Power/Knowledge: Selected Interviews and Other Writings, 1972–1977*, ed. and trans. C. Gordon, 109–33. New York: Pantheon.

——. 1982. "The Subject and Power." *Critical Inquiry* 8 (4): 777–95.

——. 1998. *The History of Sexuality: The Will to Knowledge*. London: Penguin.

Fraser, James Baillie. 1826. *Travels and Adventures in the Persian Provinces of the Southern Banks of the Caspian Sea, with an Appendix Containing Short Notices on the Geology and Commerce of Persia*. London: Royal Collection Trust.

Friedl, Erika. 2014. *The Folktales and Storytellers of Tribal Iran: Culture, Ethos and Identity*. London: I.B. Tauris.

Fukuyama, Francis. 1992. *The End of History and the Last Man*. New York: Free Press.

Germani, Gino. 1966. "Social and Political Consequences of Mobility." In *Social Structure and Mobility in Economic Development*, ed. Neil Smelser and Seymour Martin Lipset, 364–95. Chicago: Aldine.

Ghaderi, Amin, Maryam Motmaen, Iraj Abdi, and Morad Rasouli-Azad. 2017. "Gender Differences in Substance Use Patterns and Disorders among an Iranian Patient Sample Receiving Methadone Maintenance Treatment." *Electron Physician* 9 (9): 5354–62.

Ghamari-Tabrizi, Behrooz. 2009. "Memory, Mourning, Memorializing: On the Victims of Iran-Iraq War, 1980–Present." *Radical History Review* 105: 106–21.

Ghiabi, Maziyar. 2018a. "Maintaining Disorder: The Micropolitics of Drugs Policy in Iran." *Third World Quarterly* 39 (2): 277–97.

——. 2018b. "Under the Bridge in Tehran: Addiction, Poverty and Capital." *Ethnography*, https://doi.org/10.1177/1466138118787534.

Goffman, Erving. 1955. "On Face Work." In *Social Theory: The Multicultural Readings*, ed. Charles Lemert, 338–43. Philadelphia: Westview.

——. 1956. *The Presentation of Self in Everyday Life*. University of Edinburgh Social Science Research Center, Mongraph No. 2.

——. 1963. *Stigma*. London: Penguin.

——. 1967. *Interaction Ritual: Essays on Face-to-Face Behavior*. New York: Anchor.

——. 1972. *Interaction Ritual: Essays on Face-to-Face Behavior*. London: Penguin.

Goldthorpe, John, and Keith Hope. 1972. "Occupational Grading and Occupational Prestige." In *The Analysis of Social Mobility: Methods and Approaches*, ed. Keith Hope, 19–80. Oxford: Oxford University Press.

Goldthorpe, John, and Gordon Marshall. 1992. "The Promising Future of Class Analysis: A Response to Recent Critiques." *Sociology* 26 (3): 81–101.

Gregg, Gary. 2005. *The Middle East: A Cultural Psychology*. Oxford: Oxford University Press.

Gries, Peter. 2004. *China's New Nationalism: Pride, Politics, and Diplomacy*. Berkeley: University of California Press.

Gugler, Josef. 1996. "Urbanisation in Africa South of the Sahara: New Identities in Conflict." In *The Urban Transformation of the Developing World*, ed. Josef Gugler, 210–51. Oxford: Oxford University Press.

Haeri, Shahla. 1989. *Law of Desire: Temporary Marriage in Shi'i Iran*. Syracuse: Syracuse University Press.

Haim, Sulayman. 2002. *Persian-English Dictionary*. 4th printing. New York: Hippocrene.

Hajiani, Ebrahim. 1393/2014. *Jame'-Shenasi-ye Akhlaq: Tahlil-e Vazi'at-e Akhlaq-e Ejtema'i dar Jame'eh-ye Iran* [The sociology of morality: An interpretation of the conditions of social morality in Iranian society]. Tehran: Jame'eh-shenasan.

Hall, Peter, and John Hewitt. 1970. "The Quasi-Theory of Communication and the Management of Dissent." *Social Problems* 18 (1): 17–27.

Hambly, Gavin. 2008. "Āghā Muḥammad Khān and the Establishment of the Qājār Dynasty." In *The Cambridge History of Iran*, vol. 7, ed. Peter Avery, Gavin Hambly, and Charles Melville, 104–44. Cambridge: Cambridge University Press.

Hammermesh, David. 2011. *Beauty Pays: Why Attractive People Are More Successful*. Princeton, NJ: Princeton University Press.

Hammermesh, David, and Jeff Biddle. 1994. "Beauty and the Labor Market." *American Economic Review* 84 (5): 1174–94.

Harkness, Geoff, and Rana Khaled. 2014. "Modern Traditionalism: Consanguineous Marrriage in Qatar." *Journal of Marriage and Family* 76: 587–603.

Harris, Kevan. 2012. "The Brokered Exuberance of the Middle Class: An Ethnographic Analysis of Iran's 2009 Green Movement." *Mobilization: An International Journal* 17 (4): 435–55.

———. 2017. *A Social Revolution: Politics and the Welfare State in Iran*. Oakland: University of California Press.

Hashemi, Manata. 2015. "Waithood and Face: Morality and Mobility among Lower-Class Youth in Iran." *Qualitative Sociology* 38 (3): 261–83.

———. 2017. "Aspirations, Poverty and Behavior among Youth in the Middle East: Some Theoretical Considerations." *Muslim World* 107 (1): 83–99.

———. 2018. "Tarnished Work: Dignity and Labour in Iran." *British Journal of Middle Eastern Studies*. doi: 10.1080/13530194.2018.1552116.

———. 2019. "Embedded Enclaves: Cultural Mimicry and Urban Social Exclusion in Iran." *International Journal of Urban and Regional Research* 3 (5): 914–29.

Hebdige, Dick. 1979. *Subculture: The Meaning of Style*. London: Routledge.

Hedayat, Hirbohd. 2017. "The Development of the Modern Iranian Nation-State: From Qajar Origins to Early Pahlavi Modernization." Unpublished master's thesis, Virginia Polytechnic Institute and State University, Blacksburg, VA.

Hedström, Peter, and Richard Swedberg. 1998. *Social Mechanisms: An Analytical Approach to Social Theory*. Cambridge: Cambridge University Press.

Hewitt, John, and Peter Hall. 1973. "Social Problems, Problematic Situations, and Quasi-Theories." *American Sociological Review* 38 (3): 367–74.

Hewitt, John, and Randall Stokes. 1975. "Disclaimers." *American Sociological Review* 40 (1): 1–11.

Hillman, Michael. 1981. "Language and Social Distinction in Iran." In *Modern Iran: The Dialectics of Continuity and Change*, ed. Michael Bonine and Nikki Keddie. Albany: State University of New York Press.

Ho, David Yau-fai. 1976. "On the Concept of Face." *American Journal of Sociology* 81 (4): 867–84.

Holy, Ladislov. 1989. *Kinship, Honour and Solidarity: Cousin-Marriage in the Middle East*. Manchester: Manchester University Press.

Hoodfar, Homa. 1997. *Between Marriage and the Market: Intimate Politics and Survival in Cairo*. Berkeley: University of California Press.

Hooglund, Eric. 1982. *Land and Revolution in Iran, 1960–1980*. Austin: University of Texas Press.

Huntington, Samuel. 1993. "The Clash of Civilizations." *Foreign Affairs* 72 (3): 22–50.

———. 1996. *The Clash of Civilizations and the Remaking of World Order*. New York: Touchstone.

Ikhwan-us-Safa. 1999. *Letters of Ikhwan-us-Safa*. Vol. 3. Beirut: Dar Sader.

Imam Khomeini Relief Committee. n.d. "Foundation of Imam Khomeini Emdad Committee." Islamic Revolution Document Center. www.irdc.ir.

———. https://portal.emdad.ir.

International Labor Office. 1972. "Employment, Incomes and Equality: A Strategy for Increasing Productive Employment in Kenya." Geneva: International Labor Organization. www.ilo.org.

Islami, Hossein. 1372/1993. *Tarikh-e Do Hezar Saleh-ye Sari* [A 2,000-year history of Sari]. Gaemshahr: Azad University Mazandaran-Gaemshahr.

Ismail, Salwa. 2006. *Encountering the Everyday State: Political Life in Cairo's New Quarters*. Minneapolis: University of Minnesota Press.

Kamalkhani, Zahra. 1993. "Women's Everyday Religious Discourse in Iran." In *Women in the Middle East: Perceptions, Realities and Struggles for Liberation*, ed. Haleh Afshar, 85–95. Basingstoke: Palgrave Macmillan.

Karimi, Zahra. 2011. "The Effects of International Trade on Gender Inequality in Iran: The Case of Women Carpet-Weavers." In *Veiled Employment: The Political Economy of Female Employment in Iran*, ed. Roksana Bahramitash and Hadi Salehi-Esfahani, 166–91. Syracuse: Syracuse University Press.

Karpat, Kemal. 1976. *The Gecekondu: Rural Migration and Urbanization*. Cambridge: Cambridge University Press.

Kazembeyki, Mohammad Ali. 2003. *Society, Politics and Economics in Mazandaran, Iran, 1848–1914*. London: Routledge Curzon.

Kazemi, Farhad. 1980. *Poverty and Revolution in Iran: The Migrant Poor, Urban Marginality and Politics*. New York: New York University Press.

Keddie, Nikki. 2006. *Modern Iran: Roots and Results of Revolution*. New Haven: Yale University Press.

Keivani, Ramin, Michael Mattingly, and Hamid Majedi. 2005. "Enabling Housing Markets or Increasing Low Income Access to Urban Land: Lessons from Iran." Paper presented at World Bank/IPEA Urban Research Symposium, Brasilia, April 4–6.

Khamenei, Ayatollah. 2018. "The Islamic Republic Has Defeated the U.S., Continuously, for 40 Years." November 3. http://english.khamenei.ir.

Khatami, Mahmoud. 1393/2014. *Pishdaramad-e Falsafeh-i Baraye Honar-e Irani* [A philosophical introduction to Iranian art]. Tehran: Shadrang.

Kheirabadi, Masoud. 1991. *Iranian Cities: Formation and Development*. Austin: University of Texas Press.

Khosravi, Shahram. 2008. *Young and Defiant in Tehran*. Philadelphia: University of Pennsylvania Press.

———. 2017. *Precarious Lives: Waiting and Hope in Iran*. Philadelphia: University of Pennsylvania Press.

Khuri, Fuad. 1970. "Parallel Cousin Marriage Reconsidered: A Middle Eastern Practice That Nullifics the Effects of Marriage on the Intensity of Family Relationships." *Man* 5: 597–618.

Kia, Mana. 2015. "Moral Refinement and Manhood in Persian." In *Civilizing Emotions: Concepts in Asia and Europe, 1870–1920*, ed. Margrit Pernau and Helge Jordheim et al., 146–65. Oxford: Oxford University Press.

Kian-Thiébaut. 1999. "Political and Social Transformations in Post-Islamist Iran." *Middle East Report* 212: 12–16.

Kinzer, Stephen. 2008 *All the Shah's Men: An American Coup and the Roots of Middle East Terror*. Hoboken: Wiley.

Klaufus, Christien. 2012. "The Symbolic Dimension of Mobility: Architecture and Social Status in Ecuadorian Informal Settlements." *International Journal of Urban and Regional Research* 36 (4): 689–705.

Koutlaki, Sofia. 2010. *Among the Iranians: A Guide to Iran's Culture and Customs*. London: Nicholas Brealey.

Lamont, Michèle. 1992. *Money, Morals, and Manners: The Culture of the French and the American Upper-Middle Class*. Chicago: University of Chicago Press.

———. 2000. *The Dignity of Working Men: Morality and the Boundaries of Race, Class, and Immigration*. Cambridge: Harvard University Press.

Lamont, Michèle, and Virág Molnár. 2002. "The Study of Boundaries in the Social Sciences." *Annual Review of Sociology* 28: 167–95.

Lange, Christian. 2007. "On That Day When Faces Will Be White or Black." *Journal of the American Oriental Society* 127 (4): 429–45.

Lesetedi, Gwen Ntenda. 2011. "The Changing Face of Urbanisation in Botswana: 'The City Is for Work, the Village Is Home?'" In *Contemporary Social Issues in Africa: Cases in Gaborone, Kampala and Durban*, ed. Mokong Simon Mapadimeng and Sultan Khan, 79–92. Pretoria: Africa Institute of South Africa.

Levin, David. 1985. *The Body's Recollection of Being: Phenomenological Psychology and the Deconstruction of Nihilism*. Honolulu: University of Hawai'i Press.

Lewis, Bernard. 1990. "The Roots of Muslim Rage." *Atlantic Monthly* 266 (3): 47–60.

Lewis, Oscar. 1959. *Five Families: Mexican Case Studies in the Culture of Poverty*. New York: Basic Books.

Lob, Eric. 2017. "Development, Mobilization and War: The Iranian Construction Jehad, Construction Mobilization and Trench Builders Association (1979–2013)." *Middle East Critique* 26 (1).

Loeb, Laurence. 1978. "Prestige and Piety in the Iranian Synagogue." *Anthropological Quarterly* 51 (3): 155–61.

Loeffler, Reinhold. 1986. "Economic Changes in a Rural Area since 1979." In *The Iranian Revolution and the Islamic Republic*, ed. Nikki Keddie and Eric Hooglund, 93–107. Syracuse: Syracuse University Press.

———. 1988. *Islam in Practice: Religious Beliefs in a Persian Village*. Albany: State University of New York Press.

Lomnitz, Larissa. 1977. *Networks and Marginality: Life in a Mexican Shantytown*. New York: Academic Press.

MacLeod, Jay. 2008. *Ain't No Makin' It: Aspirations and Attainment in a Low-Income Neighborhood*. Boulder: Westview.

Madanipour, Ali. 1998. *Tehran: The Making of a Metropolis*. Chichester: Wiley and Sons.

Madelung, Wilferd. 1975. "The Minor Dynasties of Northern Iran." In *The Cambridge History of Iran*, vol. 4, ed. Richard Frye, 198–249. Cambridge: Cambridge University Press.

———. 1993. "Dabuyids." In *Encyclopaedia Iranica*. Vol. VI/5. Winona Lake: Eisenbrauns.

Maghbouleh, Neda. 2013. "The *Ta'arof* Tournament: Cultural Performances of Ethno-National Identity at a Diasporic Summer Camp." *Ethnic and Racial Studies* 36 (5): 818–37.

Mahdavi, Pardis. 2008. *Passionate Uprisings: Iran's Sexual Revolution*. Stanford, CA: Stanford University Press.

Mahmood, Saba. 2005. *Politics of Piety: The Islamic Revival and the Feminist Subject*. Princeton, NJ: Princeton University Press.

Majd, Hooman. 2008. *The Ayatollah Begs to Differ: The Paradox of Modern Iran*. New York: Doubleday.

Maloney, Suzanne. 2015. *Iran's Political Economy since the Revolution*. Washington, D.C.: Brookings Institution.

Management and Planning Organization of Mazandaran. n.d. "Jadval 1: Amar-e Jami'ati-ye Shahrestan-ha-ye Ostan-e Mazandaran dar Sal-e 1395" [Table 1: Population statistics of counties in Mazandaran Province in the year 2017]. https://mazandaran.mporg.ir.

Manoukian, Setrag. 2012. *City of Knowledge in Twentieth Century Iran: Shiraz, History and Poetry*. London: Routledge.

Marashi, Afshin. 2008. *Nationalizing Iran: Culture, Power, and the State, 1870–1940*. Seattle: University of Washington Press.

Matza, David, and Gresham Sykes. 1961. "Juvenile Delinquency and Subterranean Values." *American Sociological Review* 26 (5): 712–19.

Mauss, Marcel. [1925] 1990. *The Gift: The Form and Reason for Exchange in Arabic Societies*. London: Routledge.

———. 1979. "A Category of the Human Mind: The Notion of Person, the Notion of Self." In *Sociology and Psychology*, trans. Ben Brewster. London: Routledge and Kegan Paul.

Mears, Ashley. 2011. *Pricing Beauty: The Making of a Fashion Model*. Berkeley: University of California Press.

Melville, Charles. 2000. "The Caspian Provinces: A World Apart, Three Local Histories of Mazandaran." *Iranian Studies* 33: 45–89.

Mills, C. Wright. 1940. "Situated Actions and Vocabularies of Motive." *American Sociological Review* 5: 904–13.

Mofrad, Ghazaleh Haghdad. 2014. "The Emergence of 'Home Shows': The Market and Politics of Television Entertainment in Iran." Ajam Media Collective, November 17. https://ajammc.com.

Molyneux, Maxine. 2002. "Gender and Silences of Social Capital: Lessons from Latin America." *Development and Change* 33 (2): 167–88.

Momen, Moojan. 1985. *An Introduction to Shi'i Islam*. New Haven: Yale University Press.

Morgenthau, Hans, and Ethel Person. 1978. "The Roots of Narcissism." *Partisan Review* 45 (3): 337–47.

Moslem, Mehdi. 2002. *Factional Politics in Post-Khomeini Iran*. Syracuse: Syracuse University Press.

Mottahedeh, Roy. 1985. *The Mantle of the Prophet: Religion and Politics in Iran*. Oxford: Oneworld Publications.

Mulderig, Chloe. 2011. "Adulthood Denied: Youth Dissatisfaction and the Arab Spring." *Issues in Brief* 21: 1–8.

Nelson, Joan. 1979. *Access to Power: Politics and the Urban Poor in Developing Nations*. Princeton, NJ: Princeton University Press.

Newman, Katherine. 1999. *No Shame in My Game: The Working Poor in the Inner City*. New York: Vintage and Russell Sage Foundation.

Nickson, Dennis, Chris Warhurst, Anne Witz, and Anne Marie Cullen. 2001. "The Importance of Being Aesthetic: Work, Employment and Service Organization." In *Customer Service: Empowerment and Entrapment*, ed. Andrew Sturdy, Irena Grugulis, and Hugh Willmott, 170–90. Basingstoke: Palgrave.

Nikpour, Golnar. 2018. "Drugs and Drug Policy in the Islamic Republic of Iran." *Middle East Brief* 119: 1–7.

Nomani, Farhad, and Sohrab Behdad. 2006. *Class and Labor in Iran: Did the Revolution Matter?* Syracuse: Syracuse University Press.

Nooshin, Laudan. 2005. "Underground, Overground: Rock Music and Youth Discourses in Iran." *Iranian Studies* 38 (3): 463–94.

Norton, Richard. 2001. *Civil Society in the Middle East*. New York: Leiden.

Olszewska, Zuzanna. 2013. "Classy Kids and Down-at-Heel Intellectuals: Status Aspirations and Blind Spots in the Contemporary Ethnography of Iran." *Iranian Studies* 46 (6): 841–62.

———. 2015. *The Pearl of Dari: Poetry and Personhood among Young Afghans in Iran*. Bloomington: Indiana University Press.

Osanloo, Arzoo. 2006. *The Politics of Women's Rights in Iran*. Princeton, NJ: Princeton University Press.

Ossowska, Maria. 1980. *Moral Norms: A Tentative Systematization*. Warsaw: Polish Scientific Publishers.

Pamuk, Orhan. 2015. *A Strangeness in My Mind*. New York: Knopf.

Patai, Raphael. 1973. *The Arab Mind*. New York: Scribner's.

Pitt-Rivers, Julian. 1965. "Honor and Social Status." In *Honor and Shame: The Values of Mediterranean Society*, ed. Jean G. Peristiany, 19-79. London: Weidenfeld and Nicolson.

Perry, John. 1984. "Āgā Moḥammad Khan Qājār." In *Encyclopaedia Iranica*. Vol. I/6. Winona Lake: Eisenbrauns.

Portes, Alejandro, and Julia Sensenbrenner. 1993. "Embeddedness and Immigration: Notes on the Social Determinants of Economic Action." *American Journal of Sociology* 98 (6): 1320–50.

Pourshariati, Parvaneh. 2008. *Decline and Fall of the Sasanian Empire: The Sasanian-Parthian Confederacy and the Arab Conquest of Iran*. London: I.B. Tauris.

Purser, Gretchen. 2009. "The Dignity of Job-Seeking Men: Boundary Work among Immigrant Day Laborers." *Journal of Contemporary Ethnography* 38 (1): 117–39.

Ray, Debraj. 2003. "Aspirations, Poverty and Economic Change." CSIC Working Paper 03–2003, New York.

Razavi, Negar. 2014. "The Rise of 'Youth Pop' Films in Contemporary Iran." In *Iranian Cinema in a Global Context: Policy, Politics and Form*, ed. Peter Decherney and Blake Atwood, 143–64. New York: Routledge.

Rios, Victor. 2011. *Punished: Policing the Lives of Black and Latino Boys*. New York: New York University Press.

Rugh, Andrea. 1984. *Family in Contemporary Egypt*. Syracuse: Syracuse University Press.

Sa'di. [1865]. *The Gulistan or Rose Garden*. Trans. Francis Gladwin. Boston: Ticknor and Fields.

Saeidi, Shirin. 2018. "Iran's Hezbollah and Citizenship Politics: The Surprises of Religious Legislation in a Hybrid Regime." In *The Middle East in Transition: The Centrality of Citizenship*, ed. Nils A. Butenschon and Roel Meijer, 223–51. Cheltenham: Edward Elgar.

Sahlins, Marshall. 1972. *Stone Age Economics*. Chicago: Aldine-Atherton.

Salehi-Esfahani, Hadi. 2005. "Alternative Public Service Delivery Mechanisms in Iran." *Quarterly Review of Economics and Finance* 45: 497–525.

Salehi-Isfahani, Djavad. 2006. "Revolution and Redistribution in Iran: Poverty and Inequality 25 Years Later." Working Paper, Virginia Polytechnic Institute and State University, Department of Economics.

———. 2010a. "Iranian Youth in Times of Crisis." Working Paper, Dubai Initiative, Belfer Center for Science and International Affairs, Harvard Kennedy School.

———. 2010b. "Iran's Youth, the Unitended Victims of Sanctions." Policy Brief, Dubai Initiative, Belfer Center for Science and International Affairs, Harvard Kennedy School.

———. 2016. "Long Term Trends in Poverty and Inequality in Iran." *Tyranny of Numbers Blog*, March 29. https://djavadsalehi.com.

Salehi-Isfahani, Djavad, and Navtej Dhillon. 2008. "Stalled Youth Transitions in the Middle East: A Framework for Policy Reform." Working Paper, Dubai Initiative, Wolfensohn Center for Development, Brookings Institution.

Salehi-Isfahani, Djavad, and David Egel. 2007. "Youth Exclusion in Iran: The State of Education, Employment and Family Formation." Working Paper, Dubai Initiative, Wolfensohn Center for Development, Brookings Institution.

Salehi-Isfahani, Djavad, and Mohammad Mostafavi-Dehzooei. 2017. "Cash Transfers and Labor Supply: Evidence from a Large-Scale Program in Iran." Working Paper 1090, Economic Research Forum.

Sánchez-Jankowski, Martín. 1991. *Islands in the Street: Gangs and American Urban Society*. Berkeley: University of California Press.

———. 1999. "The Concentration of African-American Poverty and the Dispersal of the Working Class: An Ethnographic Study of Three Inner-City Areas." *International Journal of Urban and Regional Research* 23 (4): 619–37.

———. 2002. "Representation, Responsibility and Reliability in Participant Observation." In *Qualitative Research in Action*, ed. Tim May, 144–60. London: Sage.

———. 2008. *Cracks in the Pavement: Social Change and Resilience in Poor Neighborhoods*. Berkeley: University of California Press.

Sayer, Andrew. 2004. "Moral Economy." Department of Sociology, Lancaster University, Lancaster, UK. www.comp.lancs.ac.uk.

Schayegh, Cyrus. 2009. *Who Is Knowledgeable Is Strong: Science, Class, and the Formation of Modern Iranian Society, 1900–1950*. Berkeley: University of California Press.

Schimmel, Annemarie. 1975. *Mystical Dimensions of Islam*. Chapel Hill: University of North Carolina Press.

Schirazi, Asghar. 1993. *Islamic Development Policy: The Agrarian Question in Iran*. Boulder: Lynne Rienner.

Scott, James. 1985. *Weapons of the Weak: Everyday Forms of Peasant Resistance*. Chicago: University of Chicago Press.

Scott, Marvin B., and Stanford M. Lyman. 1968. "Accounts." *American Sociological Review* 33 (1): 46–62.

Sedghi, Hamideh. 2007. *Women and Politics in Iran: Veiling, Unveiling, and Reveiling.* Cambridge: Cambridge University Press.

Shah, Nasra. 2004. "Women's Socioeconomic Characteristics and Marital Patterns in a Rapidly Developing Muslim Society, Kuwait." *Journal of Comparative Family Studies* 35 (2): 163–83.

Shahabi, Mahmood. 2006. "Youth Subcultures in Post-Revolution Iran: An Alternative Reading." In *Global Youth? Hybrid Identities, Plural Worlds*, ed. Pam Nilan and Carles Feixa, 111–30. New York: Routledge.

Shahbazi, Shahpur. 2004. "Iraj." *Encyclopaedia Iranica*. Vol. XIII/3. Winona Lake: Eisenbrauns.

Shahrabi, Shima. 2014. "The 'Not So Rich' Kids of Tehran." *Iranwire*, October 13. https://iranwire.com.

Shams, Alex. 2015. "Sacralizing a Shia Public Sphere: Muharram Commemorations across Iran." Ajam Media Collective, December 1. https://ajammc.com.

Sherman, Jennifer. 2009. *Those Who Work, Those Who Don't: Poverty, Morality and Family in Rural America*. Minneapolis: University of Minnesota Press.

Simmel, Georg. 1906. "The Sociology of Secrecy and Secret Societies." *American Journal of Sociology* 11 (4): 441–98.

———. 1950. *The Sociology of Georg Simmel*. Edited by K. H. Wolff. New York: Simon and Schuster.

———. 1957. "Fashion." *American Journal of Sociology* 62 (6): 541–58.

Singerman, Diane. 1995. *Avenues of Participation: Family, Politics and Networks in Urban Quarters of Cairo*. Princeton, NJ: Princeton University Press.

Small, Mario. 2017. *Someone to Talk To*. Oxford: Oxford University Press.

Smilde, David. 2007. *Reason to Believe: Cultural Agency in Latin American Evangelicalism*. Berkeley: University of California Press.

Smith, Ken. 2007. "Operationalizing Max Weber's Probability Concept of Class Situation: The Concept of Social Class." *British Journal of Sociology* 58 (1): 87–104.

Smith, Sandra. 2007. *Lone Pursuit: Distrust and Defensive Individualism among the Black Poor*. New York: Russell Sage.

Sreberny-Mohammadi, Anabelle, and Ali Mohammadi. 1994. *Small Media, Big Revolution: Communication, Culture, and the Iranian Revolution*. Minneapolis: University of Minnesota Press.

Statistical Center of Iran. 2016. "Selected Results of the 2016 National Population and Housing Census." Tehran: Markaz-e Amar-e Iran. www.amar.org.ir.

Swidler, Ann. 1986. "Culture in Action: Symbols and Strategies." *American Sociological Review* 51 (2): 273–86.

———. 2000. *Talk of Love: How Culture Matters*. Chicago: University of Chicago Press.

Tartt, Donna. 2013. *The Goldfinch*. New York: Little, Brown.

Tasnim News Agency. 2019. "Rouhani: Nejat-e Jam'e-eh va Javanan az Mo'zel-e 'Etiyad Vazifeh-ye Melli Ast" [Rouhani: Saving society and youth from the problem of addiction is a national responsibility]. July 30. www.tasnimnews.com.

*Tehran Times*. 2018. "Inflation Rate Stands at 9.9%: CBI." February 25. www.tehran-times.com.

Thurfjell, David. 2006. *Living Shi'ism: Instances of Ritualisation among Islamist Men in Contemporary Iran*. Leiden: Brill.

Trouille, David. 2013. "Neighborhood Outsiders, Field Insiders: Latino Immigrant Men and the Control of Public Space." *Qualitative Sociology* 36 (1): 1–22.

Turner, Bryan. 1974. "Islam, Capitalism and the Weber Theses." *British Journal of Sociology* 25 (2): 230–43.

U.S. Department of State. 2015. *Joint Comprehensive Plan of Action*. Vienna. www.state.gov.

Vaisey, Stephen. 2009. "Motivation and Justification: A Dual-Process Model of Culture in Action." *American Journal of Sociology* 114 (6): 1675–715.

Vakil, Sanam. 2011. *Women and Politics in the Islamic Republic of Iran: Action and Reaction*. New York: Bloomsbury Publishing USA.

Varzi, Roxanne. 2006. *Warring Souls: Youth, Media, and Martyrdom in Post-Revolutionary Iran*. Durham: Duke University Press.

Veblen, Thorstein. [1899] 1953. *The Theory of the Leisure Class: An Economic Study of Institutions*. New York: New American Library.

Venkatesh, Sudhir. 1994. "Getting Ahead: Social Mobility among the Urban Poor." *Sociological Perspectives* 37 (2): 157–82.

Wacquant, Loïc. 1995. "Pugs at Work: Bodily Capital and Bodily Labour among Professional Boxers." *Body and Society* 1 (1): 65–93.

———. 2004. *Body and Soul: Notebooks of an Apprentice Boxer*. Chicago: University of Chicago Press.

Warhurst, Chris, Dennis Nickson, Anne Witz, and Anne Marie Cullen. 2000. "Aesthetic Labor in Interactive Service Work: Some Case Study Evidence from the 'New' Glasgow." *Service Industries Journal* 20: 1–18.

Waterbury, John. 1970. *Commander of the Faithful: The Moroccan Political Elite—A Study in Segmented Politics*. New York: Columbia University Press.

Weber, Max. [1922] 1978. *Economy and Society*. Berkeley: University of California Press.

Whyte, William Foote. 1955. *Street Corner Society*. Chicago: University of Chicago Press.

Wikan, Unni. 1984. *Behind the Veil in Arabia: Women in Oman*. Chicago: University of Chicago Press.

Wilensky, Harold. 1966. "Measures and Effects of Mobility." In *Social Structure and Mobility in Economic Development*, ed. Neil Smelser and Seymour Martin Lipset, 98–141. Chicago: Aldine.

———. 2002. *Rich Democracies: Political Economy, Public Policy, and Performance*. Berkeley: University of California Press.

Willis, Paul. 1977. *Learning to Labor: How Working Class Kids Get Working Class Jobs*. Aldershot: Gower.

Winchester, Daniel. 2008. "Embodying the Faith: Religious Practice and the Making of a Muslim Moral Habitus." *Social Forces* 86 (4): 1753–80.

Witz, Anne, Chris Warhurst, and Dennis Nickson. 2003. "The Labour of Aesthetics and the Aesthetics of Organization." *Organization* 10: 33–54.

World Bank. 2017. "Rural Population (% of Total Population)." https://data.worldbank.org.

———. 2018. "Islamic Republic of Iran: Overview." 11 October. www.worldbank.org.

Zaborowska, Magdalena. 2014. "A Contribution to the Persian Concept of *Āberu*." *Hemispheres: Studies on Cultures and Societies* 29 (1): 113–27.

Zeydabadi-Nejad, Saeed. 2010. *The Politics of Iranian Cinema: Film and Society in the Islamic Republic*. New York: Routledge.

# INDEX

Numbers in italic apply to photographic plates.

# ABOUT THE AUTHOR

Manata Hashemi is the Farzaneh Family Assistant Professor of Iranian Studies at the University of Oklahoma. She holds a PhD in Sociology from the University of California, Berkeley, an MA in Middle Eastern Studies from Harvard University, and a BA in Near Eastern Studies from Cornell University. She is the co-editor of *Children in Crisis: Ethnographic Studies in International Contexts* (2013) and the author of several articles on urban poverty and youth-hood in Iran.